AIRBORNE
IN VIETNAM

An officer and his RTO radioman monitor the arrival
of a flight of UH-1D Hueys as they come in to land to
pick up troops for yet another 'search and destroy'
operation. *National Archives*

ELITE ATTACK FORCES

AIRBORNE IN VIETNAM

Simon Dunstan and Michael Sharpe

CHARTWELL
BOOKS, INC.

This edition published by 2007 by

CHARTWELL BOOKS, INC.
A Division of
BOOK SALES, INC.
114 Northfield Avenue
Edison, New Jersey 08837

ISBN 10: 0-7858-2327-1
ISBN 13: 978-0-7858-2327-8

© 2007 Compendium Publishing Ltd, 43 Frith
Street, London, W1D 4SA
Previously published in the Spearhead series

Cataloging-in-Publication data is available from
the Library of Congress

Printed in China through Printworks Int. Ltd

Acknowledgements
The Author and Publisher acknowledge the help of
a number of people in the production of this
book, including Teddy Nevill of TRH Pictures and
Lolita Chizmar of Real War Photos who supplied
photographs, and Bob Aquilina of the Marine
Historical Center for the information in the
commanding generals table on page 82.

Note: Website information provided in the
Reference section was correct when provided
by the author. The publisher can accept no
responsibility for this information becoming
incorrect.

Many of the photographs reproduced in this
book clearly do not portray the correct colours.
Shot 30 years ago on print film, the colours have
deteriorated. Nevertheless, we feel that some
colour is better than reproducing them in black
and white.

Right: Troopers from the aerorifle platoon of Bravo
Troop, 1/9th Cavalry, disembark from a hovering UH-
1D during 'Operation Oregon.

CONTENTS

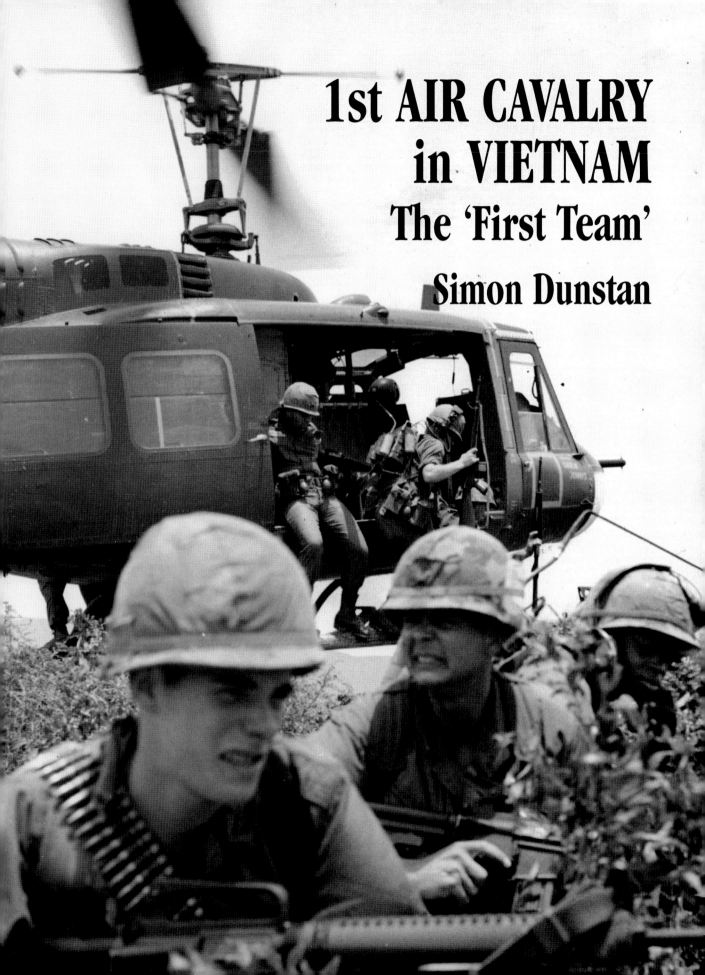

1st AIR CAVALRY
in VIETNAM
The 'First Team'
Simon Dunstan

ORIGINS & HISTORY

The enduring image of the US Army cavalryman is ingrained in the public consciousness through a thousand Hollywood movies that have made the horse soldier the stuff of legend in the history of the Wild West. Following their widespread service during the American Civil War under such dynamic leaders as Nathan Bedford Forrest, Phil Sheridan and Jeb Stuart, US cavalry regiments proved indispensable during the expansion of the United States westwards in the late 1860s and 70s. Their primary task was to protect settlers and pioneers as they ventured deep into the hinterland beyond the Mississippi/Missouri River. At the same time, the army was required to safeguard the interests of the native North American Indian nations herded into ever-diminishing reservations as more and more white farmers, trappers and prospectors encroached on their traditional hunting grounds and tribal lands. It was an impossible dichotomy and the army's role essentially became the pacification of the Indian peoples by coercion or force as necessary.

Nevertheless, the first antecedent unit of the 1st Cavalry Division (Airmobile) was formed as early as 1855 when the 2nd Cavalry Regiment was raised as the army was expanded from 10,000 to 15,000 men.[1] In 1861, this unit was redesignated as the 5th Cavalry Regiment. During the Civil War it fought in several famous battles including Bull Run, Antietam, Gettysburg and Appomattox. The 5th together with the 7th, 8th and 9th Cavalry Regiments that remain with the 1st Cavalry Division to this day, fought throughout the Indian Wars against the fearsome fighters of the Sioux, Comanche, Apache, Arapaho, Kiowa and Ute nations culminating in the death of the legendary Chief Sitting Bull and the Battle of Wounded Knee in December 1890.[2] With the crushing of the Oglala Sioux and the Ghost Dance cult, the Indian Wars ended and to the strains of their bugles playing 'Garry Owen', the 7th Cavalry marched ever westwards until their patrols reached the Pacific coast and the frozen tundra of Alaska. The United States of America now stretched from ocean to ocean.

When not acting as policemen during labour disputes, cavalry units fought in the Spanish-American War of 1898 and, in the same year, the 'Buffalo Soldiers' of the 9th Cavalry joined in the famous attack on San Juan Hill with Teddy Roosevelt's 'Rough Riders' in Cuba. Cavalry saw extensive service in the Philippines over the coming years but the majority of horsed units spent most of their time in the sun-scorched deserts of the south-western United States patrolling the border with Mexico. Following an attack by the bandit cum Mexican nationalist Pancho Villa on the town of Columbus, New Mexico, in March 1916, the US Army was directed to mount a punitive expedition into Mexico to capture Villa, dead or alive. Under the command of General 'Black Jack' Pershing, the 5th and 7th Cavalry made up part of the expeditionary force that included two thirds of the entire US air force (eight out of the 13 Curtis JN-2 'Jennies' in service). For the next 11 months and often living off the land, the cavalry units of the Punitive Expedition pursued Pancho Villa and his raiders across northern Mexico in the last great

Notes

1 The 1st Regiment of Dragoons was raised in 1833 and subsequently became the 1st Cavalry Regiment that served in the 1st Cavalry Division between 1921 and 1933.

2 The 7th, 8th and 9th Cavalry Regiments were raised in 1866 with the 12th in 1901.

cavalry campaign conducted by the US Army. On 5 February 1917, Pershing's men returned across the border having surmounted many problems and learnt new lessons in warfare. There were now more pressing commitments. On the next day, the United States joined the war against the Kaiser's Germany and troops were needed on the Western Front.

The Great War was the nemesis of horsed cavalry: the age of the tank had dawned. The great majority of US Army cavalry regiments remained in America patrolling the border with Mexico. Following the war, the cavalry arm was cut from 17 to 14 regiments. With the promulgation of the National Defense Act, the 1st Cavalry Division was formally activated at Fort Bliss, Texas, on 13 September 1921 with Maj Gen Robert Lee Howze as its first division commander. Howze was a seasoned veteran of virtually every cavalry campaign back to the Indian Wars and a recipient of the Medal of Honor. Among the units assigned to the 1st Cavalry Division were the 1st, 7th, 8th and 10th Cavalry Regiments, while the 5th Cavalry joined on 18 December 1922 replacing the 10th. On 3 January 1933, the 12th Cavalry Regiment joined the 1st Cavalry Division and relieved the 1st Cavalry to bring together the principal units within the division of the Vietnam era.[3] Life between the wars was predominantly taken up with border patrols and polo with only two cavalry regiments of the US Army becoming mechanised by 1938. Although experiments were undertaken with armoured scout cars from 1928 onwards, the 1st Cavalry Division remained firmly wedded to the horse.

After the outbreak of war following the Japanese attack on Pearl Harbor, the 1st Cavalry Division was assembled in its entirety at Fort Bliss for extensive field training. Its authorised strength rose from 3,575 to 10,110 troops. In March 1942, the office of Chief of Cavalry was eliminated by the War Department. The 1st Cavalry Division was living on borrowed time as it continued its well-worn path of border surveillance with horses and armoured cars. The horse soldiers were finally dismounted in February 1943. Many cavalrymen resented trading in their saddles to become 'cushion pounders'. However, they were allowed some memories of their glorious past with the retention of of the term 'Troops' where the infantry used 'companies' and soldiers remained 'Troopers' while proudly wearing yellow cavalry insignia and marching beneath the red and white guidons of the former horse regiments. The division was retrained as amphibious assault infantry for service in the Pacific War, departing overseas on 23 May 1943.

After six months training in the jungles of Queensland in Australia, the division was ready for battle. On 29 February 1944, the 1st Cavalry Division set sail for the Admiralty Islands and stormed ashore in an amphibious assault on Los Negros. Harking back to their involvement in the Plains Wars, the division incorporated a unique radio unit known as the 'Code Talkers' with Lakota and Dakota native American Indians who communicated with other units in the ancient tribal Sioux language that defied all enemy radio intercept attempts. After the Admiralty Islands campaign, the division joined the invasion force of the Philippines, landing on Leyte on 20 October 1944. Leyte was followed by Luzon in January 1945 when General Douglas MacArthur ordered the division: 'Go to Manila! Go around the Japs, bounce off the Japs, save your men, but get to Manila! Free the internees at Santo Tomas! Take the Malacanan Palace [the Presidential Palace] and the legislative building!' In a flying column, elements of the division cut a swathe through 100 miles of enemy-held territory to be the first US Army unit to enter the Philippine capital of Manila, releasing many Allied POWs: equally satisfactory was the liberation of the San Miguel brewery. After the 'First Team' was the first into Manila, the 1st Cavalry Division was given the honour to lead the Allied Occupational Army into Tokyo at the conclusion of World War 2. It was another notable first for the 'First Team'.

Following the Army Organization Act of 1950,[4] the 1st Cavalry Division was configured as a standard infantry division. It remained on occupation duties in Japan until

Above: A group photograph of Troop C, 3rd Cavalry taken at Fort Davis, Texas, in 1886 shows these troopers in regulation uniforms but still equipped with US Model 1860 light cavalry sabres which were rare at this late date. They are wearing 1883 campaign hats, 1884 fatigue blouses and are armed with US Model 1873 Springfield carbines and Schofield Smith & Wesson revolvers.
(*Fort Davis National Historical Site*)

Notes

3 The 1st Cavalry Division (Airmobile) assigned cavalry units in Vietnam were drawn from the 5th, 7th, 8th, 9th and 12th Cavalry Regiments.

4 On 25 March 1949, the 1st Cavalry Division was reorganised as a Triangular Division. The 5th, 7th and 8th Cavalry Regiments were retained while the 12th Cavalry Regiment was deactivated.

Above: The classic image of US cavalrymen during the Indian Wars with Sergeant J. Bouck and Corporal Sampson of Troop K, 1st Cavalry, at the Crow Agency Montana in late 1887. They feature an interesting combination of official issue and private purchase items such as the gunbelt with hunting knife and civilian slouch hat worn by Bouck (right) while Sampson wears the superannuated Civil War holster. Soon after this photograph was taken, Sampson was killed by Crow renegades. *National Archives*

Right: On the left, the standard divisional shoulder patch; on the right, the subdued patch used during the Vietnam era.

the communist invasion of South Korea by its northern neighbour on 25 June 1950. Although severely understrength as many specialist personnel and NCOs were immediately despatched to the fighting, the division was deployed piecemeal to South Korea from 18 July to bolster the hard-pressed perimeter of the 'Pusan Pocket' around the last major seaport in the south. After the front was stabilised, the United Nations counterattacked with MacArthur's brilliant amphibious landings at Inchon near the South Korean capital of Seoul. Pounded unmercifully by airpower, the North Korean army crumbled and the United Nations force forged across the 38th Parallel into North Korea on 9 October 1950. The 1st Cavalry Division gained another first by being the first unit into the North Korean capital of Pyongyang, which was captured on 19 October. The advance continued northwards to the Yalu River and the border with communist China. Then the full weight of the Chinese People's Liberation Army fell upon the overextended United Nations forces. A headlong retreat southwards ensued with heavy losses. On 1 November 1950, the 8th Cavalry Regiment was surrounded and cut off at Unsan by Chinese forces. Hand to hand fighting raged for several days: the 8th lost over half its personnel, either dead or POWs, as well as hundreds of vehicles and weapons.

Ironically, the 1st Cavalry Division was fighting in terrain more suited to horses than vehicles that were restricted to the crumbling tracks and roads in the valley floors. Time and again, the Chinese used sturdy ponies to negotiate the overlooking precipitous hills and outflank UN units. Fierce fighting continued through the bitter winter of 1950/51 until the front lines stabilised along the Han River below Seoul with over 1½ million communist soldiers facing just 250,000 UN troops. During February and March, the 1st Cavalry Division participated in the UN counterattack that recaptured Seoul. After a period in reserve, it returned to the line during the Chinese spring offensive that was thwarted by overwhelming firepower and a dogged UN defence along the Imjin River. The war then became predominantly static along the high ground astride the 38th Parallel as the two sides entered prolonged armistice negotiations at Panmunjon that finally came to fruition on 27 July 1953. Meanwhile, after 18 months of almost continuous fighting,

THE HISTORY OF THE PATCH

The shoulder patch and insignia of the 1st Cavalry Division is one of the most distinctive in the US Army, reflecting the division's proud history and cavalry heritage. Following a War Department directive on the division's formation in 1921, an insignia was designed by Mrs Ben Dorcy, the wife of the colonel then commanding the 7th Cavalry Regiment at Fort Bliss in Texas. As with so many aspects of military history, there are different interpretations as to the original inspiration for the insignia. The background yellow was the traditional colour of the cavalry and a reminder of the golden sunsets at Fort Bliss. The shape was reminiscent of the shield carried by knights in battle. Mrs Dorcy used the yellow cloth of one of her husband's old dress capes as the background for the design. The diagonal bar was originally blue to reflect the other traditional colour of the cavalry from their uniforms. The bar represented a scaling ladder to breach castle walls. In January 1969, Mrs Dorcy wrote to the division to suggest that it could also represent the Jacob's ladder suspended from Chinook helicopters during the Vietnam War. The horse's head was an obvious reference to the cavalry's mounts and was based on the observation of a trooper leading a beautiful black thoroughbred past the Dorsey household. The original specification allowed for only two colours for the divisional insignia due to economic constraints. Subsequently, the blue bar and horse's head were changed to black to represent the colour of iron and armour following mechanisation. With rounded corners and a height of 5¼ inches, the patch is the largest in the US Army and was oversized because, according to Mrs Dorcy, 'the patch had to be large enough to be seen through the dust and sand at Fort Bliss'. During the Vietnam War, the yellow background of the shoulder sleeve insignia was changed to a subdued olive drab for the battle dress uniform in order to minimise the wearer as a potential target to the enemy.

Notes

5 On 1 November 1957, the 1st Cavalry Division was converted to the Pentomic structure with five battle groups. This change brought back the 12th Cavalry Regiment and added the 4th Cavalry Regiment.

6 On 15 July 1963, the new Army Division called Reorganization Objective Army Division or ROAD brought back the triangular divisional structure. For the 1st Cavalry Division this resulted in the loss of the 12th Cavalry Regiment once again as well as the 4th Cavalry Regiment.

Below: Troopers of the 1st Cavalry Division cross the Imjin River on 6 June 1951 aboard M-24 Chaffee light tanks of the divisional reconnaissance company. One of the first US Army formations to see service in the Korean War, the 1st Cavalry Division suffered over 16,000 casualties in 18 months of heavy combat before being withdrawn in to Japan in January 1952.

the 1st Cavalry Division returned to Japan in January 1952 after being relieved by the 45th Infantry Division.

The 1st Cavalry Division remained in Japan until September 1957 when all US forces were redeployed from the main Japanese islands. It then moved to Korea to defend the Demilitarized Zone or DMZ dividing North and South Korea. By now, the 'First Team' was configured as a Pentomic Division[5] of 13,500 men divided into five integrated battle groups that were deemed more suited to the needs of a dispersed nuclear battlefield. With the division's headquarters based at Camp Howze, the 'First Team' spent the next few years patrolling 'Freedom's Frontier' on a 24-hour, seven days a week basis, suffering several fatalities and casualties in clashes with the North Korean border guards. As the only US Army formation in direct contact with the communists (there being no formal end to the Korean War), the 1st Cavalry Division was equipped in 1962 with the full panoply of the new infantry weapons then entering service including M-14 rifles, M-60 general purpose machine guns, M-79 40mm grenade launchers and Claymore anti-personnel mines as well as UH-1A Huey helicopters for front-line medical evacuation. In spring 1963, the division began extensive training with H-19, H-21 and H-37 helicopters in air assault tactics – a role pioneered ten years before during the Korean War.[6] It was a portent of things to come when the 1st Cavalry Division was redeployed to the United States in July 1965; the first time it had returned to America in 22 years. But not for long as another war in Asia was looming large.

READY FOR WAR

THE HOWZE BOARD

Following its successful use during the Korean War for troop lift and resupply on the front lines, the role of the helicopter within the US Army fell by the wayside in the postwar years. The military now concentrated its resources on nuclear weapons and their delivery systems at the expense of conventional forces within the army. However, there remained some firm advocates of the helicopter in war including General Hamilton H. Howze, the Director of Army Aviation. In June 1956, he authorised Colonel Jay D. Vanderpool to form an experimental 'Sky Cavalry' platoon with armed and troop lift helicopters. With like-minded enthusiasts, 'Vanderpool's Fools' conducted several dramatic field exercises to demonstrate the concept of 'vertical envelopment' that was subsequently termed 'airmobility'. Gradually, official approval was gained and the unit was expanded to become the 7292nd Aerial Combat Reconnaissance Company (Provisional) in March 1958.

Two years later, the Rogers Board, chaired by Lt Gen Gordon B. Rogers, was convened to study US Army requirements for all types of aircraft for observation, surveillance and transport. This led to a new generation of helicopters with greatly enhanced performance over existing types thanks largely to the introduction of the compact gas-turbine engine. Rogers also recommended that another board be set up – 'to determine whether the concept of air fighting units was practical and if an experimental unit should be activated to test feasibility and develop material requirements'. This led to the appointment of Lt Gen Hamilton Howze, then the commander of the XVIII Airborne Corps, to head a task force entitled the US Army Tactical Mobility Requirements Board or 'Howze Board' for short.

The revival of interest in the role of the helicopter was now endorsed in high places with the appointment of Secretary of Defense Robert S. McNamara in President John F. Kennedy's administration. A firm believer in a technological solution to military problems, he demanded 'a bold new look at land warfare mobility'. Within a remarkably short time, the Howze Board proposed the creation of an airmobile division[1] and, to verify the concept, the 11th Air Assault Division (Test)[2] was formed at Fort Benning, Georgia, on 7 February 1963 under the command of

Notes

1 The proposed airmobile division was to comprise 14,678 men (as against a standard infantry division of 15,799) with 920 vehicles (as against to 3,671) and 400 aircraft (as against 103).

2 This designation was a tribute to the 11th Airborne Division, the 'Blue Angels', of World War 2 fame in the Pacific and an affirmation of the need for the airborne spirit within the new formation

Below: Critical to the to the overall viability of the airmobility concept was the emergence a reliable, gas-turbine powered troop transport helicopter. The Bell Model 204 was the mainstay of the US Army helicopter fleet throughout the era. More commonly known as the Huey, it was initially designated the HU-1 Iroquois in US Army service. This UH-1B is marked with a white cross for telemetry purposes during a world record attempt: it achieved a top speed of 142.2mph (the previous record by a Soviet MIL-1 was 130.8mph). (*Bell Helicopter Company*)

Above: In the heavy lift role, the 1st Air Cavalry Division (Airmobile) employed the Sikorsky CH-54 Tarhe 'Skycrane'. This CH-54A is shown lifting a complete battery of M-102 105mm howitzers – the standard artillery piece of the Air Cav in Vietnam. The M-102 was more commonly airlifted by the CH-47 Chinook. Note the rearward-facing crewman who monitors the underslung load during flight. He also controls the Skycrane's hoist during winching operations.

Brig Gen Harry W. Kinnard, together with its associated 10th Air Transport Brigade. At first it had few assets starting with only 3,000 men but gradually the army added two more brigades of infantry with artillery and support units. It was now possible to conduct battalion and brigade exercises that tested and refined the theories of the airmobility advocates.

However, there remained a dire shortage of aircraft, both rotary and fixed wing, compounded by distinct opposition from the US Air Force as the 'Skysoldiers' took to the air. While the new Bell UH-1 Iroquois helicopter provided the bulk of the lift capability and was also adaptable as an aerial weapons platform, the medium-lift Chinook helicopter was plagued with problems. Designed by Vertol and built by Boeing, the CH-47 Chinook was chronically unreliable and several were involved in catastrophic component failures resulting in fatalities. The situation became so bad that the entire airmobility test programme was put in jeopardy until improved manufacturing and maintenance procedures were instituted and the Chinook became available in acceptable numbers.

With the Chinook up and flying, it was now possible for the 11th Air Assault Division to conduct a major exercise, codenamed 'Air Assault I', involving 120 helicopters against an objective 100 miles away, the maximum range of a laden CH-47 Chinook. On 14 October 1964, despite appalling weather thanks to Hurricane Isbell offshore in the Atlantic Ocean, the helicopters struggled through the low cloud and driving rain to achieve the objective only one hour behind schedule. The exercise had been a great success and had unreservedly proved the concept of airmobility and air assault. This was confirmed in 'Air Assault II', a division-sized field exercise stretching over two states conducted in November. In the following month, the final reports were submitted to the Pentagon where many airmobility advocates believed they would languish. Furthermore, in the spring of 1965, there was a rueful expectation that the 11th Air Assault Division would be disbanded and its new-found expertise in airmobility dissipated.

The Air Assault exercises conducted during October and November coincided with the presidential elections of 1964. As the Democratic candidate, President Lyndon Baines Johnson declared that, 'American boys will not be sent to do what Asian boys ought to be doing for themselves.' Having won the election, he promptly ordered a massive escalation of American forces in Vietnam including ground troops with units of the US Marine Corps in March 1965 followed by the US Army's 173rd Airborne Brigade in May. In the same month, senior officers of the 11th Air Assault Division (Test) were closeted in heavily guarded classrooms at the Infantry School at Fort Benning to conduct top-secret map exercises. Most of the maps covered an area in Vietnam known as the Central Highlands. On 15 June, Secretary of Defense McNamara announced the creation of an airmobile division within the army force structure.

The plan called for the 11th Air Assault Division (Test) to be inactivated and its assets absorbed into an existing regular army division, which would then be converted to the airmobile role. As the existing commanding officer, Maj Gen Kinnard favoured the conversion of his former unit, the 101st Airborne Division, but the Army Chief of Staff, General Harold K. Johnson, was a former 1st Cavalry Division trooper and rank has its privileges. As the airborne divisions were part of the strategic reserve, it was felt that the ethos of the 1st Cavalry Division was more akin to airmobile operations, despite the fact that it was currently a standard infantry division based in Korea. On 29 June 1965, the colours of the 1st Cavalry Division were flown from Korea to Fort Benning. The men remained in Korea and were presented with the 'Indianhead' shoulder patch to become the 2nd Infantry Division. On 1 July, the 11th Air Assault Division (Test) stood down but was then presented with new colours to become the 1st Cavalry Division (Airmobile). At the same time, Secretary of Defense McNamara ordered the new airmobile division to be ready for overseas deployment by 28 July 1965. Overseas meant only one destination – Vietnam.

By the summer of 1965, the military situation in South Vietnam was dire with the Army of the Republic of Vietnam (ARVN) on the ropes in its war against the insurgent communist forces, known as the Viet Cong. The Mekong Delta was the main rice growing

Below: The other essential helicopter in the execution of the airmobility concept was the Boeing-Vertol CH-47 Chinook. As a medium-lift helicopter, the Chinook Ch-47A was capable of carrying up to 44 troops in the main cabin but in Vietnam the payload was much reduced because of the hot and humid conditions and a payload of 7,000lb was normal when operating in the Central Highlands. This Chinook is lifting an M-56 Scorpion tank destroyer as an underslung load.

The first real test of airmobility was undertaken by the 11th Air Assault Division (Test) during late 1964, against stiff opposition from the US Air Force. The 11th Air Assault Division (Test) became the 1st Cavalry Division (Airmobile) on 1 August 1965 and within 90 days it was in combat in South Vietnam.

area of the country and 40% of the population was situated there. They now lived under the sway of the Viet Cong with only marginal government control of the area. It was little different in the other Corps Tactical Zones (CTZ) that divided up South Vietnam. To the north of the country in ICTZ, the US Marine Corps was fighting the 1st Viet Cong Regiment in the largest American ground operation of the war so far – Operation 'Starlite'. Meanwhile, the US Air Force and US Navy had begun extensive bombing raids against North Vietnam in Operation 'Rolling Thunder' but there were few lucrative targets in an essentially agrarian society. To General William Westmoreland, the commander of MACV (Military Assistance Command Vietnam), the answer was more US troops and in particular the 1st Cavalry Division (Airmobile).

On the evening of 28 July, President Johnson announced the deployment of the division to South Vietnam. It was the first US Army division to be despatched to the country, with the Advance Liaison Detachment leaving by air on 2 August and arriving there two days later. The advance party departed between 14 and 20 August by C-124 and C-130 transport planes and landed in Vietnam with nine UH-1B helicopters and 152 tons of equipment between 19 and 27 August. They set up the division's base at An Khe, 36 miles (57km) inland from the coastal city of Qui Nhon, in the heart of IICTZ. The remainder of the division departed Fort Benning in mid-August and embarked on six troop transports, four aircraft carriers and 11 cargo ships of the Military Sea Transport Service at ports on the Atlantic and Gulf coasts. Together they carried more than 15,000 soldiers; 470 rotary and fixed-wing aircraft; 3,100 vehicles and 19,000 tons of supplies. Some of the ships sailed via the Mediterranean Sea and the Suez Canal, while the others made the western passage through the Panama Canal and across the Pacific Ocean. The long journey was largely uneventful with only the division's white mule mascot, Maggie, being inconvenienced when she was branded on the left flank by some sailors with the letters 'USN'. The time was spent undergoing further training, particularly with the new M-16 assault rifle, and preparations for jungle warfare. On 14 September, the USNS *Buckler* carrying the 2nd Brigade dropped anchor in the harbour of Qui Nhon and the first combat elements were flown directly to An Khe. Within 90 days of formal activation, the 'First Team' had been trained, equipped and transported 12,000 miles to a combat zone. The 1st Cavalry Division (Airmobile) was the first complete US Army division to be committed to the Vietnam War. The concept of airmobility and the Air Cavalry were soon to undergo trial by combat. Although the 1st Cavalry Division (Airmobile) was its official title, the formation was also known as the 'First Team'; the Air Cav; Skytroopers or Sky Soldiers; the 1st Cav and the 1st Cavalry Division during its service in Vietnam.

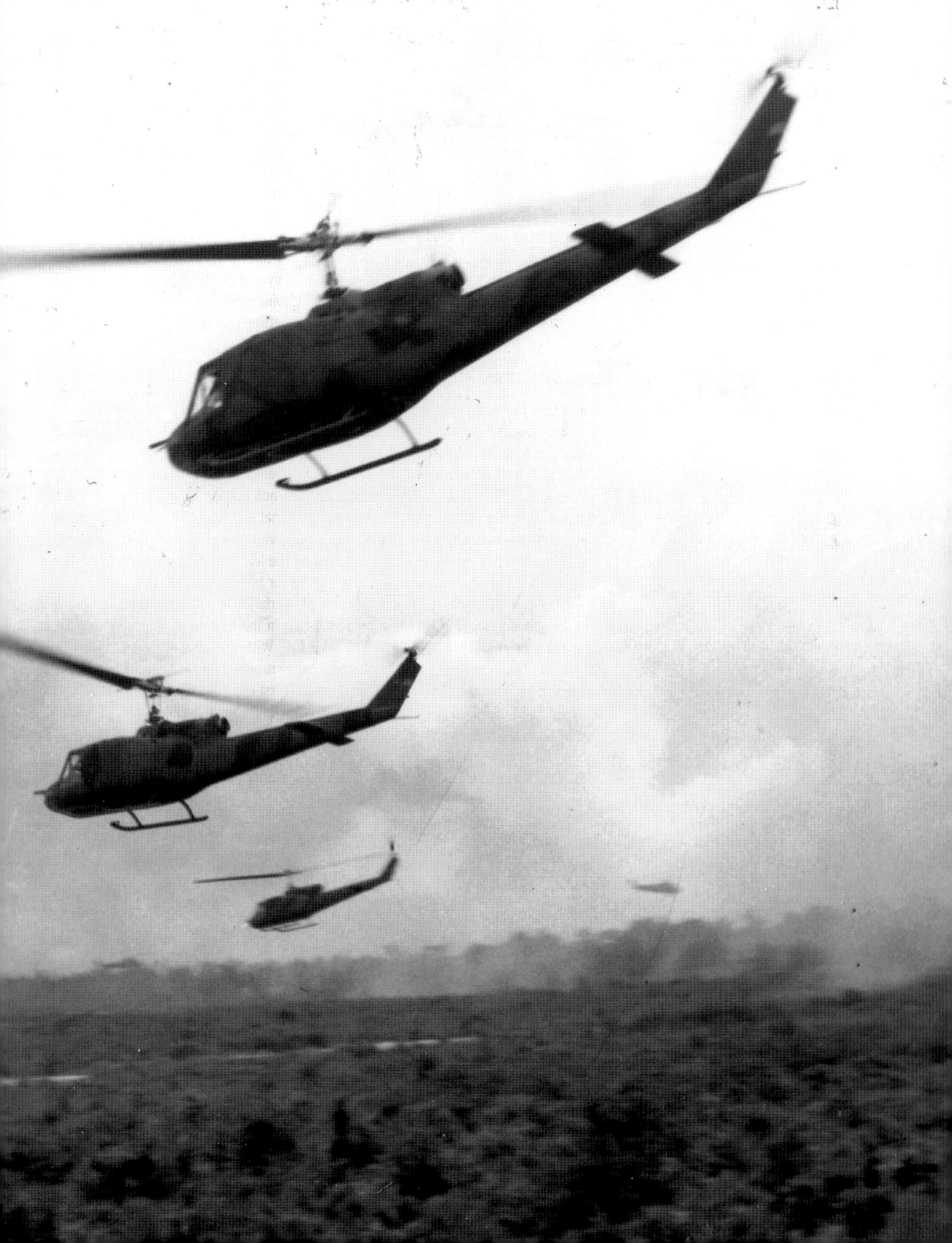

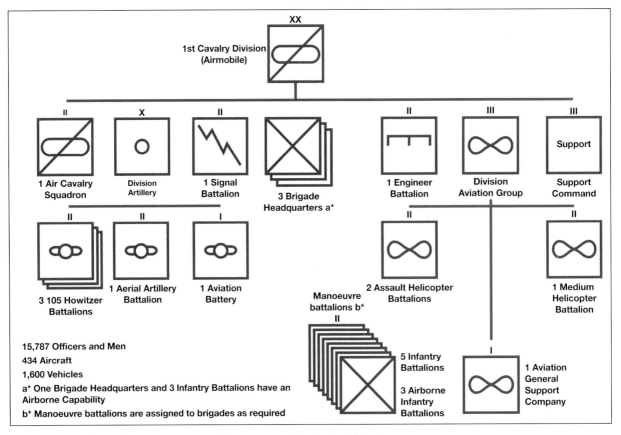

Above: Organisation of 1st Cavalry Division
(Airmobile) – Summer 1965.

Below: Organisation of 1st Squadron, 9th Cavalry –
Summer 1965.

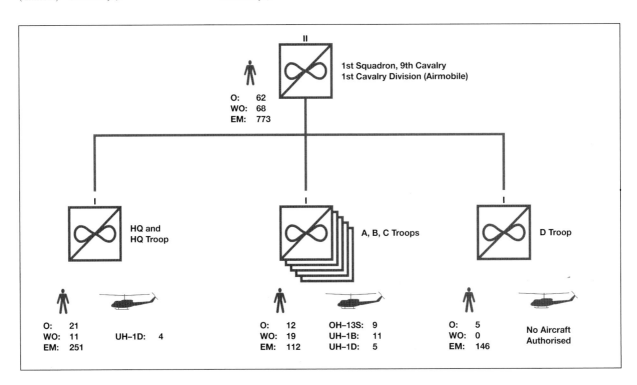

1st CAVALRY DIVISION (AIRMOBILE)
Assigned and attached units

1st Brigade
- 1st Battalion (Airborne), 8th Cavalry
- 2nd Battalion (Airborne), 8th Cavalry
- 1st Battalion (Airborne), 12th Cavalry

(Airborne capability terminated 1 Sept 1967)

2nd Brigade
- 1st Battalion, 5th Cavalry
- 2nd Battalion, 5th Cavalry
- 2nd Battalion, 12th Cavalry

3rd Brigade
- 1st Battalion, 7th Cavalry
- 2nd Battalion, 7th Cavalry
- 5th Battalion, 7th Cavalry

Division Artillery
- 2nd Battalion, 17th Artillery (105mm)
- 2nd Battalion, 19th Artillery (105mm)
- 2nd Battalion, 20th Artillery (Aerial Rocket)
- 1st Battalion, 21st Artillery (105mm)
- 1st Battalion, 30th Artillery (155mm)
- 1st Battalion, 77th Artillery (105mm)
- Battery E, 82nd Artillery (Aviation)

Division Reconnaissance
- 1st Squadron, 9th Cavalry (Air)
- 11th Pathfinder Company (Provisional)

- Company E, 52nd Infantry (Long Range Recon)
- Company H, 75th Infantry (Ranger)

Division Aviation
- 11th Aviation Group
- 227th Aviation Battalion (Assault Helicopter)
- 228th Aviation Battalion (Assault Support Helicopter)
- 229th Aviation Battalion (Assault Helicopter)
- 11th Aviation Company (General Support)
- 17th Aviation Company (Fixed Wing)
- 478th Aviation Company (Heavy Helicopter)

Division Support
- 1st Personnel Service Battalion
- 8th Engineer Battalion
- 13th Signal Battalion
- 15th Medical Battalion
- 15th Supply & Service Battalion
- 15th Administrative Company
- 15th Transportation Battalion
- 27th Maintenance Battalion
- 191st Military Intelligence Detachment
- 371st Army Security Agency Company
- 545th Military Police Company

Units temporarily attached
- 1st Battalion, 50th Infantry (Mechanized)
- 2nd Battalion, 2nd Infantry (Mechanized)
- 1st Squadron, 11th Armored Cavalry
- 2nd Squadron, 11th Armored Cavalry

The standard light observation helicopter (LOH) at the outset of the Vietnam war was the Bell OH-13 Sioux. A veteran of the Korean War when it was used primarily for front-line casualty medevac, the Sioux was replaced by the definitive LOH of the Vietnam War — the Hughes OH-6 Cayuse, more commonly known as the Loach.

IN ACTION

Right: Topographical map of South Vietnam showing the four different Corps Tactical Zones or Military Regions.

Below: Elements of the Blues – the Rifle Platoon of Troop B, 1st Squadron 9th Cavalry, known as the 'Eyes and Ears of the Division' – conduct a combat assault mission against VC and NVA troops in the An Lao Valley during Operation 'Pershing' on 28 July 1967. The antenna of the radio set makes this RTO a conspicuous target to enemy snipers; it was often shortened to reduce such exposure.

THE GOLF COURSE

While the main body of the division was on the high seas during the month-long voyage, the advance guard was busy preparing the base camp at An Khe guarded by the 1st Brigade of the 101st Airborne Division conducting Operation 'Highland'. The site chosen was a former French airstrip from the First Indochina War in the strategically important Central Highlands that form the spine of South Vietnam. There is an old Vietnamese military maxim, 'He who controls the Central Highlands controls South Vietnam'. Camp Radcliff lay astride Highway 19 and protected two vital mountain passes in an area where the Viet Minh had ambushed and defeated the French Groupement Mobile 100 just 11 years before. Anyone in control of Highway 19 had the capacity to cut South Vietnam in half: it was to be the chosen invasion route of the North Vietnamese Army (NVA) in the spring of 1975. Detritus of the battle and of the earlier French presence was all too apparent as the men cleared a new helicopter landing port under the direction of Brig Gen John M. Wright Jr, the assistant divisional commander. He decreed that heavy earth-moving equipment should not be used as this would displace the soil and create unacceptable dust clouds in the dry season and catastrophic erosion during the monsoons. Clasping a machete, Gen Wright led by example and the site was cleared of scrub by hand until, in the words of the general, 'it was as smooth as a golf course'. The name stuck and throughout the division's service in Vietnam, the helipad at the An Khe base camp was known as the Golf Course. It was surrounded by a fortified defence perimeter, some 12 miles long and 100 yards deep, called the Barrier Line.

Enemy reaction to the new camp was limited to a few light probes by some local VC guerrillas. Nervous sentries returned fire into the treeline and tragically the division suffered its first casualty in the form of the cavalry mascot, Maggie the Mule, when she was challenged and failed to impart the password. On 19 September, air and ground elements of the division supported the paratroopers of the 1st Brigade, 101st Airborne Division, during Operation 'Gibraltar'. The division was declared operational on 28 September 1965 and assumed complete responsibility for the defence of the An Khe complex. On the following day, the 1st Battalion (Airborne), 8th Cavalry, the 'Jumping Mustangs', conducted

18

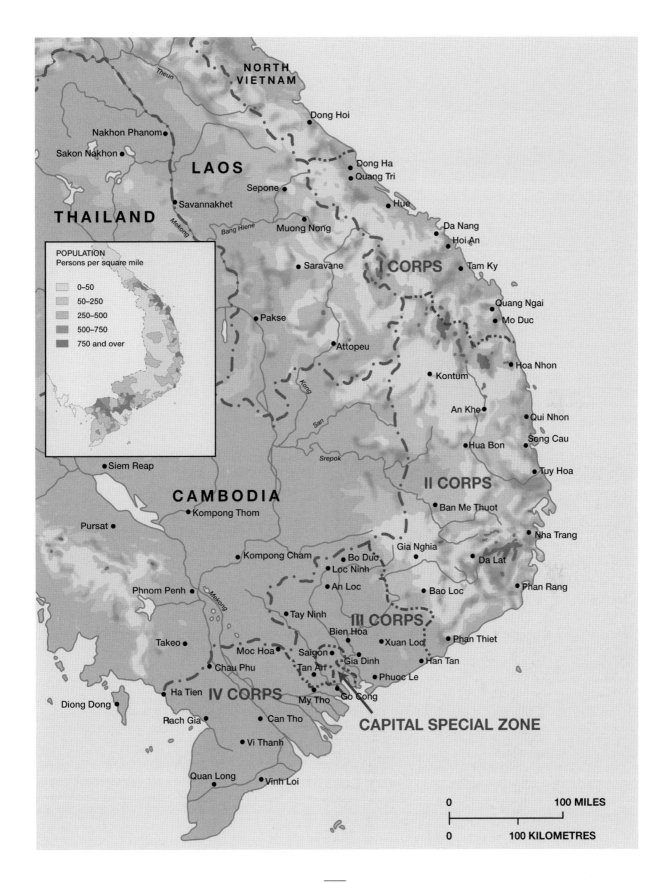

NORTH
VIETNAM

LAOS

THAILAND

Nakhon Phanom

Sakon Nakhon

Dong Hoi

Dong Ha
Quang Tri

Sepone

Savannakhet

Bang Hiene

Muong Nong

Hue

Da Nang
Hoi An

I CORPS

Tam Ky

Saravane

Quang Ngai
Mo Duc

Pakse

Attopeu

Hoa Nhon

Kontum

An Khe

Qui Nhon

Song Cau

Hua Bon

Tuy Hoa

II CORPS

Ban Me Thuot

Nha Trang

Gia Nghia

Da Lat

Phan Rang

POPULATION
Persons per square mile

0–50
50–250
250–500
500–750
750 and over

Siem Reap

CAMBODIA

Kompong Thom

Pursat

Kompong Cham

Bo Duc
Loc Ninh

An Loc

Bao Loc

Phnom Penh

Tay Ninh

III CORPS

Bien Hoa

Xuan Loc

Phan Thiet

Takeo

Moc Hoa

Saigon
Gia Dinh

Han Tan

Chau Phu

Tan An

Phuoc Le

Ha Tien

IV CORPS

My Tho

Go Cong

Diong Dong

CAPITAL SPECIAL ZONE

Rach Gia

Can Tho

Vi Thanh

Quan Long

Vinh Loi

Theun

Mekong

Kong

San

Srepok

Mekong

0   100 MILES

0   100 KILOMETRES

Left: *Combat troops are unloaded from* USS Boxer *on 14 September 1965 as the 15,800 men and 424 aircraft of the 1st Air Cav arrive in South Vietnam.* Boxer *carried a total of 239 aircraft comprising 57 CH-47 Chinooks, 50 UH-1 Hueys, 122 OH-13s, four CH-54 Tarhes and six OV-1 Mohawks.*

Far Left: *After landing at Qui Nhon, troops of 1st Air Cav disembark from a CV-2B Caribou at An Khe on 14 September 1965. The Caribou was an extremely versatile STOL utility aircraft with a remarkable rate of climb and high manoeuvrability – vital assets when trying to avoid enemy ground fire.*

Below Left: *An aerial view of 10 December 1965 shows the tented encampment of the living quarters and operations area at An Khe before the construction of buildings to house the command elements.*

Right: *Within days of the establishment of Camp Radcliff, numerous shops and bars sprang up to serve the needs of the troops and no doubt intelligence for the Viet Cong. The base camp at An Khe was named Radcliff after the division's first fatality in Vietnam.*

Below: *In one of the first operations by the 1st Air Cav, troops of Co A, 1/5th Cavalry, wade through a rice paddy during a sweep for the Viet Cong on 15 October 1965.*

Right: *The disparity in height between SFC John Lutz and his interpreter is a graphic reminder of the impact that the Americans had on their arrival. Here a peasant is questioned on the 15 October patrol.*

The First of the Ninth – the 'Cav of the Cav'

The unit was formed as the air cavalry squadron of the 1st Cavalry Division (Airmobile) on 1 July 1965 drawn from equipment and personnel of 3rd Squadron, 17th Cavalry, that had been part of the 11th Air Assault Division (Test). With 62 officers, 68 warrant officers and 733 enlisted men, the air cavalry squadron comprised a Headquarters and Headquarters Troop, three air cavalry troops (Alpha, Bravo and Charlie) and a ground reconnaissance troop (Delta). Each air cavalry troop consisted of an infantry platoon known as the 'Blues' – hence Blue Platoon – transported in five UH-1D Huey 'slicks'; a White Platoon of ten OH-13 Light Observation Helicopters (LOH) that acted as reconnaissance scouts and a Red Platoon of ten Huey gunships that provided fire support to the other elements of the troop. Scout and gunship helicopters customarily flew in pairs or 'teams' for mutual support; thus two scout helicopters formed a 'White Team' and two gunships a 'Red Team'. This was the minimum for any type of operation and subsequently it was common practice to combine a scout helicopter and a gunship to become a 'Pink Team'. The Standard Operating Procedure or SOP was for the scout helicopter to fly low and slow to reconnoitre the ground while the gunship circled at altitude but ready to strike at anytime at the direction of the LOH. These initials gave rise to the term 'Loach' that usually referred to the successor to the OH-13 – the Hughes OH-6A Cayuse that was the definitive scout helicopter of the Vietnam War. Similarly the earlier gunships were superseded by the purpose-designed Huey Cobra with a much enhanced payload and performance. The combination of the Loach and Cobra made

a formidable partnership and gave rise to the 'Hunter Killer Team' with the Loach acting as the Hunter and the Cobra as the Killer. The Blues were commonly employed for ground reconnaissance, ambushes and to recover downed helicopters and rescue their crews. The Delta Troop comprised three 'Rat Patrol' platoons mounted in jeeps equipped with machine guns and recoilless rifles as well as truck-mounted mortar teams. Later in the war it was customary to absorb these assets into the Blues as the air cavalry troops proved so effective in the area war that characterised Vietnam.

It is no exaggeration to say that the helicopters of the First of the Ninth initiated over three-quarters of all contacts of the 1st Cavalry Division (Airmobile) during its service in Vietnam. The First of the Ninth – 1/9th – were the elite within an elite and an air cavalry trooper often saw more action in a month than a 'ground-pounder' did in the whole of his 365-day tour of duty in Vietnam. The air cavalry squadron was intended by the Howze Board to be the basic building block of the airmobile division. It remains intriguing that so few were actually activated when they proved so effective during the Vietnam War and none more so than the First of the Ninth – the Eyes and Ears of the Air Cav.

the first major air assault mission into the Vinh Thanh Valley supported by 16 UH-1D helicopters of the 227th Assault Helicopter Battalion. Employing the full panoply of USAF tactical air support, tube artillery, aerial rocket artillery and helicopter gunships, the battalion executed a successful landing but no enemy were encountered although 22 Skytroopers were wounded due to punji sticks: these were sharpened bamboo stakes that were capable of penetrating the jungle combat boot, being concealed as booby traps for the unwary. They were often tipped with excrement to cause infection of the wound, requiring extensive medical treatment. The 'Jumping Mustangs' had proven the concept of Combat Air Assault. On 10 October, the first brigade-sized airmobile assault was conducted with Operation 'Shiny Bayonet' involving the 1st and 2nd Battalions, 7th Cavalry, and 1st Battalion, 12th Cavalry, supported by the 1st Battalion, 21st Artillery, and the divisional air reconnaissance group – the 1st Squadron, 9th Cavalry, under the dynamic leadership of Lt Col John B. 'Bullwhip' Stockton. As so often during the war, the VC/NVA declined to join battle and only minor contacts occurred before the enemy slipped away to its sanctuaries in Cambodia and elsewhere.

THE BATTLE OF THE IA DRANG VALLEY

On arrival in Vietnam, the divisional commander, Maj Gen Harry W. Kinnard, was instructed, 'Harry, your job with your division is to prevent the enemy from cutting the country in two.' A major enemy offensive was expected in the Central Highlands with the intention of splitting South Vietnam before the build-up of American ground forces became too powerful. On 19 October, a potent force of the B-3 Front comprising the 33rd and 320th NVA regiments under the command of General Chu Huy Man, launched a concerted assault against the US Special Forces camp at Plei Me in western Pleiku province while setting ambushes for any relief forces. The offensive was also intended to lure the newly arrived American 'Sky Soldiers' into battle so as to learn their fighting techniques. The official historian of the People's Army of Vietnam, Maj Gen Hoang Phuong, was a lieutenant colonel at the time of the Ia Drang campaign and he recalls:

'When we received the news that the 1st Air Cavalry had come to Vietnam, the commanders of our divisions in the South were very nervous, very worried by what they were hearing about this strong, mobile unit so well equipped with helicopters. The liberation forces moved mainly by foot, were poorly equipped. Our hospital and food services were not good. How could we fight and win against the cavalry?...We foresaw that the coming battle would be very fierce. First, we evacuated the population and prepared training camps. We improved our positions, dug shelters, and prepared caches of food and underground hospitals. We knew sooner or later that you would attack our zones and we tried

Below: Pleiku campaign October to November 1965.

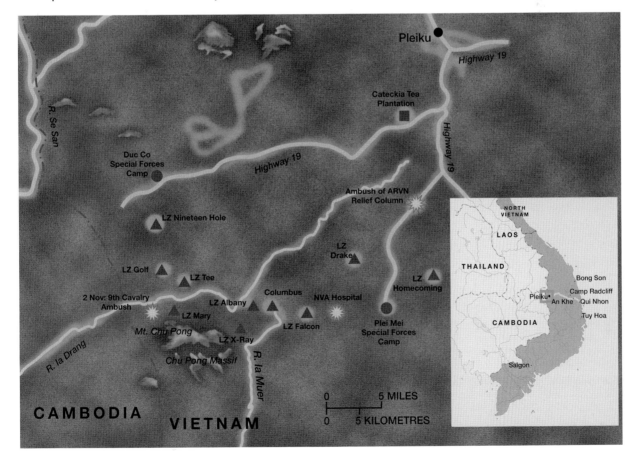

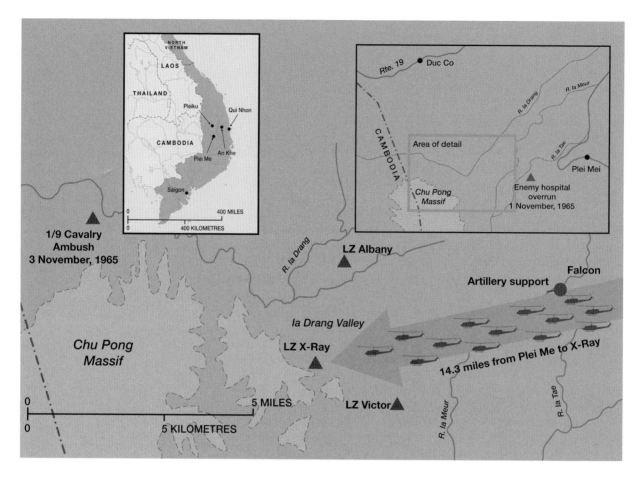

Above: Combat air assault of 1/7th Cavalry into the Ia Drang Valley, 14 November 1965.

Right and Far Right: The standard weapon carried by Huey slicks was the M-23 Armament Subsystem, Helicopter, 7.62mm Machine Gun, Door Mounted. It comprised two 7.62mm M-60D machine guns and two mounts, one on each side of the aircraft. A 500-round ammunition box was attached to the base tube assembly. Rounds were fed to the weapon by flexible chuting or else the belt was free, as shown here. A B-3 size C-ration can was usually fitted to the assault bag-fastening slide as a feed guide to reduce the likelihood of stoppages.

to prepare positions that would neutralise you. We knew that it would not be enough just to make propaganda saying that we were winning. We had to study how to fight the Americans.'

Following ferocious fighting, the attack on Plei Me was thwarted and the two NVA regiments retired to regroup at their base camp below the Chu Pong Mountain. There they met up with newly arrived 66th NVA Regiment that was near its full strength of three battalions; each of 40 officers and 513 enlisted men. The three battalions were dispersed around a large clearing near the base of the mountain.

At that time, the code letter of the 66th Regiment was X to shield its identity. On the evening of 13 November, the operations officer of 1st Battalion, 7th Cavalry, Capt 'Matt' Dillon, identified the same clearing as the landing zone for the battalion in its forthcoming operation against the NVA and gave it the codename LZ X-Ray.

Throughout their retreat from Plei Me, the 33rd and 320th NVA Regiments were pursued by the OH-13 LOHs of Lt Col 'Bullwhip' Stockton's 1/9th Cavalry, who directed the infantry battalions of the 1st Brigade into blocking positions as the enemy fled westwards. On 1 November, LOHs of 1/9th Cavalry spotted unusual activity five miles (8km) west of Plei Me camp and the squadron quickly committed its rifle platoons – the Blues – supported by its gunships – the Reds. It was soon apparent that an enemy hospital complex had been discovered and a fierce firefight developed with the NVA losing 78 KIA and 57 captured as against five troopers KIA and 17 WIA. Inserted by UH-1 helicopters, the airmobile infantry of the 1st Brigade scored some notable successes over the next few days such as the action on the night of 3 November when Blue team riflemen of Troop C, 1/9th Cavalry, ambushed an NVA heavy weapons company only to be attacked in force by the 8th Battalion of the 66th NVA Regiment. The situation was dire and only relieved by the first night-time use of aerial rocket artillery support by the gunships of the 2nd Battalion, 20th Artillery (Aerial Rocket), firing in close support. Even so the NVA continued the assault. The Blues called for reinforcements and Dustoff medical evacuation helicopters. Illuminated by a circling flareship, Company A of 1/8th Cavalry – the 'Jumping Mustangs' – made the first nocturnal helicopter combat assault in warfare soon after midnight. Together, they fought off repeated NVA attacks until the enemy withdrew as daylight dawned. Over 150 enemy casualties were inflicted at a cost of four US soldiers dead and 25 wounded.

Further fierce fighting occurred on 6 November when Company B of 2/8th Cavalry clashed with the 6th Battalion, 33rd NVA Regiment. The enemy was heavily entrenched and the attacking platoons were soon pinned down until reinforced by the battalion's Charlie Company. All the while intensive supporting fire from tube artillery and gunships pounded the enemy. But the NVA was learning quickly and moved in as close as possible to the American positions so that it became nigh on impossible to direct fire support without hitting US troops. These 'hugging' tactics were to become a familiar methodology to negate American superior firepower and were known to the NVA as 'grabbing the enemy by the belt buckle'. It was a costly firefight with 26 US dead and 53 wounded. Further sweeps around Plei Me now netted only stragglers and confirmed that the NVA had withdrawn to the Chu Pong Mountain. On 9 November, the 1st Brigade was relieved by the 3rd under the command of Col Thomas W. Brown. He was given the mission to pursue the enemy into the Ia Drang Valley. Colonel Thomas decided to commit the 1st Battalion, 7th Cavalry, commanded by Lt Col Harold 'Hal' G. Moore, into the fray. It was time for the Air Cavalry to go on the offensive.

At 1048 hours on Sunday 14 November, the first of 16 UH-ID Hueys of the 229th Assault Helicopter Battalion flared and landed among the high swaying elephant grass of Landing Zone X-Ray. The area was interspersed with anthills up to eight feet high that afforded excellent cover. Bravo Company under the command of Capt John D. Herren

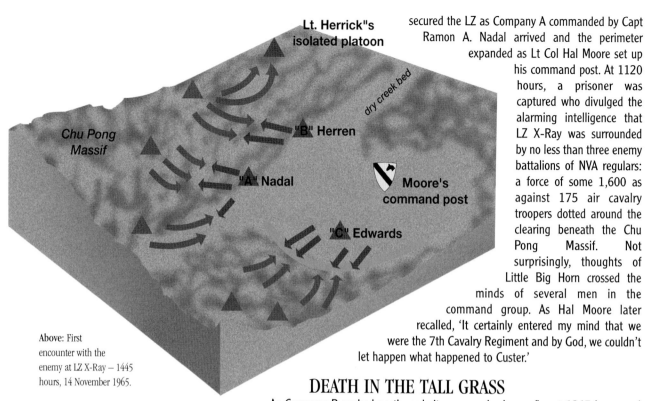

Lt. Herrick"s isolated platoon

Chu Pong Massif

dry creek bed

"B" Herren

"A" Nadal

Moore's command post

"C" Edwards

Above: First encounter with the enemy at LZ X-Ray – 1445 hours, 14 November 1965.

Below: 1/7th Cavalry fights for its life at LZ X-Ray – 0725 hours, 15 November 1965.

Lt. Herrick"s isolated platoon

Chu Pong Massif

dry creek bed

"B" Herren

"B" 2/7 Diduryk

"A" Nadal

Moore's command post

"D" Litton

"C" Edwards

secured the LZ as Company A commanded by Capt Ramon A. Nadal arrived and the perimeter expanded as Lt Col Hal Moore set up his command post. At 1120 hours, a prisoner was captured who divulged the alarming intelligence that LZ X-Ray was surrounded by no less than three enemy battalions of NVA regulars: a force of some 1,600 as against 175 air cavalry troopers dotted around the clearing beneath the Chu Pong Massif. Not surprisingly, thoughts of Little Big Horn crossed the minds of several men in the command group. As Hal Moore later recalled, 'It certainly entered my mind that we were the 7th Cavalry Regiment and by God, we couldn't let happen what happened to Custer.'

DEATH IN THE TALL GRASS

As Company B probed northwards it came under heavy fire at 1245 hours and mortar bombs began to rain down on to LZ X-Ray. Within minutes 2nd Platoon was surrounded. Capt Herren ordered his 3rd Platoon up in support but it too was soon engaged in a fierce firefight. Monitoring the situation, Col Moore called up air strikes and artillery support but the smoke of battle and lack of well-defined terrain features made the task of fire support co-ordination extremely difficult for the forward air controllers and artillery observers. The NVA however had excellent observation points on the Chu Pong Massif and the enemy mortar fire was now repeatedly hitting the landing zone. Several helicopters ferrying Company D were hit but none was actually shot down. Col Moore was forced to halt further helicopter landings so no more reinforcements or medical evacuation flights were possible for the time being. To the south of LZ X-Ray Company C under Capt Robert H. Edwards was staving off repeated enemy attacks. He radioed to Colonel Moore, 'We are in heavy contact. These guys are good!' The fighting was now intense but gradually the weight of fire support began to tell and enemy action slackened. Col Moore ordered Alpha and Bravo Companies to pull back to the landing zone and set up a defensive perimeter for the coming night.

During the withdrawal, the 2nd Platoon of Company B remained surrounded. A desperate counterattack was mounted to relieve the isolated men but to no avail. Many acts of gallantry occurred during the course of the attack including the action of Lt Walter J. Marm Jr who single-handed destroyed an NVA machine gun position with hand grenades resulting in the first of 25 Medals of Honor to be awarded to the 1st Air Cavalry Division (Airmobile) in Vietnam.

Meanwhile the remainder of the battalion was inserted by helicopters as well as Company B of 2nd Battalion, 7th Cavalry, that landed by 1800 hours. At the same time, 2nd Battalion, 5th Cavalry, conducted an air assault into LZ Victor some five miles southeast of LZ X-Ray with the intention reinforcing overland in the morning. During the evening, a pathfinder team was inserted to set up a night landing zone to allow reinforcement and medical evacuation of the many wounded throughout the hours of darkness.

During the night, the remnants of the surrounded 2nd Platoon of Company B suffered repeated attacks. With the platoon commander and platoon sergeant dead, the survivors were under the command of Sgt Clyde E. Savage who displayed cool and determined leadership throughout. Each assault was defeated by rifle and fire support directed by Sgt Savage. When daylight broke, the numerous bodies of enemy dead surrounded the position. The 2nd Platoon itself had suffered eight killed and 12 wounded in action. Only seven men remained unhurt. With daylight the battle was joined with renewed ferocity.

The enemy struck from the south inflicting heavy casualties on Company C of 1st Battalion, 7th Cavalry, followed by a furious assault against Company D to the east, resulting in fierce hand-to-hand combat with shovels and bayonets. Every single one of Company C's officers was either killed or wounded. With heavy fire sweeping the LZ, reinforcements arrived by helicopter and overland as the 2nd Battalion, 5th Cavalry, marched from LZ Victor. Against such odds the NVA slipped away and Col Moore ordered his depleted companies to sweep the area and search for their dead and wounded littering the perimeter. During the afternoon of 16 November, Col Moore's 1st Battalion, 7th Cavalry, was relieved and returned by helicopter to Camp Holloway near Pleiku – the battle for LZ X-Ray was over and the area was abandoned on the

Below: The last enemy attacks on LZ X-Ray – 0600 hours, 16 November 1965.

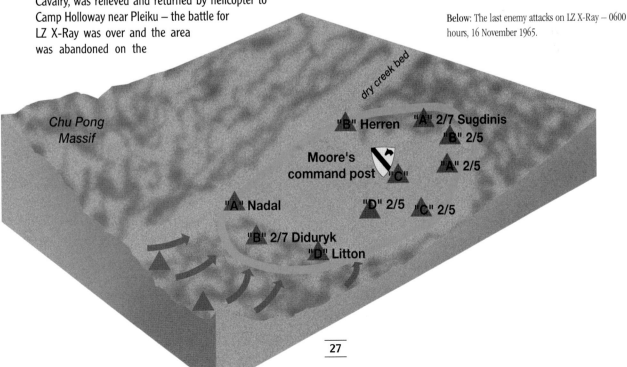

Notes
1 This and subsequent quotes are from *Time* magazine of 26 November 1965.

following day prior to a B-52 airstrike against the Chu Pong Massif, the first time this awesome weapon was used in the tactical support role under the codename 'Arclight'. A contemporary article in *Time* magazine[1] stated:

> 'Four days and nights the battle of X-Ray raged, while a remarkable concentration of American firepower kept the estimated two attacking NVA battalions at bay. The 1st Air Cav's artillery poured more than 8,000 rounds into the area, firing so fast that their barrels often glowed red with heat. By day and night, tactical air pounded the enemy, and for the first time, the giant B-52s from Guam were used in tactical support, blasting suspected enemy concentrations in the lowering mountains around X-Ray.'

THE AGONY OF ALBANY

The enemy lost a confirmed 834 soldiers at LZ X-Ray and an estimated 1,200 more of the 66th NVA Regiment in the immediate vicinity. American losses were 79 killed and 121 wounded but the campaign was not over yet. On the morning of 17 November, 2nd Battalion, 7th Cavalry, under the command of Lt Col Robert A. McDade Jr, with the attached Company A of the 1st Battalion, 5th Cavalry, moved out northwards to avoid the 'Arclight' strike area, scheduled for 1117 hours. The troopers marched towards a clearing codenamed LZ Albany from where they were to be extracted by helicopter. As the article in *Time* magazine said:

> 'Wednesday morning [17 November], X-Ray proudly theirs, the "First Team" split into two units and moved on. For one unit, some 500 men from the 5th and 7th Regiments, it was a move towards near disaster. Barely three miles north of X-Ray, the long column crossed the Ia Drang River. There lay two North Vietnamese soldiers sleeping in the grass, a sure sign that more trouble was not far away. It wasn't. Suddenly from all sides came a deadly hail of gunfire. The enemy seemed to be everywhere – slung in trees, dug into anthills, crouching behind bushes. It was a classic horseshoe trap, the fields of fire obviously meshed in perfect ambush.
>
> 'As the US force scattered and took cover, a Communist battalion sliced through its middle, cutting the Americans into two isolated halves. "After that," said an officer later, "it was man-to-man, hand-to-hand fighting between two very well-disciplined and very determined outfits." Though artillery and air support were soon on the way, and reinforcements were rushed from Pleiku (where many were abruptly called out of a memorial service for their dead at Chu Pong), Ia Drang quickly succeeded Chu Pong as the costliest battle of the war in human lives.'

Below: With its characteristic single rotor blade secured, a UH-1D is recovered by a Chinook of Bravo Company, 228TH Assault Support Helicopter Battalion. The helicopters of the ``US Army during the Vietnam War period were named after native North American Indian tribes.

Indeed, the battle of LZ Albany resulted in one of the highest day's casualty rates of the entire Vietnam War with 151 troopers killed and 121 wounded out of a total of some 400 men.

The Ia Drang campaign lasted some 35 days and to the US high command it was a resounding success and a total vindication of airmobility. Whole brigades were deployed successively by helicopter into otherwise inaccessible terrain to find, fix and destroy the enemy through superior firepower. The full panoply of American weapons was brought to bear against the enemy from the innovative M-16 assault rifle to the fearsome B-52 bomber. The divisional artillery fired 40,464 rounds and rockets during the campaign and the worth of the Aerial Rocket Artillery gunships was proven to the full, often firing within 165ft (50m) of American positions.

Yet the cost was high with the 1st Air Cavalry Division (Airmobile) suffering 334 dead, 726 wounded with 364 non-battle injuries and 2,828 succumbing to diseases such as malaria and scrub typhus. This represented a casualty rate of over 25% of the division's authorised strength of 15,955. Many of the sick and injured returned to service as 5,211 replacement troopers joined the division before the end of the year. NVA casualties were estimated to be some 3,561 dead out of a total force of 6,000.

This ratio of enemy dead was deemed to be unsustainable to the US high command at 11:1 as compared to US losses. Thus was born the concept of attrition and the 'body count' as an appalling measure of success on the battlefield. At the same time, despite claiming victory, the Americans left the battlefield to be reclaimed by nature. In an 'area war' or a 'war without fronts', there was no strategic imperative to seize and hold territory. It was a type of warfare that the American public found hard to understand. It was to have significant repercussions as the years went by and discontent with the conduct of the war grew at home.

After the first major encounter of the US Army and the NVA of the Vietnam War, both sides drew their own conclusions. The battle of the Ia Drang Valley was of considerable significance and set the pattern of military operations for much of the war. It was the first full division-scale air assault in military history augmented by an unprecedented level of co-ordinated fire support throughout the campaign. General Westmoreland was now a firm convert to airmobility and vertical envelopment thanks to the efficacy of the gas-turbine-powered helicopter, even in the hostile hot and humid environment of Vietnam. Combat air assaults were now to be one of the prime means to find and fix the enemy in ever larger 'search and destroy' missions. Fifty-nine helicopters were damaged by enemy fire during the campaign but only four were shot down, of which three were

Below: The withdrawal from LZ X-Ray to LZ Albany – Morning, 17 November 1965.

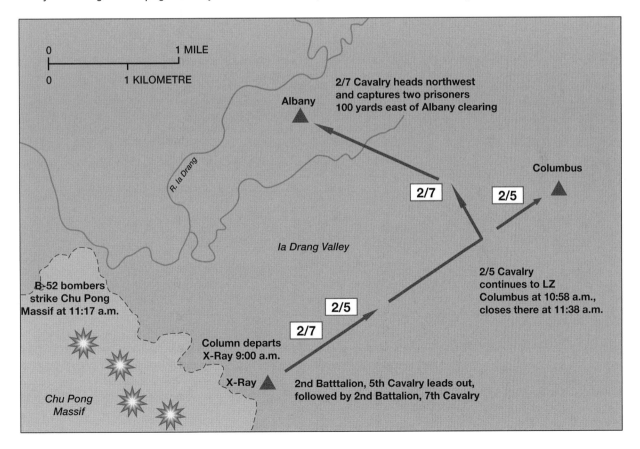

A SURVIVOR OF LZ ALBANY

Vietnam Veteran Jack P. Smith gave this speech on 8 November 2003, at the Ia Drang Survivors Banquet in Crystal City, Virginia

I have pancreatic cancer. If it is Agent Orange, it's not the first time this damned war has tried to kill me.

Let me tell you about the first time. In fact, the whole and true story of my journey home from Vietnam. But before I do, let me set the scene for you.

It is November 1965. The Ia Drang Valley. The nearest town was Pleiku, a remote Vietnamese province capital. And west of town, beyond the stilted long-huts of the Montagnards, flat scrub jungle covers the hills by the Cambodian border. A smugglers' haven, and now the infiltration route for the first North Vietnamese regulars to invade South Vietnam.

American regular infantry, the first sent to Vietnam as the war escalates, have come to this border country to hunt the People's Army of Vietnam. They are the men of the First Air Cav, the first Army infantry division to ride into war in helicopters. The leading unit is Lt Col Hal Moore's 1st Battalion, 7th Cavalry Regiment. Driving their choppers into a Landing Zone designated X-Ray, a few miles from the Cambodian border, on 14 November 1965, they land on top of a North Vietnamese Army base. A ferocious battle ensues that lasts three whole days. Hal Moore's battalion several times comes within inches of being overrun. In the end, reinforced to brigade strength, the US troops destroy the better part of a North Vietnamese division at X-Ray. Seventy-nine Americans are killed, 121 wounded, a total of 200 US casualties, the highest toll of the war till then... but there are roughly two thousand North Vietnamese casualties.

I came in on the last day of the battle. I remember the NVA bodies were piled so thick around the foxholes you could walk on them for 100 feet in some places. The American GIs were the same colour as the dirt and all had that thousand-yard stare of those newly initiated to combat.

The next day, after a restless night, my battalion, the 2/7th, walked away from X-Ray toward another clearing called LZ Albany. Around lunchtime, we were jumped by a North Vietnamese formation. Like us, about 500-strong.

The fighting was hand-to-hand. I was lying so close to a North Vietnamese machine-gunner that I simply stuck out my rifle and blew off his head. It was, I think, the only time during the war that a US battalion was ever overrun. The US casualties for this fourth day of battle: 155 killed, 121 wounded. More dead than wounded. The North Vietnamese suffered a couple of hundred casualties.

The fight at LZ Albany was largely overlooked as an aberration – poor leadership, green troops. In this first encounter between their main force regulars, the two sides focused instead on X-Ray. Interestingly, both drew the same conclusion: that each could win using the tactics of attrition.

The ferocity of the fighting during those four days was appalling. At one point in the awful afternoon at Albany, as my battalion was being cut to pieces, a small group of enemy came upon me, and thinking I had been killed (I was covered in other people's blood), proceeded to use me as a sandbag for their machine gun. I pretended to be dead. I remember the gunner had bony knees that pressed against my sides. He didn't discover I was alive because he was trembling more than I was. He was, like me, just a teenager.

The gunner began firing into the remnants of my company. My buddies began firing back with rifle grenades, M-79s, to those of you who know about them. I remember thinking, 'Oh, my God. If I stand up, the North Vietnamese will kill me; and if I stay lying down, my buddies will get me.' Before I went completely mad, a volley of grenades exploded on top of me, killing the enemy boy and injuring me.

It went on like this all day and much of the night. I was wounded twice and thought myself dead. My company [Company C] suffered about 93 percent casualties – 93 percent.

This sort of experience leaves scars. I had nightmares. For years afterwards I was sour on life, by turns angry, cynical, and alienated.

Then one day I woke up and saw the world as I believe it really is, a bright and warm place. I looked afresh at my scars and marvelled, not at the frailty of human flesh, but at the indomitable strength of the human spirit. This is the miracle of life. Like other Vietnam veterans, I began to put the personal hurt behind me, and I started to examine the war itself and to make sense of it.

When I went back to Vietnam a few years ago, I met General Vo Nguyen Giap, the man who engineered the defeat of the French at Dien Bien Phu and then commanded North Vietnamese forces in the war with South Vietnam and us. He conceded that because of the Ia Drang his plans to cut Vietnam in half and take the capital had been delayed ten years. But then, he chuckled, it didn't make a difference, did it?

We won every battle, but the North Vietnamese in the end took Saigon. What on earth had we been doing there? Was all that pain and suffering worth it, or was it just a terrible waste? This is why Vietnam veterans often have so much trouble letting go, what sets them apart from veterans of other wars...

Jack Smith died of cancer on 7 April 2004, probably due to exposure to the dioxin-based defoliant Agent Orange.

recovered. Typically, the helicopters delivered 500 tons of supplies a day and consumed 50,000 gallons of aviation fuel. Aviation units transported 5,048 tons of cargo to the troops in the field while a further 8,216 tons was despatched to Pleiku from supply depots on the coast, primarily Qui Nhon and Nha Trang.

General Westmoreland said, 'The ability of the Americans to meet and defeat the best troops the enemy could put into the field of battle was once more demonstrated beyond any possible doubt, as was the validity of the Army's airmobile concept.' But the assessment from 'the other side of the hill' was equally confident. Following the Ia Drang campaign, Senior General Vo Nguyen Giap wrote, 'After the Ia Drang battle we concluded that we could fight and win against the Cavalry troops. We learned lessons from this battle and disseminated the information to all our soldiers. These were instructions on how to organise to fight the helicopters. We thought that the Americans must have a strategy. We did. We had a strategy of people's war. You had tactics, and it takes very decisive tactics to win a strategic victory. You planned to use Cavalry tactics as your strategy to win the war. If we could defeat your tactics – your helicopters – then we could defeat your strategy. Our goal was to win the war.' In essence, Westmoreland remembered LZ X-Ray; Giap remembered Albany.

Yet the North Vietnamese plan to split South Vietnam in half had been thwarted and was not to succeed for another decade in a costly and protracted struggle. Despite suffering appalling casualties, the NVA had proved to be a formidable enemy – highly disciplined, adept at night fighting with well-rehearsed and executed assault plans and with excellent morale and esprit de corps to match that of the Sky Soldiers. Whereas the typical American unit needed tons of supplies each day, the NVA equivalent required just a few pounds of rice and *nuoc mam* (fish sauce) beyond a basic scale of ammunition and ordnance. This gave the NVA significant tactical mobility on the battlefield as against the detailed planning that was needed prior to any combat air assault by US forces. The 'hugging' tactics refined during the Ia Drang battles of closing with the Americans so as to negate the superiority of their fire support was decisive during the vicious hand-to-hand fighting at LZ Albany and was a lesson for future battles.

But Giap is somewhat disingenuous in his assessment: the crucial lesson of the battle of the Ia Drang Valley was the realisation that US forces were unable or unwilling to pursue the battered remnants of Giap's B-3 Front into Cambodia and defeat them utterly. Denied by political decree from hot pursuit of enemy units into the supposedly neutral countries of Cambodia and Laos, US forces were fatally hamstrung throughout the Vietnam War. With sanctuaries in Cambodia, Laos and their own homeland that were immune from US ground attack, NVA formations were able to rest and recuperate at their leisure and then resume the conflict at a time and place of their own choosing on the battlefields of South Vietnam. It was a decisive strategic advantage.

Postscript: For their part in the battle of the Ia Drang Valley, the Sky Soldiers of the 1st Cavalry Division (Airmobile) were awarded a Presidential Unit Citation – the first division of the Vietnam War to be so honoured. The deep blue streamer states simply: PLEIKU PROVINCE. It was another first for the 'First Team'.

COMBAT AIR ASSAULT
'Happiness is a cold LZ' Airmobile Combat Assault

The principal purpose of helicopter-borne airmobility was to place combat rifle units and supporting troops on or within close assault distance of their tactical objectives. Furthermore, airmobile assault made it possible to deliver fresh riflemen at the decisive point in the battle zone unwearied by long ground approach marches, while maintaining

tactical cohesion irrespective of time, distance and terrain factors.

Airmobile operations in Vietnam were conceived in a reverse sequence known as 'backward planning'. Firstly, the ground tactical plan was prepared including the assault tactics to seize objectives, artillery and aerial fires to be employed, resupply, medical evacuation, and the extraction by air or other means of the manoeuvre elements at the completion of the mission. Secondly, a landing plan was devised to place the troops on the ground in the right order and location, integrated with their own fire support scheme. Next, an air movement plan was prepared to ferry troops and supplies by air to the landing zone (LZ). A loading plan was then developed to put troops and equipment on the correct aircraft in the right sequence at the designated pickup zone (PZ). Finally the staging plan ensured that all the elements of the Airmobile Task Force (AMTF) arrived at the PZ on time and in the proper condition to begin loading.

The majority of airmobile combat assaults were organised at battalion level with a command group comprising the AMTF commander (the ground commander who exercised control of all elements of the airmobile force); the air mission commander (controlling the aviation elements participating in the operation); and the fire support co-ordinators (both artillery and air force). Together, they devised the detailed plans that incorporated each other's contributions and requirements in the support of the ground commander's mission. During

Above: Ho Chi Minh Trail and communist infiltration routes into South Vietnam.

Above Left: An officer and his RTO radioman monitor the arrival of a flight of UH-1D Hueys as they come in to land to pick up troops for yet another 'search and destroy' operation.

Left: Troopers of the 1st Air Cav's 3rd Brigade run from a CH-47A Chinook on LZ5 during Operation 'Masher' in February 1966. Such was the political micro-management of the war that President Johnson objected to such a bellicose term as 'Masher' so the operational name was changed to 'White Wing'.

execution, the command group rode in a command and control (C&C) helicopter which was not normally integrated in the tactical flight formation but was free to move wherever the two commanders could best control the operation. If time and security considerations allowed, an aerial reconnaissance was carried out to determine approach and departure routes, the size and state of the landing zone and the most appropriate flight pattern.

The first important phase in the execution of an airmobile operation was the loading plan. Loading was essentially a matter of having troops and equipment organised into individual helicopter loads and waves so that helicopters could land directly beside each load, take troops and equipment aboard and take off in the minimum time. Once airborne, the AMTF assumed its flight formation. Dependent on the size of the force and, as importantly, the size and shape of the LZ, the formation most often adopted was a stepped V or a variation with 'heavy left' or right echelon, these being the most versatile and easy to control. Others included diamond and arrowhead formations. The helicopters flew at forty-five degrees to the side and rear of the lead ship. Flying as level as possible, helicopters in close formation were separated by one rotor diameter, in normal formation by two diameters, and in open formation by three. Flight routes were selected to minimise interference by enemy forces and to maintain cover and concealment.

Since it had to be assumed that the enemy was defending every landing zone, it was highly desirable that airmobile landings be made within range of supporting artillery. As a rule, all combat assault landings were preceded by preparatory artillery bombardment and airstrikes or, on occasions, by small reconnaissance parties acting as pathfinders to mark the landing zone. The security thus gained for the assault force outweighed any attendant loss of surprise. The enemy offered three main threats to airmobile assault

Above: A CH-47A Chinook of the 228th Assault Support Bn prepares to lift an M-101A1 105mm howitzer of Bty B, 2nd Bn, 17th Artillery, at An Khe in March 1966. A battery of 105mm howitzers complete with a basic load of ammunition could be airlifted to a range of 100 miles in 11 Chinook sorties.

forces. First, claymore mines and improvised explosive devices were placed in the landing zone itself and in the adjacent treeline, to be detonated either electrically or by pressure on the approach of helicopters and troops.

Second, enemy personnel and weapons were located in prepared positions around the edge of the landing zone and several yards back into the surrounding vegetation.

Third, enemy forces positioned several hundred yards from the landing zone could deploy to attack the assault forces during or immediately after the landings.

Direct fire support was crucial to deal with each of these potential threats and included mortar, artillery, naval gunfire, tactical aircraft, strategic bombers and armed helicopters (the latter to be discussed later). During a specific operation the AMTF could be supported by any or all of these means which were controlled by the command group in the C&C helicopter. A combination of air strikes and artillery was used on enemy emplacements around the perimeter of the landing zone to a depth of 150-225ft (45–70m) back into the vegetation. Medium and heavy artillery was preferred because 105mm rounds were largely ineffective in destroying well-built bunkers. Similarly, bombs weighing at least 500lb (225kg) were necessary to destroy landing zone defences, while 750lb (340kg) or 1,000lb (450kg) weapons were better. Aircraft also flew runs perpendicular to the treeline, dropping napalm to splash back under the jungle canopy and into the embrasures and firing apertures of enemy bunkers. These same fires often disrupted the mines and explosive devices placed in the treeline. The deeper targets located in areas several hundred yards from the landing zone were engaged by artillery.

Air strikes and artillery had to be planned and co-ordinated so that both forms of attack were employed simultaneously and continuously. The standard and simplest method was to divide the landing zone through its centre – the fire support co-ordination line – and to assign airstrikes to one side and artillery to the other. All the while consideration had to be given to the artillery gun target lines (it was not uncommon for several artillery units to be firing on the target from more than one fire support base), and also to the direction of attack and break-away of the tactical air support aircraft, so as to prevent the helicopter formation from flying through its own artillery barrage or the flight pattern of high-performance aircraft which required considerable airspace to manoeuvre. Preparatory barrages around the landing zone were usually brief but intense, typically of five to ten minutes duration, and ended with a last WP (White Phosphorous) round to signal artillery 'tubes clear' one or two minutes prior to the troop lift transports crossing the LZ threshold. The armed helicopter gunships then made rocket and strafing runs and marked the landing points for the lead helicopters with smoke.

As the landing zone was approached, the helicopters of the AMTF moved into close formation and dropped in altitude. In most combat assaults the preferred approach was a high speed letdown (for maximum rate of descent) with a right turn into the landing zone, which allowed the flight leader to observe the LZ throughout the manoeuvre. This straight-in approach was most frequently used to effect the initial landing in the minimum space and time. A spiralling approach in formation was considered the least desirable for an assault landing because it could less effectively be supported by gunships, but was sometimes necessary, especially in hilly terrain.

During final descent further suppressive fire was delivered to the edges of the LZ by the door gunners of the troop transports. If space permitted all aircraft attempted to land simultaneously, with the lead helicopter well forward on the landing zone. Landings were effected with the minimum of hovering so as to allow each helicopter to move in as undisturbed air as possible, thus deriving maximum lift at minimum power under the existing circumstances – especially important when operating under critical load conditions. Furthermore, when landing troops, they and their equipment were less affected by rotor wash and the resulting wind-blown debris.

While on the landing zone and prior to take-off, the flight commander issued a typical radio message: 'Lift off in 15 seconds.' The other pilots were thus prepared to depart the LZ at the same time so as to reduce the possibility of fire being concentrated on a single helicopter. On take-off, the flight commander radioed, 'Lift-off, breaking right' or 'breaking left' if different from the briefing. This allowed the transport helicopters to anticipate the manoeuvre and also notified the gunships of the flight's intention. Any terrain features that might conceal enemy positions such as villages, river banks or ridge lines were avoided, whenever possible, during departure. Military power was used until a safe altitude was reached.

Below: CH-47A Chinooks of the 228th Assault Support Bn carrying members of the 1st Air Cav lift off under the covering fire support of M-114A1 155mm howitzers during Operation 'Masher' near Bong Son on 25 January 1966.

Above: In difficult terrain it was common practice to jump from a hovering Huey – often causing sprained or broken ankles. Here, troopers of the aerorifle platoon of Bravo Troop, 1/9th Cavalry, disembark from a UH-1D during Operation 'Oregon'. The trooper in the foreground has an XM-148 rifle which incorporated a grenade launcher below his M-16 assault rifle that fired 40mm grenades out to a range of 100 yards.

A typical combat air assault mission as described by Robert Sisk, formerly a warrant officer with C Company, 229th Assault Helicopter Battalion, 1st Cavalry Division (Airmobile), took place on 1 August 1966, when the 'First Team' provided support to the 3rd Brigade, 25th Infantry Division during Operation 'Paul Revere II' when it made contact with four NVA regiments. It was the 50th operation for the Air Cav since its arrival in Vietnam:

'My company, "Charlie" or C Company, 229th Assault Helicopters, was despatched to Landing Zone "Oasis", a forward firebase southwest of Pleiku. Our area of operations extended from Pleiku to the Cambodian border and included the Chu Pong Mountains and the Ia Drang Valley, all covered by thick, triple-canopy jungle. At LZ "Oasis", the first battalions of the 7th and 12th Cavalry plus units of the 2nd Battalion, 7th Cavalry, were massing for air assaults.

'During our briefings, we were told all of the landing zones would probably be "hot" and booby-trapped. The weather was exceedingly bad: torrential rains, low-lying clouds and ground fog. This was to be my first combat air assault. I was nervous and excited.

'The door gunners and crew chief made last minute checks on their machine guns and loaded belts of ammo into the gun chutes. The infantrymen were busy

writing letters and preparing for the air assaults, checking packs, cleaning weapons and hooking hand grenades to their belts.

'Several LZs were to be assaulted simultaneously. Slicks from the 227th and 229th Assault Helicopter Battalions were to air-assault the grunts into the LZs while the big Chinooks of the 228th would sling the artillery into place once the LZs were secured.

'We lifted off in flights of four. Once airborne, the helicopters joined up in a diamond formation. Chief Warrant Officer Neil Stickney was the aircraft commander, I was the co-pilot. Our flight would be the second wave into the landing zone, following four slicks from the 1st Platoon of Charlie Company. We were to maintain a one-minute spacing between formations. Behind us were two more flights of four ships each, for a total "gaggle" of 16 helicopters. On each side of the gaggle, B-model Huey gunships from Delta Company flew shotgun for the assault helicopters.

'Each helicopter was assigned a colour code with a number-small plates on each side for easy identification. This helped the infantrymen find their assigned helicopter and it also determined the position in the formation we would be flying. "Wagonwheel Six" was designated the codename for Maj Williams, who was flying the lead ship. Yellow One. He gave orders to the aircraft commanders

Above: Several experiments were conducted to allow helicopters to land in heavily wooded terrain such as this steel mesh netting laid across the treetops. It did not prove successful and it was easier to lower combat engineers who cleared an LZ using explosives and chainsaws to remove the trees and vegetation.

to have their door gunners test-fire the M-60 machine guns. From the open doors of the ships ahead, I could see short bursts of tracer rounds spewing from the guns. Stickney told our gunners to fire a burst. The rapid chatter of each weapon was reassuring.

' "Two minutes out," the flight leader said on the UHF radio. Up ahead I could see smoke and explosions in the intended landing zone. The dark smoke and bright reddish-orange flashes of the explosions stood out against the low clouds and patches of fog. An artillery battery from a distant firebase was pounding the landing zone with high-explosive rounds.

' "Last round on the way," a voice suddenly blurted over the UHF. One ship in the flight was usually assigned to monitor the artillery FM radio frequency to advise the flight leader when the barrage was ended. The last round was "Willie Peter" (white phosphorous).

'The WP burst in the centre of the clearing, a billowing cloud of thick, white smoke. "One minute out," the flight leader said. Two aerial-rocket-artillery helicopters suddenly appeared and made firing runs down both sides of the landing zone. The ARA ships broke off their rocket runs and went into a daisy-chain holding pattern, west of the LZ. The first wave of slicks touched down. I could see the door gunners raking the jungle with machine-gun fire. Soldiers spilled out both side of the choppers and crawled for the nearest cover.

'The gunships had made the initial approach with the first flight, firing machine guns and rockets. They then swung around and escorted the next flight into the LZ. One of them was fitted with an M-5 grenade launcher, and I could see it firing into the tree line. It looked like a fat kid spitting watermelon seeds.

' "White flight short final," the platoon leader of our flight said. The first flight of slicks was still holding in the LZ while more grunts exited. Timing was critical because the following flights were on final approach.

Above: Troopers of the 1st Air Cav move warily along a river bed, constantly checking for booby traps – the cause of many casualties to US troops in Vietnam.

Above Right: Members of Co A, 2/5th Cavalry, prepare to jump from a hovering UH-1D of Co B, 227th Assault Helicopter Bn, during an operation some six miles (10km) from Quang Tri on 13 October 1968.

Right: Troops pause in a paddy field as the RTO communicates with higher HQ. Typically, the troops remain vulnerable to enemy fire from the treeline – this illustrates how the vast majority of contacts were initiated by the enemy with the intention of inflicting a few debilitating casualties. The enemy then quickly withdrew before retaliatory artillery fire and gunship support.

' "If they don't get the hell out of there, we'll have to make a go-around," said Stickney. Then the flight on the LZ lifted slowly and began to accelerate straight ahead and away. I locked my shoulder harness and lowered the visor on my helmet. A few weeks earlier, another assault helicopter company had lost an aircraft when the windshield was shot out. Neither pilot had his visor down; the shredded plexiglass blinded them both. The helicopter crashed, killing the crew chief.

' "We're in contact; the LZ is hot, the LZ is hot," an excited voice suddenly blurted over the FM radio. As we touched down I could see grunts lying flat behind rotting trees and giant ant hills. To the northeast of the clearing a steady stream of tracers poured from the dense tree line of the jungle.

' "We've got automatic-weapons fire east side," the same excited voice said. "We're pinned down. Wagonwheel Six, can we get those ARA ships back in here?"

' "Affirmative, Blue Fox. Do you want just the east side hit?" Wagonwheel Six asked.

' "Roger, for now. We've got a heavy machine gun in the north-east corner and small-arms fire all along the east side," replied Blue Fox.

' "White flight is up," Stickney said, meaning all of the grunts were clear of the helicopters.

' "Lifting," the platoon leader replied. All four helicopters lifted off, still in diamond formation.

'A long stream of tracers arced up at White Two, the helicopter on the right point of the diamond. "We're taking a lot of fire," the aircraft commander of White Two said in a calm, matter-of-fact voice.

' "Green and red flights, go to a staggered trail formation. We've got room in the LZ to do it. It will give you better coverage," Wagonwheel Six said.

' "Blue Fox, this is Black Knight Six. Do you want your reserve platoon brought in?" asked the battalion commander, orbiting in the command-and-control helicopter. Normally the C&C helicopter would orbit high over the LZ. But because of the low clouds, it had to remain low-level, well off to one side of the battle.

' "If we can get that heavy gun knocked out, I think we'll be okay," Blue Fox replied.

'"Blue Fox, this is Hog One; we're starting our run now," the ARA flight leader said. "We've got enough fuel for about two runs apiece," he added.

'"Okay, concentrate on the north-east side," said Blue Fox.

'White Flight made a left 180-degree turn and I could see the next flight of helicopters lifting from the landing zone. Streams of tracers continued to pour from the dense foliage on the east side.

'The first ARA ship was just pulling up after its rocket attack on the heavy machine gun. As the helicopter broke to the right, I saw a flash of fire from the right rocket pod. Smoke trailed from the pod and the flames were getting bigger. "We've got a pod on fire and I can't jettison it," said the pilot of Hog One. "I'm going to put down on the LZ."

'The ARA ship continued in a right turn. The last flight of slicks was just lifting off as the burning ship rolled out level and approached the landing zone. Suddenly, the flaming rocket pod exploded. The helicopter rolled violently to the left. A large piece of rotor blade broke off as the ship went inverted. Losing forward momentum, it plummeted straight down.

' "We've bought it," the pilot of Hog One said just before the ship hit the ground. It lay partially on the LZ, its broken tailboom sticking out of the heavy jungle growth. The whole aircraft was in flames. Several soldiers ran in a low crouch toward the wreckage. They were still being fired at from the tree line. "I'm going to land", said the pilot of the other ARA ship.

' "Negative; stay on station. We've got people on the ground that will get the crew out," said the battalion commander.

' "Black Knight Six, three of the crew are dead. The fourth one was thrown clear but he's hurt real bad," said Blue Fox.

' "Okay, we'll get Dust Off in there to get him out," replied Black Knight. "Also, I'm going to send your reserves in. Wagonwheel Six, pick up the ready reaction force at 'Oasis' and assault them into the same landing zone," he added.

' "Roger," said Wagonwheel Six.

' "We can't get a medevac right now; they're all busy." Black Knight said a

Below: On 16 October 1965 members of Co A, 1/5th Cavalry, conduct one of the division's first patrols in the sweltering heat and lush vegetation that was so typical of operations in South Vietnam.

Above: With a bottle of 'bug juice' and C-ration matches tucked into his helmet band, a squad leader points to an enemy position during a search and destroy mission conducted by the aerorifle platoon of Troop B, 1/9th Cavalry, west of Duc Pho in Quang Ngai Province during Operation 'Oregon' on 24 April 1967. Attached to the AN/PRC-25 radio of the RTO in the foreground are M-18 smoke grenades to mark friendly positions to tactical air support aircraft.

Left: A CH-47 Chinook medium-lift helicopter of the 228th Assault Helicopter Bn is loaded with ammunition crates at Camp Holloway near Pleiku that served as a forward supply point for the 1st Air Cav during Christmas 1965.

minute later. "Wheel Six, can you send one of your ships in to get that crewman out?"

' "Affirmative, sir. Green Four, break out of formation and do the medevac. Keep both gunships with you," said Wagonwheel Six.

'Green Four broke from the formation and made a left turn back into the landing zone. The two gunships continued to make firing runs on the east side of the clearing. The remaining ARA ship had knocked out the heavy machine gun and was returning to "Oasis" with its fuel critically low.

'We returned to Landing Zone "Oasis" and picked up the ready reaction force. We air-assaulted them into the same LZ, this time receiving very little ground fire.'

THE YEAR OF THE HORSE

The 1st Cavalry Division returned to its original base of operations at An Khe on Highway 19. Soon the intelligence section recommended a return to the Western Highlands early in 1966 in the hope of encountering the enemy reassembling in the unpopulated jungles. However, a new threat emerged in the Province of Binh Dinh, a region of abrupt mountains and populated coastal plains. The ARVN 22nd Division responsible for the area was spread thin as it tried to keep Highway 19 open and secure. The intelligence staff of the 1st Cavalry Division (Airmobile) confirmed that the Vietcong Main Force 2nd Regiment and 18th and 19th NVA Regiments of the 'Sao Vang' Division were operating in the area.

All the elements of a fire mission are shown in these four photographs. First (**Far Left**), the M-3 armament subsystem of a gunship of Bty A, 2nd Bn, 20th Artillery Regt, is reloaded prior to a mission.

Although the 2.75-inch FFAR (Free Flight Aerial Rocket) was deemed to be an area weapon, the pilots of 2/20th Aerial Rocket Artillery were so adept that they were able to place the 24 rockets from a pod accurately within close proximity to friendly troops to engage the enemy who commonly got as near as possible to US troops to negate the effects of fire support. As well as the rockets, the 'Hogs' were also armed with M-60D machine guns

Next (**Left**), with a 'Prick 25' on his back, an RTO of Bravo Troop, 1/9th Cavalry, directs the 'Hog' gunship to a target. (The three action photos were taken during Operation 'Pershing', a search and destroy mission in the An Lao Valley, on 28 July 1967.)

The 'Blues' of Bravo Troop take cover (**Below Left** and **Below**) as the gunship makes a firing pass at the target.

Operation 'Masher'/'White Wing' began on 25 January 1966, following the truce for the Tet holiday and Lunar New Year. These were the codenames for the operations to be launched in Binh Dinh Province by the 3rd Brigade, which began to move by road and air to staging posts in the eastern part of the province. The opening phase of the mission included 1st and 2nd Battalions, 12th Cavalry and 1st Squadron, 9th Cavalry which reconnoitred ahead of the convoy and along both sides of the road, searching for potential ambushes.

The first phase of Operation 'Masher' began on 28 January. The 3rd Brigade attacked north of Bong San from LZ Dog and quickly ran into heavy NVA resistance. However, in the first two days of February, contact with the enemy fell away as the North Vietnamese withdrew to the north and west. In the first week of combat, 1st Cavalry Division (Airmobile) lost 77 troopers while enemy losses amounted to an estimated 1,350 KIA, rendering two battalions of the 22nd NVA Regiment ineffective.

On 7 February, Operation 'White Wing' initiated the second phase of the search and destroy mission. Nine days later, on 16 February, the battle-weary 3rd Brigade returned to the division's home base of An Khe and was replaced in the field by the 1st Brigade. While 1st Brigade patrolled in the valleys around LZ Bird, the 1st and 2nd Battalions, 5th Cavalry, and 2nd Battalion, 12th Cavalry, of the 2nd Brigade encircled the Iron Triangle. With air and artillery support, the three battalions fought for four days against a tenacious enemy defence which finally collapsed after a B-52 strike.

The final phase of 'White Wing' began on 1 March with a move into the jungle-covered Cay Giep Mountains. B-52s blasted openings in the thick jungle canopy, enabling engineer teams to descend from helicopters to clear out landing zones for the 2nd Brigade. Sweeping down the slopes of the Cay Giep Mountains, the 2nd Brigade met little resistance as the main body of the NVA's 6th and 18th Battalions had pulled back immediately after the first air assault. Operation 'Masher'/'White Wing' came to an end on 6 March. By all tactical measures it was pronounced a success, having destroyed the enemy's grip on Binh Dinh Province. Once again the 1st Cavalry Division (Airmobile) had successfully combined mobility and air power. Helicopters airlifted entire infantry battalions a total of 78 times and moved artillery batteries 55 times. In 41 days of enemy

Left: A White Team of OH-6A Loaches flies low and slow, showing how dangerous the aeroscout role was when enemy groundfire could be expected at any moment. Aeroscout pilots and crew chiefs gained an uncanny sense to uncover enemy positions and then expose them to the full panoply of divisional firepower.

Below Left: A trooper is lowered into a suspected VC tunnel complex as the aerolift platoon of Bravo Troop, 1/9th Cavalry, takes part in Operation 'Oregon' on 24 April 1967.

Below: Troops search a house on 6 October 1966 during Operation 'Irving' in the area of Qui Nhon where two battalions of NVA regulars were believed to be massing for an attack on Hammond airstrip

Above: Lines of 1st Air Cav helicopters undergo maintenance on the Golf Course at the base camp at An Khe on 16 March 1966.

contact, the Air Cav engaged all three regiments of the Sao Vang Division and rendered five of its nine battalions ineffective for combat.

On 16 May, Operation 'Crazy Horse', another search and destroy mission, was launched in the jungle hills between the Suoi Ca and Vinh Thanh valleys. Initial contact was made by Company B, 2nd Battalion, 8th Cavalry and soon the entire the 1st Brigade was involved in heavy fighting with a VC regiment in tall elephant grass and heavily canopied jungle. Once the enemy was surrounded, all available firepower was concentrated on the area. The enemy regiment was hit with artillery, aerial rockets, tactical air strikes by F-4 Phantoms and bombs from high-flying B-52s. Many of its troops were cut down in ambushes as they attempted to flee the devastation and a number of important documents, detailing the Viet Cong infrastructure in Binh Dinh, were discovered.

The aim of Operation 'Paul Revere II', launched on 2 August and concluded on 15 August, was to deny areas of rich rice fields to the famished Viet Cong. Significant contact with the enemy was made on 8 August at LZ Juliett, where Company A, 1st Battalion, 7th Cavalry, came under heavy fire from a reinforced enemy battalion. In several hours of fierce fighting, Alpha Company drove off successive mass attacks. Timely artillery and air strikes prevented the enemy from surrounding the Skytroopers and the roar of helicopters arriving at LZ Juliett forced them to flee.

At the end of 'Paul Revere II', which resulted in a total of 861 enemy KIA, a task force of 2nd Battalion, 7th Cavalry, was committed to Operation 'Byrd' and despatched to Binh Thau Province, in the southern sector of II Corps, to support the Revolutionary Development Program. The heavily populated province of Binh Thau was effectively controlled by two Viet Cong battalions. The South Vietnamese government's writ ran to little more than the provincial capital, Pham Thiet, a coastal town whose economy depended on fishing and associated industries. In the previous 16 months, the 2nd Battalion, 7th Cavalry had fanned out from Phan Thiet, clearing the enemy from the populous triangle area extending to the north and west of the provincial capital and reopening the road net closed by the Viet Cong. Most significantly, the troopers reopened Highway 1, restoring the commercial link between Phan Thiet and Saigon.

One of the largest air assaults launched by the 1st Cavalry Division (Airmobile), Operation 'Thayer I', started on 13 September. Its aim was to clear Binh Dinh Province once more of NVA and VC troops and to destroy the political infrastructure of the Viet Cong. On 16 September, troops of the 1st Brigade discovered an enemy regimental hospital, a factory for making grenades, antipersonnel mines and a variety of weapons. Three days later, elements of 2nd Battalion, 8th Cavalry, exchanged fire with two NVA combat support companies.

In the opening phases of Operation 'Thayer I', elements of the 7th and 8th Battalions, 18th NVA Regiment, had been reported in the village of Hoa Hoi. The 1st Battalion, 12th Cavalry was deployed to encircle the village, and on 2 October, Company B was the first unit to be landed, some 330yd (300m) east of Hoa Hoi. It immediately came under intense small arms and mortar fire. Company A landed to the southwest to begin a move on Hoa Hoi, while Company C landed north of the village to strike south. By this time Alpha and Bravo Companies had joined up to establish positions which prevented the enemy slipping out of Hoa Hoi under cover of darkness.

During the course of the evening, Alpha and Charlie Companies of the 1st Battalion, 5th Cavalry Regiment, were airlifted into an area east of Hoa Hoi to further contain the enemy. Artillery forward observers from Battery A, 2nd Battalion, 19th Artillery, provided further assistance as enemy positions were identified and called in during the night. On the morning of 3 October, Company C, 1st Battalion, 12th Cavalry, and Company C, 1st Battalion, 5th Cavalry, attacked south to drive the remaining enemy forces towards Alpha and Bravo Companies, 1st Battalion 12th Cavalry, which were braced in strong blocking positions to receive the attack. This last action broke the enemy's resistance and the mission was completed. The pacification drive in Binh Dinh Province was stepped up with Operation 'Thayer II'. On 1 November troopers of Apache Troop, 1st Squadron, 9th Cavalry, and elements of the 5th Battalion, 7th Cavalry, were drawn into a sharp fight with Viet Cong forces in the vicinity of National Route 1 and south of the Cay Giep mountains. In Operation 'Thayer II' the enemy suffered heavy losses of 1,757 KIA.

As 1966 drew to a close, a two-day Christmas truce was observed. On 27 December, three battalions from the 22nd NVA Regiment exploited the truce to move from their usual haunts in the Hoai Nhon Delta into position for a surprise attack on LZ Bird. Three

Below: 1st Cavalry Division (Airmobile) area of operations 1965–6.

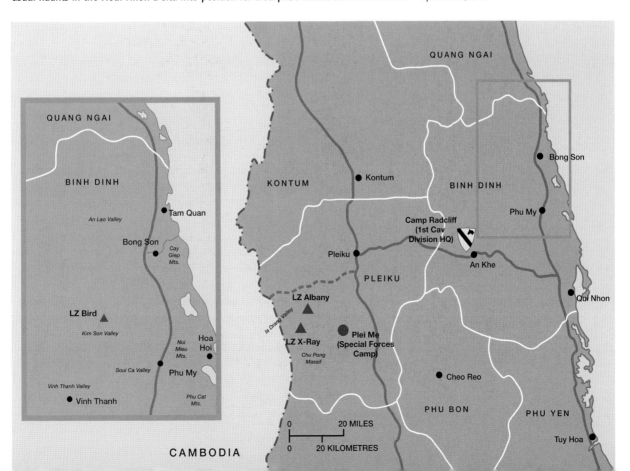

enemy units mounted a fierce infantry and mortar attack at Landing Zone Bird in the Kim Song Valley. The LZ was defended by just three understrength units: C Company, 1st Battalion, 12th Cavalry, and two artillery batteries, Battery B, 2nd Battalion, 19th Artillery and Battery B, 6th Battalion, 16th Artillery. However, the LZ was within the artillery range of two other fire support batteries. Initially, bad weather restricted air support operations and the NVA broke through the perimeter to occupy a number of gun positions. Hand-to-hand fighting ensued until some of artillery's 105mm howitzers were cranked down to pointblank range to pour 'beehive rounds into the enemy, taking a heavy toll.

For the next two days, troopers of the 1st Cavalry Division (Airmobile) pursued the fleeing NVA and made contact several times. At least 266 NVA died in this battle, in which many ARA and armed C-47 'Puff the Magic Dragon' sorties were flown. SSgt Delbert Jennings, C/2/12th Cavalry, earned the Medal of Honor for his valour in this action and went on to become the Command Sergeant Major of the 1st Cavalry Division

Below: The gun crew of the 6th Gun Section, Battery C, 1/77th Artillery, fire their M-101 105mm Light Howitzer (Towed) against VC targets in the Bong Son District during Operation 'White Wing' on 19 February 1966.

Right: One of the prime roles of the CH-47 Chinook was the creation of fire support bases to support the manoeuvre battalions in the field. The CH-47B was able to lift an M-102 105mm howitzer externally with 60 rounds of ammunition slung below and the seven-man crew carried inside the helicopter. By these means, the gun crew were ready to fire within minutes of landing while the Chinooks returned with more ammunition and ground troops to defend the newly established fire base.

in 1983. For their part in the fighting of 27 December 1966, Company C, 12th Cavalry, was awarded a Presidential Citation. Shortly afterwards the site of LZ Bird was deemed too vulnerable, and a new LZ was built on a hogback several miles to the east.

SEARCH AND DESTROY

On 13 February 1967, Operation 'Pershing' was launched in the Bong Son Plain in northern Binh Dinh Province, territory familiar to many Skytroopers. For the first time, 1st Cavalry Division committed all three of its brigades to a single battle area. ARVN troops who were familiar with Viet Cong tactics in the Bong Son Plain helped the Skytroopers to locate and eliminate the many caves and tunnels built by the enemy. For nearly a year, 1st Cavalry Division (Airmobile) scoured the Bong Son Plain, An Lo Valley and the hills of coastal II Corps Tactical Zone, seeking out enemy units and their sanctuaries. Operation 'Pershing' became a tedious and unglamorous 11-month mission which resulted in 18 major engagements and many minor skirmishes. It came to an end

Above: A battery of M-102 105mm Light Howitzers (Towed) of 2nd Bn, 19th Artillery, perches on a hilltop to provide fire support to ground troops of the 1st Air Cav during Operation 'Crazy Horse' on 15 May 1966. The M-102 weighed 3,298lb—as against 4,466lb for the earlier M-101—and was capable of firing three rounds a minute out to a range of 12,576 yards.

Above: The gun crew of an M-114A1 155mm Medium Howitzer (Towed) reposition their artillery piece at Fire Support Base Grant in October 1969. It is mounted on a 'speedjack' that allowed the rapid traverse of the weapon which weighed 12,950lb. The M-114A1 was the heaviest weapon in the Divisional Artillery so much fire support was provided by the helicopter gunships of the Aerial Rocket Artillery.

on 21 January 1968 and was the longest of the First Cav's actions in Vietnam. It accounted for 5,401 enemy soldiers killed and 2,400 captured. In addition some 1,300 individual and 137 crew weapons were destroyed.

Moving to I Corps. Vietnam's northernmost tactical zone, the division established its base at Camp Evans. On 31 January 1968, amid the celebrations of the Vietnamese New Year, the enemy launched the Tet Offensive, a major effort to overrun South Vietnam. Some 7,000 well-equipped and experienced NVA regulars blasted their way into the imperial city of Hue, overpowering all but a few pockets of resistance held by ARVN troops and US Marines. Within 24 hours, the invaders were joined by a similar number of reinforcements, while to the north of Hue five North Vietnamese and Viet Cong battalions attacked Quang Tri City, the capital of South Vietnam's northern province.

The Cavalry's immediate response was to despatch four companies of Skytroopers from the 1st Battalions of, respectively, 5th and 12th Cavalry Regiments to the village of Thorn An Thai, east of Quang Tri. Under heavy rocket attack, the enemy quickly broke off the assault on Quang Tri, split up into small groups and attempted to escape. Quang Tri was liberated within ten days.

After fierce fighting at Thorn La Chu, the 3rd Brigade moved on the embattled city of Hue. The southwest wall of the city was quickly taken after the 1st Battalion, 7th Cavalry, overcame fierce enemy resistance to link up with the 5th Battalion. By late February, the invaders were driven from Hue and the Tet Offensive was over. With some 32,000 killed and 5,800 captured, the Viet Cong and NVA had suffered a massive defeat.

After the Tet Offensive, the 1st Cavalry Division (Airmobile) embarked on Operation 'Pegasus' to relieve the 3,500 US Marines and 2,100 ARVN soldiers besieged at Khe Sanh by an enemy force of some 20,000 men. On 1 April 1968, the 3rd Brigade made a massive air assault within five miles of Khe Sanh Combat Base, followed by 1st and 2nd Brigades and three ARVN battalions. Company A, 2nd Battalion, 7th Cavalry, led the way, followed by Company C, 2nd Battalion, 7th Cavalry. After four days of hard fighting, they marched into Khe Sanh and assumed the defence of the battered base. Pursuing the retreating North Vietnamese, 1st Battalion, 12th Cavalry, recaptured the Special Forces camp at Lang Vei, uncovering large stockpiles of supplies and ammunition. In Operation 'Pegasus', 1,259 enemy soldiers were killed and more than 750 weapons were captured.

On April 19 1968, Operation 'Delaware' was launched into the cloud-shrouded A Shau Valley, near the Laotian border and 28 miles (45km) west of Hue. None of the Free World forces had been in the valley since 1966 which was now being used as a way station on the supply route known as the Ho Chi Minh Trail (see map on page 33). The first engagements were made by the 1st and 3rd Brigades. Under fire from mobile 37mm cannon and 0.50-calibre machine guns, they secured several landing zones. For the next month the brigades scoured the valley floor, clashing with enemy units and uncovering huge enemy caches of food, arms, ammunition, rockets and Russian-made tanks and bulldozers. By the time that Operation 'Delaware' was ended on 17 May, the Viet Cong sanctuary was thoroughly disrupted.

At the end of June, the 3rd Squadron, 5th Cavalry (Armored) of the 9th Infantry Division was assigned to support the Skytroopers during Operation 'Jeb Stuart III'. Operating under the tactical control of the 2nd Brigade, 1st Cavalry Division (Airmobile), it was given the mission of securing the Wunder Beach complex and the access road to Highway I, near Camp Evans in Quang Tri Province. At 0900 hours on 27 June, Troop C,

3rd Squadron, 5th Cavalry (Armored) came under rocket-propelled grenade (RPG) fire as it was undertaking a detailed search of an area known as the 'Street Without Joy'.

Anticipating the onset of heavy fighting, the inhabitants of the nearby coastal village of Binh An, began to flee the area. An NVA soldier, hiding in the column of refugees, was captured and interrogated. He revealed that the entire 814th NVA Infantry Battalion was in the village. A and B Troops of the 3rd Squadron, 5th Cavalry, along with D Troop, 1st Squadron, 9th Cavalry, closed on the village, joining C Troop, 3/5th Cavalry, and trapping the enemy within a cordon of overwhelming firepower in clear daylight and good weather conditions.

Besides Division Artillery, fire support was supplemented by Marine artillery fire from Quang Tri, Tactical Air Control (TAC) aircraft from Da Nang and the five-inch guns of a US Navy destroyer. The NVA battalion in Binah An was subjected to a seven-hour pounding. During the afternoon, Company D, 1st Battalion, 5th Cavalry and Company C, 2nd Battalion, 5th Cavalry were airlifted into an adjacent LZ and closed on the village. To deny the enemy the opportunity to infiltrate their lines under the cover of darkness, it was decided to overrun the enemy positions during the night. The guided missile cruiser, USS

Below: The ground crew rearm an AH-1G Cobra gunship with 2.75-inch FFAR and 7.62mm ammunition for the XM-28 Armament Subsystem. This weapon system comprised either two 'miniguns' or two XM-129 40mm grenade launchers or one of each.

Right: Drinking water was a precious commodity in the field and there was never enough for washing so troops took every opportunity to wash themselves and their sweaty uniforms when they encountered a river.

Below: 1Lt James Graham, the Executive Officer of Co C, 2nd Bn, 12th Cavalry, distributes mail during Operation 'Thayer I' on 19 September 1966. Mail was and will always be vital to the morale of troops in the field and it was one of most important items delivered by resupply helicopters.

Left: Aircraft maintenance was a constant task to keep the helicopter fleet of the 1st Air Cav aloft. Here, SP4 Auburn Lemon Jr repairs an ammunition linker of a UH-1C 'red ship' of B Troop, 1/9th Cavalry.

Below: Sgt George Nemosbatho, a mortar platoon squad leader of 1/12th Cavalry, takes a break with a drink of fresh coconut milk in the village of Troun Lan, Binh Dinh Province, during Operation 'Pershing' on 9 June 1967.

Average Monthly Combat Stores	
Ammunition	4,609 tons
Fuel	4,010,700 gallons
Defence stores	749 tons
Clothing and equipment	1,082 tons
Foodstuffs	1,005 tons
Rations	597,311 meals
Milk	944,780 pints
Ice cream	11,430 pints
Ice	2,777 tons

Boston, arrived at dusk and in an all-night bombardment her basic load of eight-inch shells was exhausted. It was an appalling night for the enemy troops trapped within the tight cordon. Disorganised, some of the survivors attempted individual escapes and were soon rounded up by tanks mounting searchlights and two US Navy 'Swift' patrol boats operating close to the shoreline. At 0930 hours on the following morning, a final assault was made on the enemy. In the after battle assessment, 253 of the 814th NVA Infantry Battalion were KIA and 44 were taken prisoners while the 5th Cavalry suffered only three casualties.

In late 1968, the Division moved southwards and set up operations in III Corps Tactical Zone with Divisional Headquarters at Phuoc Vinh. The Air Cav assumed a tactical area of responsibility embracing four provinces: Phuoc Long, Binh Long, Tay Ninh and Binh Duong. The beginning of 1969 found the First Cavalry Division (Airmobile) and ARVN forces engaged in Operation 'Toan Thang II'. During the first three weeks of the operation, the Skytroopers uncovered one of the largest caches of munitions found in the Vietnam War.

In February 1969, Operation 'Cheyenne Sabre' was launched with the aim of straddling and cutting enemy infiltration routes to the northeast of Bien Hoa. The rest of the summer was relative calm — until the night of 12 August when the VC unleashed simultaneous attacks against Quan Lai, LZ Becky, LZ Jon, LZ Kelly and LZ Caldwell. The VC assaults were repulsed suffering heavy losses as they fled in retreat. In the final months of 1969, the 'First Team' blocked enemy infiltration along the roads, trails and narrow paths of the Serges Jungle Highway which was hidden beneath the canopy of heavy jungle growth. The year 1969 ended on a high note for the 1st Cavalry Division: the enemy's domination of the northern areas of III Corps had been decisively smashed.

On 1 May 1970, the 'First Team' spearheaded the incursion into Cambodia striking what was previously an inviolable Communist sanctuary. Pushing through the 'Fish Hook' region of the border area, 1st Air Cav occupied the towns of Mimot and Snoul, scattering the enemy forces and depriving them of large quantities of supplies and ammunition. On 8 May, the Skytroopers of the 2nd Brigade found an enemy munitions base that they dubbed 'Rock Island East'.

Ending on 30 June, the incursion into Cambodia far exceeded all expectations and proved to be one of the most successful operations conducted by the 'First Team'. All aspects of ground and air combat elements were utilised to the full. The enemy lost enough men to field three NVA divisions and weapons to equip two. A year's supply of rice and corn was seized. The Skytroopers and ARVN forces discovered huge quantities of ammunition, including 1.5 millions small arms rounds, 200,000 anti-aircraft rounds and 143,000 rockets, mortar rounds and recoilless rifle rounds as well as 300 trucks.

The campaign had severe political repercussions in the United States for the Nixon Administration. Domestic pressure was mounting to remove America's fighting men from the war in Vietnam. Although there would be further combat assault operations, the conflict was beginning to wind down for many US Army units.

VIETNAMISATION

In July 1970, the 1st Cavalry Division continued the task of clearing NVA combat elements from the region of III Corps Tactical Zone, to the north, east and west of Saigon, an immense area of approximately 4,500 square miles. In addition, the process of Vietnamisation accelerated with many Skytroopers devoted to the task of passing the bulk of the ground fighting to the ARVN forces. As other US Army units departed from

Above Right: An AH-1G Cobra gunship rolls into the attack during the incursion into Cambodia of 1970 with the terrain feature in the background marking the border with Vietnam. The narrow profile of the Cobra as compared as compared to the UH-1B/C/M models made it a more difficult target to hit and the VC/NVA showed great respect for what they termed the 'skinny helicopter'.

Right: A Red Team of AH-1G Cobra gunships resplendent with fearsome shark mouth markings conducts another fire-support mission during the incursion into Cambodia in May 1970.

Vietnam, some of their equipment passed to the Air Cav. In particular, the First of the Ninth received a significant infusion of Loaches to augment its strength; many of these were fitted with miniguns to give them an offensive capability. In October 1970, this force was augmented by the attachment of the 3rd Squadron, 17th Cavalry, to the division, together with other elements such as the Rangers of Company H, 75th Infantry, to form a provisional Air Cavalry Combat Brigade, as had been originally been recommended by the Howze Board.

Above: A CH-47A Chinook of Co B, 228th Assault Support Helicopter Bn, comes to the hover to pick up another slung load of 105mm ammunition for the guns of 2/19th Artillery firing in support of ground elements of the 1st Air Cav during Operation 'Thayer I' on 28 September 1966.

The 9th Air Cavalry Brigade (Combat) was officially authorised on 5 December 1970 with the mission of supporting ARVN units on an area basis. In February, the brigade supported an ARVN operation in Cambodia but the Vietnamese lacked the flexibility and military skills to conduct swift moving airmobile combat assaults. Accordingly, with no American troops fighting on the ground, the brigade never realised its full potentiality and it was gradually allowed to wither on the vine.

Although 26 March 1971 officially marked the end of operations in Vietnam for the 1st Cavalry Division (Airmobile), President Nixon's programme of Vietnamisation required the continued presence of a strong US fighting force. The 2/5th Cavalry, 1/7th Cavalry, 2/8th Cavalry and 1/12th Cavalry along with specialised support units such as Troop F, 9th Cavalry, and Delta Company, 229th Assault Helicopter Battalion remained in Vietnam to become the 3rd Brigade, 1st Cavalry Division (Separate) with its headquarters at Bien Hoa and an assigned strength of 7,632 men. Subsequently known as Task Force Garry Owen, its primary mission was to interdict enemy infiltration and supply routes in War Zone D, encompassing some 3,500 square miles. On 5 May 1971, the colours of the 1st Cavalry Division (Airmobile), except those of the 3rd Brigade, were furled in Vietnam and flown to Fort Hood, Texas. Meanwhile, the 3rd Brigade (Separate) was now defending the Saigon/Long Binh US military complex and acting as a regional ready reaction force.

On 1 April 1972, the North Vietnamese Army began a major offensive across the DMZ and from the Fishhook area of Cambodia. By 3 April, these thrusts became a full-scale attack. More than 48,000 NVA troops hit Loc Ninh. Two days later, on 5 April, the North Vietnamese threw heavy assaults against An Loc and the brigade's air assets were heavily involved in containing the onslaught. In April and May, massive bombing missions by B-52s blunted the North Vietnamese invasion. Large groups of enemy soldiers were caught in the open fields and entire NVA units were destroyed. Helicopters and gunships from the 3rd Brigade saw heavy action at An Loc and Loc Ninh, engaging tanks as well as ground troops.

On 15 May, relief units advanced down Highway 13 and broke through to help lift the bitter siege of An Loc. The NVA was reeling after suffering huge losses and began to withdraw to sanctuaries in Cambodia and Laos. The 1972 Easter offensive aimed at cutting South Vietnam in half had failed. The helicopter air effort of the 3rd Brigade had turned in a magnificent performance in support of the remaining advisors with the ARVN units. During the period from 5 April through to 15 May 1972, numerous T-54 tanks, armoured personnel carriers and anti-aircraft guns were knocked out in the area around An Loc.

In June 1972, the stand-down ceremony for the 3rd Brigade (Separate) was held in Bein Hoa and its colours were returned to the United States. The last Skytrooper left Tan Son Nhut Airbase on 21 June, completing the division withdrawal that had started on 5 May 1971. With the departure of the 3rd Brigade, the 1st Cavalry Division (Airmobile) had been the first US Army division to be deployed to Vietnam and was the last to leave.

Above: Purple Haze – a radioman of Bravo Troop, 1/9th Cavalry, sets off a smoke grenade to mark a pick up zone for a Huey to extract his aerorifle team after an operation. The blue scarf was an obvious unofficial item worn by the 'Blues' of the 1/9th.

Right: Sgt William Patterson, the squad leader of 1st Pl, Co D, 1/8th Cavalry, and SP4 Hugh Shipp, an artillery FOO, search a well in the village of Mi Duc on 9 August 1967. Note the standard yellow divisional patch worn at this date while the soldier on the right has the subdued patch on his left shoulder but the full colour insignia of the 82nd Airborne Division on his right, indicating an earlier combat tour. In the background is an M-42A1 'Duster' twin 40mm anti-aircraft gun used in the ground-support role.

INSIGNIA, CLOTHING & EQUIPMENT

Above: Being 10in shorter and 1.5lb lighter than the M-16, the XM-177E2 or Colt Commando was favoured by specialised troops such as this K-9 dog handler with his German Shepherd preparing to move out on an operation.

UNIFORMS

Trooper, 1st Cavalry Division (Airmobile), 1970 (right)

The US armed forces in Vietnam were well equipped for jungle warfare with improvements in weapons and clothing being introduced throughout the conflict. Beside his personal weapon, the most important item was the Tropical Combat Uniform as worn by this Air Cavalry Trooper depicted during the Cambodian incursion of 1970. From top to bottom, he wears an M-1 helmet with reversible camouflage cover although by this stage of the war individual additions such as beads and a 'peace medallion' were commonplace to accompany the cigarette pack and insect-repellent 'bug juice' bottle in the helmet band. Around his neck is the chinstrap of his soft 'boonie hat' that sits atop his heavily laden rucksack. This type is the nylon Tropical Rucksack that was based on the ARVN model with an X-frame but of larger dimensions with a third external pocket. It was introduced for US troops in late 1968. The rucksack has attachment points for other pieces of equipment including a one-quart water canteen and the Lightweight Entrenching Tool in its M-1967 nylon carrier. Tucked into the top flap of the rucksack is a 66mm M-72 Light Anti-Tank Weapon or LAW. This one-shot disposable weapon was highly effective against enemy bunker systems. The Tropical Rucksack is suspended from the M-1967 Modernized Load Carrying Equipment or MLCE that was essentially identical to the previous M-1956 web gear but with nylon substituted for canvas and plastic for metal fittings. These allowed quicker drying and were unaffected by the mildew prevalent in Vietnam. Here, two M-1967 ammunition

From top to bottom: First, a 1st Air Cav badge with hanger manufactured by the Vietnamese and sold to the Skytroopers in the shops around camp. Next a cavalry flash; third, a belt buckle also manufactured locally by the Vietnamese.

pouches as well as two M-26 fragmentation grenades are attached to the web equipment belt fitted with a quick-release 'Davis' buckle. Below his belt is a cotton bandolier holding seven 20-round M-16 ammunition magazines, although experienced soldiers invariably loaded only 18 or 19 rounds into each clip to minimise the risk of jamming. In his right hand is an M-1942 machete and in his left an XM-177 or CAR-15 (Colt Automatic Rifle). This was a shorter and lighter version of the M-16 assault rifle. On the left shoulder of the tropical coat is the subdued sleeve insignia of the 1st Cavalry Division (Airmobile). The trouser cargo pockets are typically full of gear and are bound around the lower leg with bootlaces to prevent snagging on foliage. The tropical combat boots are the improved 1966 version with the 'Panama' pattern tread to prevent the build-up of mud between the cleats and with a spike-resistant insole to defeat punji sticks.

Pilot, 227th Aviation Battalion (Assault Helicopter), 1970 (right)

The integral aviation assets and their personnel were the key to the success of the 1st Cavalry Division (Airmobile) in Vietnam. There was a constant shortage of pilots and aircrew to serve the thousands of aircraft in Southeast Asia. At the height of US involvement, in March 1970, there were 3,926 US Army helicopters in South Vietnam. As early as January 1966, lack of aviators was threatening the entire viability of airmobility in Vietnam. Officer pilots were withdrawn from US Army and US Marine Corps formations across the world for service in Vietnam and veterans of the conflict were returned on further tours of duty with increasing regularity. Helicopter qualification courses were shortened but, even so, by June 1966 there were still only 9,700 pilots as against an Army requirement of 14,300. By now, the US Army's aviation school at Fort Rucker was working at full pitch to produce as many officer pilots as possible for immediate deployment to Vietnam. As in World War 2, the solution to the problem lay in allowing other ranks to become aviators, drawing on a generation of young and daring warrant officers that proved to be ideally suited to flying in the dangerous and demanding environment of South East Asia alongside commissioned pilots. Between 1961 and 1973, a total of 1,045 Army aviators was killed on flying duties in Vietnam. The most common type of aviation unit was the Assault Helicopter Company or AHC. When not flying, the most common form of headgear was the baseball utility cap obtained locally in theatre complete with embroidered captain's bars and aviator's wings. Introduced in 1969, the Shirt and Trousers, Flying, Hot Weather Fire Resistant was manufactured from 4.4oz Nomex synthetic material. The shirt featured two chest pockets and a pen pocket on the upper left sleeve. The trousers had two large thigh pockets for maps and both the wrists and ankles incorporated Velcro fastenings to enhance fire resistance. All flight crews were advised to avoid any form of nylon clothing as such garments could melt into the flesh in the event of fire. Accordingly, flight personnel were instructed to fly with their sleeves rolled down and hands protected by Nomex flying gloves. Similarly, tropical combat boots were eschewed as they were reinforced with nylon. Instead, most crewmen wore leather boots for increased fire protection. Subdued rank and branch collar insignia are worn on the shirt as are US Army and name tapes as well as the wings of an Army aviator. On the upper left arm is the oversize Shoulder Sleeve Insignia in US Subdued Twill of the 1st Cavalry Division (Airmobile). On the right chest pocket is the unit insignia of Company B, 227th Aviation Battalion (Assault Helicopter). The cowboy-style leather belt and holster for the .45-inch automatic pistol is a typical affectation of aviation personnel. This Vietnamese-made example features bullet loops on the belt, a twin magazine pouch at the rear and an additional one on the holster itself.

Far Left: An Air Cav trooper braces himself against the rotor downwash of a UH-1H as it takes off from an LZ northeast of Fire Support Base Gladiator during May 1971.

Above Left: With the Ranger flash and divisional patch prominent on his shoulder, Capt William E. Taylor communicates by radio to the C&C helicopter circling overhead. The standard radio for ground troops was the PRC-25, known to troops as the 'Prick 25'.

Left: Crew chief SP4 James M. Ralph refuels his UH-1D of Co A, 229th Helicopter Assault

Bn, on 14 March 1966. The helicopters of the helicopter assault battalions came under the centralised control of the 11th Aviation Group within the 1st Air Cav.

Above: PFC Roger D. Goon of Co A, 2nd Bn, 12th Cavalry Regt, takes a swig of water during a patrol from Camp Evans in January 1968. The Air Cav often carried less equipment and ammunition than standard line infantry as they could rely on rapid resupply by their own helicopter units. Even so, this rifleman carries a belt of 7.62mm ammunition for the squad M-60 machine gun.

DUST OFF – AEROMEDICAL EVACUATION

Although the helicopter was used extensively during the Korean War, the Vietnam War will forever be remembered as the helicopter war and the single machine that epitomised that more than any other was the Bell Iroquois UH-1. This remarkable aircraft was the first helicopter to be produced in large numbers that featured a gas-turbine engine. This compact and efficient powerplant was the technological breakthrough that allowed the helicopter to come of age. Design of the new helicopter began in 1955 under the designation H-40 which became the HU-1 or Helicopter Utility from which the nickname of Huey derived. The first flight of the new aircraft powered by a Lycoming T-53 engine took place in October 1956. Although classified as a utility helicopter, one of the main design parameters was for the helicopter to be able to accommodate four standard stretchers across the width of the hull for the aeromedical evacuation role. In previous designs, patients were carried in external pods that afforded little protection from the elements and did not allow any medical attention to be administered beyond a plasma drip bottle. The Bell Model 204 provided sufficient space for the stretchers as well as a medical corpsman to provide in flight emergency treatment besides the two pilots and crewchief. Production of the UH-1, as it was finally designated by the US Army, began in 1959 with the first model delivered on 30 June 1959. In its standard configuration, the UH-1A was capable of lifting two crewmen and seven passengers.

The first Huey helicopters were deployed to Vietnam in April 1962 with the arrival of the 57th Medical Detachment (Helicopter Ambulance) comprising five UH-1A helicopters in support of the 8th Field Hospital at Nha Trang. These were replaced by five UH-1Bs in March 1963 with flights spread across South Vietnam. Shortly afterwards, the 57th adopted the radio call sign 'Dust Off' that has become synonymous with aeromedical evacuation units ever since. On its arrival in September 1965, the 1st Cavalry Division (Airmobile) incorporated an air ambulance platoon. As part of the division's 15th Medical

Below: Wounded troopers of Company C, 2nd Bn, 8th Cavalry, are evacuated by a UH-1D Huey of the Air Ambulance Platoon, callsign 'Medevac', 15th Medical Bn on 5 November 1965 at the outset of the Pleiku Campaign.

Battalion, this comprised 12 UH-1D Hueys with a medical evacuation section of eight helicopters and a crash rescue section of four. Three of the latter were equipped with Kaman 'Sputnik' fire-suppression systems to enable firefighters to enter burning aircraft. However, the extra equipment so overloaded the firefighting Hueys in the hot and humid conditions of Vietnam that the system had to be abandoned and the helicopters reverted to standard helicopter ambulances.

The platoon adopted the call sign 'Medevac' and was soon heavily involved in the battle of the Ia Drang valley. With casualties averaging between 70 and 80 wounded a day, the 'Medevac' helicopters were hard pressed to meet such a commitment and, on occasions, troop lift Hueys were employed to carry the less seriously injured from the fireswept landing zones. In the first three months of operations the platoon lost two pilots killed,[1] one flight crewman wounded and nine Hueys hit by enemy fire with one shot down and destroyed on 10 October.

The fundamental purpose of the helicopter ambulance was to bring the combat casualty from the battlefield to the operating table in the shortest possible time. The seriously injured were taken directly from the field to a base hospital, often bypassing the battalion aid and clearing stations.

Dustoff crews flew some of the most hazardous combat missions of the war in their unarmed helicopters. Medical evacuation missions were received either at the divisional base at An Khe, at a stand-by area close to a particular formation conducting an operation or even in flight. Precise information had to be given to the 'Medevac' crew to effect evacuation such as co-ordinates of location, nature and number of casualties and the tactical security of the Pickup Zone. Casualties were either classified as 'urgent', 'priority' or 'routine'. 'Urgent' demanded immediate response from any helicopter ambulance in order to save life or limb, while 'priority' were those casualties who had serious but not critical wounds and were likely to remain stable for up to four hours. In practice many casualties were understandably overclassified as 'urgent'. Similarly, the security of the Pickup Zone was often exaggerated by ground units anxious to evacuate their casualties.

Once the casualties were loaded aboard, the medical corpsman identified the most serious patient, applied first aid as appropriate and reported the nature of his wounds to the aircraft commander. He in turn radioed the local medical regulating officer, who advised him of the nearest hospital with the necessary surgical capability to deal with the condition. Since most pickups were made within range of a surgical, field or evacuation

Above: Hanging on to the helicopter hoist, the crewchief of a UH-1H ambulance guides his pilot into a jungle clearing to effect an medevac.

Notes

1 Captain Charles F. Kane Jr. on 12 October 1965 and WO George W. Rice on 18 December 1965. Both were killed by single shots to the head while loading casualties in contested LZs prompting the fitting of extra armour protection to the pilots' seats of the air ambulance UH-1Ds. An additional 28 members of the Air Ambulance Platoon were killed during the Vietnam War undertaking aeromedical evacuation missions in support of the 1st Cavalry Division (Airmobile).

Above: The aeromedical evacuation helicopters of the 'Dustoff' units were a significant morale booster to the troops fighting a protracted and frustrating war against a determined enemy that rarely stood and fought except at times and places of his own choosing and when he enjoyed a local tactical advantage. Too often, troopers were injured by devious and devastating booby traps resulting in dreadful blast injuries. Whatever the cause, the casualty was assured that a dustoff helicopter would arrive as soon as humanly possible and fly him directly to hospital.

hospital, the air ambulance often flew directly to whatever facility offered the best medical care. Although the less seriously injured were sometimes evacuated too far back, the practice saved the lives of the critically wounded who required immediate life-saving surgery. By these means some 97.5% of the wounded who were airlifted from the combat zone survived their wounds. On average, the elapsed time between being injured and surgery was an hour and 40 minutes as compared to ten hours during World War 2. More than 900,000 US and allied sick and injured were evacuated between 1964 and 1973. Helicopters on aeromedical evacuation missions were three times more likely to be shot down than on all other types of flights combined. Almost a third of the 1,400 pilots that flew dustoff missions in Vietnam were killed or wounded due to hostile fire or accidents. The courage and fortitude of the 'Medevac' flight crews made an immeasurable contribution to troop morale as every trooper knew that if he was wounded he would soon be picked up by an air ambulance whatever the conditions.

DISTRIBUTION OF HELICOPTERS

The 428 authorised helicopters of the 1st Air Cavalry Division (Airmobile) were distributed as follows:

- The three infantry brigades each had eight LOHs and two UH-1Bs.
- The Air Cavalry Squadron had 30 LOHs, 38 UH-1B gunships and 20 UH-1Ds.
- Division Artillery had 12 LOHs and 43 UH-1Bs, including 36 rocket-firing Hueys and three UH-1Bs in the ARA battalion.
- The Aviation Group comprised two Aviation Battalions (Assault Helicopter). Each battalion had three LOHs and was divided into three lift companies of 20 UH-1Ds each and an armed helicopter company of 12 UH-1B gunships.
- The Aviation Battalion (Assault Support Helicopter) had 48 CH-47 Chinooks divided into three companies with 16 in each and three LOHs.
- The General Support Company had 16 UH-1Ds and 10 LOHs.
- The Support Command incorporated the Medical Battalion with 12 UH-1Ds and the two Maintenance Battalions had eight LOHs and eight UH-1Ds between them.
- From 1967, the OH-13 LOHs were replaced by OH-6A Loaches and, from 1968, the UH-1B/C gunships were superseded by AH-1G Cobra attack helicopters. All UH-1D Hueys were progressively replaced by the improved 'Hotel' model. During 1966, helicopter availability averaged 68% for Hueys, 63% for Skycranes and 43% for Chinooks reflecting the harsh operating conditions in Vietnam.

Below: UH-1D 'slicks' of the 229th Assault Helicopter Battalion lift off after inserting troopers of the 1st Air Cav. The term 'slick' was given to troop lift helicopters as distinct from the gunships that were festooned with gun and rocket pods giving rise to a host of other nicknames such as 'Hogs'.

Left: A UH-1D of Co B, 229th Assault Helicopter Bn, lifts off after dropping off supplies for Co A, 1st Bn, 7th Cavalry, during Operation 'Pershing' on 27 May 1967.

Opposite, Above: The Hughes OH-6A Cayuse was the most successful light observation helicopter of the Vietnam War. Named the Cayuse, the OH-6A was commonly known as the Loach. In White Teams of two, the Loaches scoured the countryside at low level searching for any signs of the enemy. In the 1st Air Cav, Loaches served with the 1st Sqn, 9th Cavalry, and initiated most of the division's contacts with the enemy.

Opposite, Below: UH-1D Hueys of Bravo Troop, 1/9th Cavalry, flare as they land to pick up members of the 'Blues' from the aerorifle platoon during Operation 'Pershing' on 28 May 1967, some 30 miles (50km) northeast of the divisional base camp at An Khe.

Below: A CH-54A 'Skycrane' of the 478th Aviation Co lowers a badly damaged CH-47 on to the Golf Course. The drogue parachute attached to the Chinook stabilised the underslung load in flight and prevented it from rotating. During the war, the Skycrane retrieved hundreds of aircraft valued at over $200 million.

Above: Sgt Edward A. Shelby sets the fuse of a 106mm recoilless rifle 'Beehive' round held by SP4 Melvin R. Munoz on 31 January 1967. The XM-581 anti-personnel round contained thousands of 'flechettes', small 2¼-inch arrow-like projectiles, that spread out on firing to create a devastating cone of steel against troops in the open. On Boxing Day 1966, the 22nd NVA Regiment attacked Firebase Bird held by some 100 1st Air Cav troops protecting two artillery batteries. The position was almost overrun by the NVA when the defenders responded with 'Beehive' rounds that slaughtered the attackers in their tracks. Although the Air Cav suffered significant casualties, the NVA lost 266 KIA and Firebase Bird was saved from destruction.

Right: A classic image of a Huey door gunner in action as crew chief SP4 James M. Ralph of Co A, 229th Assault Helicopter Bn, engages the enemy with his M-60D machine gun during a combat air assault on 16 March 1966.

Right: The principal weapon of the OH-6A Loach was the M-27 Armament Subsystem comprising an M-134 GAU-2B/A 7.62mm minigun with a phenomenal rate of fire – either 2,000 or 4,000 rounds per minute with an effective range of 1,000 yards. 2,000 rounds of ammunition were commonly carried inside the helicopter.

Below: An 81mm mortar crew engages the enemy in support of a 1st Air Cav operation in the Bong Son District on 19 February 1966. The 'Eighty One' was the standard infantry mortar throughout the Vietnam War and was integral to every infantry company. With a range of up to three miles, it was an area weapon with a rapid fire capability of 25 rounds a minute.

M-16 versus AK-47

The 1st Air Cav was the first major US Army formation to be equipped with the M-16 assault rifle. Indeed, the weapon was so new that much of the initial training with the rifle took place on the ships sailing for Vietnam. The M-16 was designed by Eugene Stoner of the Armalite Corporation. In 1954, the company was asked to produce a survival rifle for pilots of the US Air Force who were shot down – to kill small game for food rather than defending themselves against attack. Although the AR-5 (Armalite Five) proved perfectly effective, the USAF did not procure it in quantity although it was adopted by Special Forces units for clandestine operations in .22in Long Rifle calibre. Stoner continued development of his innovative lightweight designs combined with the advent of the 5.56mm (.223in) Fireball cartridge resulting in the Armalite AR-15. The first customer to buy the new rifle in quantity was the British Army followed by the US Air Force in 1961 as the M-16. Two years later the US Army chose the design as its new standard infantry rifle. Production was undertaken by the Colt Firearms Company and the M-16 entered widespread service with the US Army in 1965 although Special Forces units in SE Asia procured the new weapon earlier. During acceptance trials, the M-16 proved to be highly accurate and reliable with formidable wound ballistics. The weapon proved so efficient that troops were told that it was unnecessary even to clean it. With its black plastic furniture, the M-16 was significantly lighter than its 7.62mm predecessor, the M-14, and more ammunition could be carried for the same basic load. However, once in combat in Vietnam alarming faults arose. The M-16 often suffered stoppages and jamming in combat resulting in the deaths of combat infantrymen. This provoked a scandal in Congress and a subsequent investigation soon discovered the root cause. During trials, the 5.56mm cartridge used was commercial ammunition with a propellant known as IMR or Improved Military Rifle. Once full-scale manufacture began, a different propellant known as ball powder was used that caused a sticky residue after firing that on cooling could cause the bolt head to jam solid. A modification programme was quickly implemented together with a cleaning kit for the troops in the field and the resulting weapon was designated the M-16A1. Thereafter it gave satisfactory service for the remainder of the Vietnam War.

Calibre: 5.56mm (.223in)
Length: 990mm (38.98in)
Weight: 3.64kg (8.02lb)
Magazine: 20 or 30-round box
Cyclic rate of fire: 700 rpm
Muzzle velocity: 1,000m (3,280ft) /sec

Conversely, the weapon of choice of the Viet Cong and the North Vietnamese Army suffered no such difficulties in the field. The legendary AK-47 assault rifle, named after its inventor Mikail Kalashnikov, has proved to be one of the most widespread and successful personal weapons in military history. Much of the design is borrowed from the German Sturmgewehr 44 assault rifle and the 7.92mm kurz (short) round of World War 2. Easy to mass-produce with few moving parts for maximum reliability, the AK-47 is a rugged and robust weapon that can absorb much hard use with the minimum of maintenance and training by the operator. Accordingly, it was the ideal rifle for a guerrilla army in the hostile environment of Vietnam where weapons had frequently to be secreted underground or even underwater for long periods. Although the Viet Cong were often equipped with the 7.62mm SKS rifle or captured French and American weapons, the NVA used both the AK-47 and the Chinese derivative, the Type 56, in huge numbers. Firing the 7.62mm x 39 cartridge, the round combines high lethality and hitting power at the typical combat ranges encountered in Vietnam of under 300yd (275m), frequently less than 100 (90m).

Calibre: 7.62mm (0.3in)
Length: 869mm (34.21in)
Weight: 5.13kg (11.31lb)
Magazine: 30-round box
Cyclic rate of fire: 600rpm
Muzzle velocity: 710m (2,330ft) /sec

Above Right: A member of Co B, 5/7th Cavalry, demonstrates the telescopic stock of the CAR-15 or XM-177E2 version of the M-16 assault rifle. Popular with Special Forces – hence its name of Colt Commando – the CAR-15 was rarely issued to line infantry in Vietnam except for elite units such as the 1st Air Cav. Despite being more compact inside helicopters, the CAR-15 provided no great advantage over the standard M-16 to Sky Soldiers and it was not adopted in quantity.

Right: Rock and Roll – a trooper fires his M-16 assault rifle which has an XM-148 grenade launcher mounted underneath. This is an early model of the rifle/grenade launcher combination which was subsequently standardised as the M-203.

RPG-7 versus LAW

Although the VC/NVA were highly adept in their use of mortars and free-flight rockets, their principal infantry support weapons were the 75mm recoilless rifle and the RPG-7 rocket launcher. The 75mm recoilless rifle was mounted on a two-wheel carriage to provide a more stable and, therefore, more accurate firing platform. Because of its distinctive backblast, mortar sights were often attached to the weapon to allow indirect fire against US positions and firebases up to a maximum range of 2,000yd (1,830m). Although designed as an anti-tank weapon and derived from the German Panzerfaust of World War 2, the RPG-2 and RPG-7 were also used in the indirect role as surrogate artillery pieces. In the direct role, the RPG-7 fired a five-pound B-41 fin-stabilised rocket with an accurate range of 500yd (460m) and an area capability out to 1,000yd (920m). Both weapons were capable of knocking out APCs and bunkers and were also highly effective against helicopters, many of which were lost to RPGs. Tank and APC crews quickly learned to counter the RPG by erecting chain-link fencing as 'RPG Screens' around their vehicles when stationary to disrupt the warhead prior to its striking the AFV. No such measures could be taken to protect a hovering helicopter or one on short finals into a hot LZ.

At the outset, the Americans had no equivalent to the RPG although some units still used the old M-20 3.5in Bazooka and the M-79 40mm grenade launcher fulfilled part of the same role. Accordingly, the M-72 Light Anti-armour Weapon or LAW was developed. The 66mm warhead was housed in a telescopic tube housing that was extended prior to firing. As the launcher was opened, simple flip-up sights appeared and the trigger mechanism was primed. Once the rocket had been fired at the target, the launcher was discarded and another LAW was primed to continue the action. Weighing just 5.5lb (2.5kg), the LAW was accurate out to 300yd (275m) and capable of penetrating 6in (152mm) of armour or destroying a bunker system. In comparison, the RPG-7 weighed 18.7lb (8.5kg) with its attached 4.4lb (2kg) warhead. The principal difference was that the RPG could be reloaded whereas the LAW was a one-shot disposable weapon but then US forces in Vietnam could call on heavier firepower when necessary as this account by an Air Cav trooper affirms.

Private Mark M. Smith of 1st Battalion, 5th Cavalry served with the 1st Cavalry Division (Airmobile) between February 1967 and February 1968 and was on an operation in Binh Dinh Province.

'On patrol in August, my platoon found a dud butterfly bomb and determined to blow it up in place. We spent 20 frustrating minutes without managing to set it off, using hand grenades – pull the pin and run like hell for cover – and well aimed shots with M-79s. Finally one of the grenadiers, who had fired at it five or six times was fed up and snapped. "Fuck the motherfucker – call a B-52 strike in on it!" That was always the solution – wipe things out. Run into an enemy scout, call in the gunships; meet an enemy patrol, send for the fighter-bombers; take a burst of sniper fire, radio the howitzers.

'When I achieved a position of real responsibility in Nam, platoon sergeant and platoon leader, I always told the new guys as they came to the field: "Forget everything they taught you except how to use your weapons, and follow your squad leaders." What this indicated, of course, is not that the training was that awful but that in actual combat nothing goes according to the book. Everything is hellishly confused, you can't remember hand and arm signals, you haven't the time to yell out formations, so you just yell, "Let's go, let's go! This way, let's go!" and hope your people come along.'

Nevertheless, in a typical firefight, the weapons of an infantry squad from NVA or Viet Cong Main Force units were on a par with their American counterparts

Opposite, Above: The 1st Air Cav were pioneers in the use of night vision equipment. This soldier has an AN/TVS-2 starlight scope mounted on his M-16 – allowing targets to be acquired at night out to a distance of 100 yards depending on weather.

Opposite, Below: PFC James Darwin checks out the M-134 'minigun' on the M-21 Armament Subsystem of a 'Gunfighter' UH-1B of the aeroweapons platoon, Bravo Troop, 1/9th Cavalry prior to a mission. The M-21 comprised a combination of a 'minigun' and an M-158 seven-tube 2.75-inch rocket pod.

Left: A UH-1B of the 'Red Scorpions', the aeroweapons platoon of Apache Troop, 1/9th Cavalry, completes hot refuelling during an operation on 28 May 1968.

PEOPLE

GENERAL HAMILTON H. HOWZE

Hamilton Hawkins Howze was born in West Point, New York, on 21 December 1908. The son of Maj Gen Robert L. Howze (who served under Theodore Roosevelt and his 'Rough Riders'), he attended the US Military Academy at West Point and graduated in the class of 1930, commissioned in the Cavalry.

Howze saw action in numerous European campaigns during World War 2. He earned his Army Aviator wings in 1955. He is recognised as the intellectual force behind the concept of airmobility and current Army Aviation doctrine.

While serving as the first Director of Army Aviation, Department of the Army, from 1955 to 1958, he developed new tactical principles for the employment of Army Aviation, and was instrumental in helping the Aviation Center and School become fully established in its new home at Fort Rucker, Alabama.

As Chairman of the Tactical Mobility Requirements Board in 1961, he cited the need for the development of airmobile theory and doctrine. The army's adoption of the Howze Board recommendations revolutionised mobile warfare concepts based on the use of organic aviation in much the same manner as the introduction of the tank affected mobility concepts almost 50 years earlier.

The 11th Air Assault Division (Test) was formed in 1963 to test and validate these concepts. As a result of his leadership, foresight, and perception, two airmobile divisions were eventually established in the army force structure. These divisions successfully provided the full spectrum of mobile, combined arms capabilities which are requisite to successful ground combat and which have become fundamental to modern airmobility doctrine. Later, General (then Lt Gen) Howze served as the Commander of the XVIII Airborne Corps. His last assignment was as Commander-in-Chief, US Forces Korea.

LT GEN JOHN L. TOLSON III

Colonel (later Lt Gen) John J. Tolson became actively involved with Army Aviation in 1953 while serving as Chief, Doctrine and Combat Developments, G3, Headquarters, Department of the Army. At that time he initiated the first study dealing with the tactical application of Air Cavalry. From this assignment, he moved to Fort Benning, where he was the Director, Airborne-Army Aviation Department, Infantry School, from 1955 to 1956.

During his tenure, he completed the development of initial aviation doctrine and subsequently published the first field manual governing the tactical employment of Army Transport Aviation on the battlefield. This work was validated in Vietnam and remains a basic reference for the tactical employment of Army Aviation.

In 1957, Tolson completed Fixed & Rotary Wing Qualification at Fort Rucker, and subsequently served for two years as the Assistant Commandant of the Aviation School. This was a very formative period in the School, particularly in the developing of armed helicopter concepts and the formation of the provisional air cavalry unit, the 7292nd Aerial Combat Reconnaissance Company (Provisional).

Studies by the School's Combat Developments Office produced concepts for the Air Cavalry Division. Also, lasting innovations in pilot and mechanic training were initiated during this period. From 1959 until 1961 Col Tolson served as Deputy Director of Army Aviation. It was during this period that he participated in key decisions in consolidating the family of Army aircraft for future development which later became the workhorses of the Vietnam Conflict. From April 1967 to July 1968 he served as Commanding General, 1st Cavalry Division (Airmobile), Vietnam. General Tolson subsequently became Deputy Commanding General, Continental Army Command.

Above: Lt Gen John L. Tolson III.

LT GEN HARRY W. KINNARD

Lt Gen Harry Kinnard was born in Texas and graduated from West Point in 1939. He joined the 101st Airborne Division and was the G-3 Operations Officer to Brig Gen Tony McAuliffe at the siege of Bastogne during the Battle of the Bulge. It was Kinnard who suggested that Gen McAuliffe should respond to the German demand for surrender with the single word – 'Nuts'. Kinnard became a full colonel at the age of 29 and was a seasoned authority in airborne operations before he became an Army Aviator in 1962. In the following year, he was appointed as the commanding officer of the 11th Air Assault Division (Test) to explore the concept of airmobility. Under his expert guidance, he established the feasibility of airmobility during exercises against his former unit — the 82nd Airborne Division. Using many of the assets of the 11th Air Assault Division (Test), he formed the 1st Cavalry Division (Airmobile) and within 90 days took this radically new formation into combat. Under his leadership, highly innovative techniques and ideas, such as aerial rocket artillery and night vision equipment, were refined and used to devastating effect against the enemy in Vietnam. During his year of command, the 1st Cavalry Division (Airmobile) proved its worth repeatedly and he sought to extend airmobility doctrine in his subsequent appointment as Commander US Army Combat Development Command. Ironically, Kinnard had displayed the merits of airmobility to General William Westmoreland in Vietnam but the latter was now the Chief of Staff and seemed to forget the lessons of the past. Westmoreland ordered the 1st Air Cavalry (Division) to become a Triple Capability or TRICAP division, a configuration that proved unworkable and the 'First Team's' experience as the exemplar of airmobility was lost.

Below: Lt Gen Harry W. Kinnard.

COL HAROLD G. MOORE

The word 'hero' is a much debased term through overuse and inappropriate application but for Col Hal Moore it is utterly appropriate. Born on 13 February 1922, Moore was not academically gifted and his time at West Point was a constant trial except on the rifle range where he proved to be an outstanding marksman with the M-1 rifle. After graduation in 1945, he joined the 187th Airborne Regiment and then tested parachutes at Fort Bragg, North Carolina, where on his first jump, his parachute got caught in the tailplane of a C-46 and he was dragged behind the plane at 110mph at a height of

Above: Colonel Harold G. Moore.

Right: Lt Col John 'Bullwhip' Stockton.

STOCKTON   U.S. ARI

1,500ft (460m) until he cut himself free and deployed his reserve. From June 1952, he served in the Korean War and saw heavy action at Pork Chop Hill and elsewhere. After a posting to the Pentagon in the Air Mobility Division, he was personally chosen by Brig Gen Kinnard to serve as a battalion commander in the 1st Cavalry Division (Airmobile). He was given Col George Custer's old command of the 1st Battalion, 7th Cavalry with whom he won undying fame during the battle of the Ia Drang Valley. As the first Skytrooper to place a foot on LZ X-Ray, he was also the last to leave. He was soon promoted to full colonel and took command of the 3rd Brigade of the 1st Cavalry Division (Airmobile). He subsequently commanded the 7th Division and ended his military career as Deputy Chief of Staff Personnel, retiring in 1977 after 32 years of service. Despite his undistinguished tenure at West Point, Hal Moore was the first in his class to achieve one, two, and three stars. He was a true warrior.

LT COL JOHN B. STOCKTON

Lt Col John 'Bullwhip' Stockton was one of the outstanding cavalrymen of the Vietnam War and as such commanded the elite First of the Ninth on the deployment of the 1st Cavalry Division (Airmobile) to South Vietnam. Previously, as the commander of 3/17th Cavalry at Fort Benning in Georgia, Stockton adopted the Stetson hat based on the 1876 pattern campaign hat as the 'Cav hat' to instil esprit de corps in his troops. In addition, he favoured colourful silk cravats – the 'Cav scarf' – and decreed that his officers carry their orders in cavalry saddlebags. All these affectations were carried over to the 1st Cavalry Division (Airmobile) when the 3/17th Cavalry became 1/9th Cavalry and they subsequently spread throughout the air cavalry units in Vietnam. Through his brilliant leadership, the First of the Ninth became the premier air cavalry squadron of the Vietnam War (see separate box) and Stockton was the inspiration for the character of Colonel Kilgore played by Robert Duvall in the movie *Apocalypse Now*.

COMMANDING GENERALS VIETNAM		COMMAND SERGEANTS MAJOR VIETNAM	
Commander	**Date**	**Sergeant Major**	**Date**
Maj Gen Harry W. O. Kinnard	July 1965–May 1966	CSM Chester R. Westervelt	July 1965–June 1966
Maj Gen John Norton	May 1966–Mar 1967	CSM Kenneth W. Cooper	June 1966–June 1967
Maj Gen John J. Tolson	Mar 1967–Aug 1968	CSM William O. Marshall	June 1967–May 1968
Brig Gen Richard L. Irby	Aug 1968–Aug 1968	CSM Jack B. Moore	May 1968–Oct 1968
Maj Gen George T. Forsythe	Aug 1968–Apr 1969	CSM Vern O. Peters	Oct 1968–Dec 1969
Maj Gen E. B. Roberts	May 1969–May 1970	CSM Lawrence E. Kennedy	Jan 1970–May 1971
Maj Gen George W. Casey	May 1970–July 1970	CSM Arnold E. Orr	May 1971–Jan 1972
Maj Gen George W. Putnam	Aug 1970–May 1971	CSM William Corn	Jan 1972–July 1973
Maj Gen James C. Smith	May 1971–Jan 1973		
Maj Gen Robert M. Shoemaker	Jan 1973–Feb 1975		

MEDAL OF HONOR RECIPIENTS VIETNAM

Capt Ed W. Freeman	A Co, 229th Assault Bn	14 November 1965
2Lt Walter J. Marm	A Co, 1/7th Cavalry Reg	14 November 1965
SSgt Jimmy G. Stewart	B Co, 1-12th Cavalry Reg	18 May 1966
Sgt David C. Dolby	B Co, 1/8th Cavalry Reg	21 May 1966
PFC Billy L. Lauffer	C Co, 2/5th Cavalry Reg	21 September 1966
PFC Lewis Albanese	B Co, 5/7th Cavalry Reg	1 December 1966
SSgt Delbert O. Jennings	C Co, 1/12th Cavalry Reg	27 December 1966
PFC James H. Monroe	C Co, 1/8th Cavalry Reg	16 February 1967
Sp5 Charles C. Hagemeister	A Co, 1/5th Cavalry Reg	20 March 1967
Sp4 George A. Ingalls	A Co, 2/5th Cavalry Reg	16 April 1967
Sp5 Edgar L. McWethy, Jr.	B Co, 1/5th Cavalry Reg	21 June 1967
Sp4 Carmel B. Harvey, Jr	B Co, 1/5th Cavalry Reg	21 June 1967
Sgt Allen J. Lynch	D Co, 1/12th Cavalry Reg	15 December 1967
Sgt William D. Port	C Co, 5/7th Cavalry Reg	12 January 1968
CW2 Frederick E. Ferguson	C Co, 227th Aviation Bn	31 January 1968
Capt James M. Sprayberry	D Co, 5/7th Cavalry Reg	25 April 1968
1Lt Douglas B. Fournet	B Co, 1/7th Cavalry Reg	4 May 1968
Sp4 Hector Santiago Colon	B Co, 5/7th Cavalry Reg	28 June 1968
Sgt John N. Holcomb	D Co, 2/7th Cavalry Reg	3 December 1968
SP4 Donald R. Johnston	D Co, 1/8th Cavalry Reg	21 March 1969
1Lt Robert L. Poxon	B Trp, 1/9th Cavalry Reg	2 June 1969
Sgt Rodney J. Evans	D Co, 1/12th Cavalry Reg	18 July 1969
Sgt Donald S. Skidgel	D Co, 1/9th Cavalry Reg	14 September 1969
2Lt Robert R. Leisy	B Co, 1/8th Cavalry Reg	2 December 1969
Sp4 John P. Baca	D Co, 1/12th Cavalry Reg	10 February 1970
Sgt Peter C. Lemon	E Co, 2/8th Cavalry Reg	1 April 1970
Capt Jon E. Swanson	B Trp, 1/9th Cavalry Reg	26 February 1971

ASSESSMENT

Right: Cav Country – Principal battle areas of 1st Cavalry Division (Airmobile) from 1965 to 1971.

Most of the original units of the 1st Cavalry Division were raised in the 19th century for service in the Indian wars where they fought possibly the finest light cavalry since the Golden Horde. Whether through superior firepower or starvation, they prevailed in the harshest circumstances and a tradition of fortitude was born. In the Vietnam War, the troopers of the 1st Cavalry Division (Airmobile) fought possibly the finest light infantry of the 20th century, usually on battlefields of the enemy's own choosing. Again they prevailed, although at a high cost in men and matériel. Even though many observers dismissed and despised these respective foes as savages or racially inferior 'gooks', they were redoubtable opponents and highly skilful soldiers. It is a testament to the troopers of the 1st Cavalry Division (Airmobile) that they succeeded so often and so comprehensively against such committed antagonists. The latter's martial skills had been honed over years of warfare whereas the average trooper did his 365 days and then went home: hopefully whole in mind and body. To the trooper in a Huey or a foxhole, the Viet Cong or North Vietnamese Army soldier was a formidable fighter and worthy of respect. Although subsumed in an odious communist regime, the VC/NVA fought for a nationalist cause by the creed of their enlistment 'Death or Victory'. The 'First Team' ensured that for many it was the former and that the latter only came at an awful price.

It is one of tragedies of the Vietnam War that to the political establishment and the military high command that there was no real measure of success on the battlefield other than the repugnant 'body count' that gave an utterly unreliable kill ratio of the enemy to American dead. It is not surprising that the American public could neither understand nor support such a pusillanimous strategy as the war dragged on without resolution. Nevertheless, what was totally unacceptable was the treatment meted out to many soldiers on their return from Vietnam. Ignored by government and vilified by fellow citizens in turn, they deserved better. They had followed the demands of their country to fight in a distant alien land for a culture and cause they did not understand but they did their duty. Many paid the ultimate sacrifice with their lives and more were cruelly mutilated and scarred. As the first complete division into Vietnam and the last to leave, the 1st Cavalry Division (Airmobile) endured 82 months of combat. During that time, over 150,000 troops served with the division. They suffered a total of 32,036 killed or wounded – 5,444 KIA; 26,592 WIA. That is half as many again as the combined casualties of World War 2 (4,055) and the Korean War (16,498). The Air Cav was the only US division to fight in all four Corps Tactical Zones. It also took part in the invasion of Cambodia in 1970.

Vietnam was no minor brushfire war and Johnson's strategy of 'guns and butter' without committing the Reserves or National Guard was deeply flawed. The regular US Army and Marine Corps were bled to death in the quagmire of Vietnam to be replaced by an inadequately trained and poorly led band of draftees with no corporate experience.

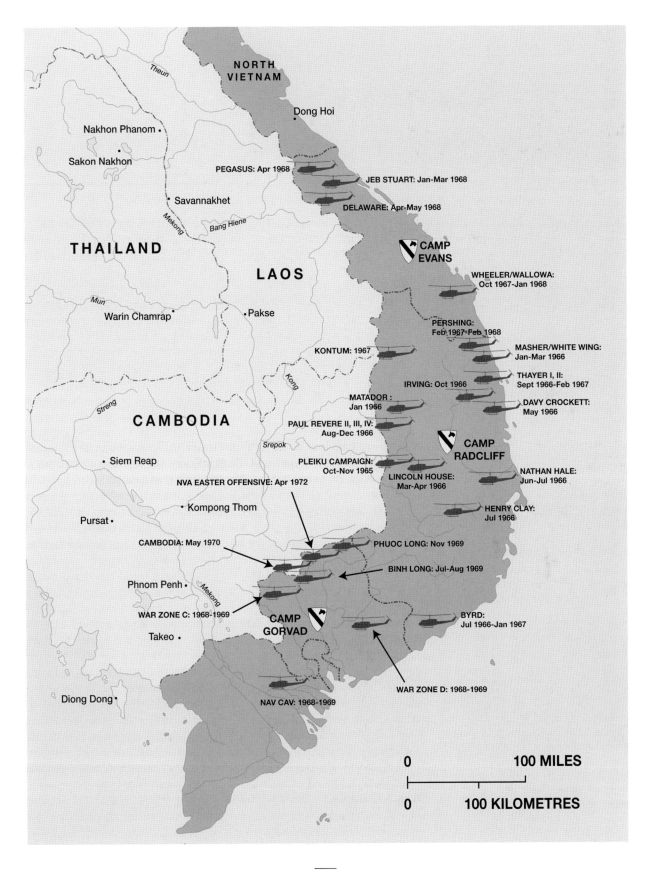

NORTH
VIETNAM

Dong Hoi

Nakhon Phanom •

Sakon Nakhon •

PEGASUS: Apr 1968

JEB STUART: Jan-Mar 1968

• Savannakhet

DELAWARE: Apr-May 1968

THAILAND

LAOS

CAMP
EVANS

WHEELER/WALLOWA:
Oct 1967-Jan 1968

Warin Chamrap •

• Pakse

PERSHING:
Feb 1967-Feb 1968

KONTUM: 1967

MASHER/WHITE WING:
Jan-Mar 1966

IRVING: Oct 1966

THAYER I, II:
Sept 1966-Feb 1967

MATADOR :
Jan 1966

DAVY CROCKETT:
May 1966

CAMBODIA

PAUL REVERE II, III, IV:
Aug-Dec 1966

CAMP
RADCLIFF

• Siem Reap

NVA EASTER OFFENSIVE: Apr 1972

PLEIKU CAMPAIGN:
Oct-Nov 1965

LINCOLN HOUSE:
Mar-Apr 1966

NATHAN HALE:
Jun-Jul 1966

• Kompong Thom

HENRY CLAY:
Jul 1966

Pursat •

CAMBODIA: May 1970

PHUOC LONG: Nov 1969

Phnom Penh •

BINH LONG: Jul-Aug 1969

WAR ZONE C: 1968-1969

CAMP
GORVAD

BYRD:
Jul 1966-Jan 1967

Takeo •

Diong Dong •

WAR ZONE D: 1968-1969

NAV CAV: 1968-1969

0   100 MILES

0   100 KILOMETRES

Above: When a Loach was combined with the gunships of a 'Red Team', it became a 'Pink Team' but later in the war it became known as a 'Hunter-Killer Team' with the Loach flying low while the gunships remained at altitude ready to sweep down on any targets directed by the Loach. The 'Blue Max' insignia on the 'doghouse' of these AH-1G Cobras identifies the 2/20th Aerial Rocket Artillery that supported the 1st Air Cav throughout the Vietnam War.

It has been said that the US Army did not fight in Vietnam for eight years but eight separate armies each fought for one year or 365 days: that magic number before DEROS and a return to 'The World'. It is all the more remarkable that some formations maintained their combat effectiveness and discipline to the end. Army units such as the 'Herd', the 173rd Airborne Brigade, and the 'First Team', the 1st Cavalry Division (Airmobile), displayed commendable professionalism with much less of the indiscipline, racial tension and accusations of atrocities that bedevilled some other formations. During its service in Vietnam, the division was awarded 27 Medals of Honor; 120 Distinguished Service Crosses; 2,766 Silver Stars; 2,697 Distinguished Flying Crosses; 8,408 Bronze Stars for Valor, 2,910 Air Medals for Valor and 5,328 Army Commendation Medals for Valor.

The concept of air mobility was conceived in an earlier Asian war. It came to fruition with the arrival the 1st Air Cavalry (Division) Airmobile in Vietnam in 1965 and in the words of the divisional history, *Memoirs First Team*, air mobility was fundamental to the success of Air Cav operations during the war: 'Perhaps this is the one message that comes across louder and clearer than all others. From the Ia Drang to the A Shau to War Zone C, the 1st Air Cav, successfully and repeatedly, changed its tactics and techniques to meet the challenges of terrain, weather and the enemy.

'It is this very adaptability – this inherent propensity for doing precisely the right thing at the right time by a finely-tuned combination of men and machines – that was has made the First Team a consistent winner.

'It has been said that the Pleiku Campaign was the triumph of the airmobile concept. In truth, every battle, every campaign, every year, has been the triumph of the concept.'

Left: The opposition – the Viet Cong with their Russian-supplied AK-47s and other munitions – proved tough opponents.

Below: The Bell Huey was the workhorse of airmobility operations in Vietnam flying hundreds of sorties a day. Here, troopers of Charlie Company of 2/8th Cavalry of 3rd Brigade (Separate) load supplies on to a Huey UH-1H during the final months of 1st Air Cav operations in the Vietnam War.

Far Left: A skytrooper of 1st Air Cav whose helmet shows he is a short-timer – he's counting off the days before DEROS: Date Eligible for Return from Overseas. Photo taken during Operation 'Pershing' in 1967.

Left: The majority of helicopter losses during the Vietnam War was due to flying accidents and mechanical failure. This Huey of the 11th Aviation Company (General Support) crashed on takeoff at the Golf Course at An Khe on 5 May 1967.

Below: A spectacular method of creating an instant LZ was by dropping a 10,000lb (4,500kg) M-121 bomb with an extended fuse to detonate it above ground level for maximum blast effect and minimum cratering – here a CH-54A of 478th Aviation Co carries an M-121.

Bottom: Blues of the Aerorifle Platoon of Bravo Troop, 1/9th Cavalry, disembark from their 'Blue Lift' UH-1H during a snatch operation on 13 October 1968.

POSTWAR

RETURN TO CONUS AND REORGANISATION

Despite its success during the Vietnam War, the future of the division in its airmobile configuration remained uncertain in early 1971. The former divisional commander, Lt Gen Harry Kinnard was now the head of the Army Combat Developments Command and he wished to expand the capabilities of airmobility with further testing of the Air Cavalry Combat Brigade as first espoused by the Howze Board. However, General William Westmoreland was now the Chief of Staff and, despite being won over to the concept of airmobility in Vietnam, he decreed otherwise. The division was now converted to a 'triple capability' or TRICAP formation comprising armour, airmobile and cavalry brigades that were essentially ground based. Now based at Fort Hood in Texas, the colours of the 1st Cavalry Division (TRICAP), minus those of the 3rd Brigade (Special) still in Vietnam, were transferred to the commander of the former 1st Armored Division under the command of Maj Gen James C. Smith. The division consisted of the 1st Armored Brigade, the 2nd Air Cavalry Combat Brigade and the 4th Airmobile Infantry Brigade as well as Division Artillery and Support Command.

Field trials of the new divisional configuration were held at Fort Hood beginning in February 1972. The purpose was to investigate the effectiveness of the TRICAP concept at company and battalion level in a European mid-intensity warfare environment. By the end of June 1972, the last of the units of the 3rd Brigade (Separate) had returned from Vietnam and several famous battalions and squadrons were inactivated. The Vietnam War was over for the 1st Cavalry Division (Airmobile). The evaluation of the TRICAP concept continued until 21 February 1975 when the 1st Cavalry Division was reorganised and reconfigured as an armoured division. During 1977, it evaluated the concept of the future 'heavy division' with additional support units.

In 1979, the 2nd Blackjack Brigade of the 1st Cavalry Division deployed to Europe by sea to undertake a major NATO Reforger or REturn of FORces to GERmany exercise in the defence of Western Europe against a Soviet invasion. In the following year, the same brigade conducted Operation 'Desert Horse' at Fort Irwin in California. The exercise lasted some six weeks and was the first time that the Multi Integrated Laser Engagement System or MILES was used on a major scale. In September 1980, the 2nd Battalion, 5th Cavalry Regiment was selected to field test the new XM-1 main battle tank that was named Abrams after General Creighton Abrams who succeeded General Westmoreland as the overall army commander in Vietnam.

Reforger exercises continued throughout the 1980s but on a reducing scale as the threat from the Warsaw Pact diminished. New equipment was absorbed such as the M-1 Abrams, the M-2 Bradley Infantry and M-3 Cavalry Fighting Vehicles as well as the MLRS (Multiple Launched Rocket System) and the AH-64 Apache attack helicopter. In addition, the HEMETT (Heavy Expanded Multi-purpose Tactical Truck) and the HMMWV (High Mobility Multi-purpose Wheeled Vehicle), better known as the Hummer, were

Left: An early production M-577 command vehicle is unloaded from a C-130 Hercules transport plane during a Reforger (Return of Forces to Germany) exercise in West Germany. During Exercise 'Reforger '83', 9,000 soldiers of the 1st Cavalry Division deployed to Holland, drew pre-positioned equipment and then moved to Germany where they conducted Exercise 'Certain Strike' on the North German Plains.

Below Left: The M-1 Abrams main battle tank entered service with the 1st Cavalry Division in 1980 and it remains the principal weapon system of the division to this day, albeit a much-enhanced uparmoured and upgunned model with the latest digital battle management equipment. The M-1 was named after General Creighton Abrams, the US Army commander in Vietnam, who was a great admirer of the First Air Cav and he once said, 'The big yellow patch does something to an individual that makes him a better soldier, a better team member, a better American than he otherwise would have been.'

introduced as was the equally important improvements in communications with the fielding of MSE (Mobile Subscriber Equipment) for secure voice and data transmission. This was augmented by SINGARS (Single Channel Ground to Air Communication System) which provides much enhanced security using frequency hopping technology. All this new equipment was assimilated by the division in large scale exercises at Fort Hood and at the National Training Center at Fort Irwin in the Mojave Desert. It was most opportune as the division received an order on 7 August 1990 for overseas deployment. The destination was Saudi Arabia following the Iraqi invasion of Kuwait five days before.

OPERATION 'DESERT SHIELD'/'DESERT SABER'

The personnel of 1st Cavalry Division flew to Dhahran on the shores of the Persian Gulf to await their equipment. Once it had arrived by sea, the division deployed to Assembly Area Horse some 160 miles westward where they acted as the principal counterattack force in the face of an Iraqi invasion of Saudi Arabia. After four months of intensive training in the desert, the 1st Cavalry Division was attached to VII US Corps for the coming offensive astride the Wadi al Batin. On 15 January 1991, a ferocious air assault was mounted against Iraq and its occupation forces in Kuwait. After a 38-day onslaught, the ground war was launched on 24 February. The mission of the 1st Cavalry Division was to conduct a feint attack up the Wadi al Batin as a diversion for the main attack by VII and XVIII Airborne Corps further westwards. Under a firestorm created by the MLRS of Battery A, 21st Field Artillery and the guns of the 3rd Battalion, 82nd Field Artillery, the 2nd 'Blackjack' Brigade advanced along the wadi ensnaring four Iraqi divisions as the main assault by VII Corps plunged into Iraq.

As the offensive developed, the 1st Cavalry Division struck the Iraqi 27th Infantry Division as well as elements of five other Iraqi divisions in an area that became known as the 'Ruqi Pocket'. By the afternoon of 27 February, the 1st Cavalry Division had advanced some 190 miles northeastwards slicing into the enemy's rear echelons. After 100 hours of combat, President George Bush ordered a ceasefire. The Iraqis had lost some 3,847 of their 4,280 tanks, over half of their 2,880 APCs and almost all of their 3,100 artillery pieces. It was a consummate victory but political considerations did not allow a hot pursuit to the capital Baghdad and the overthrow of Saddam Hussein. Over the coming years, elements of the 1st Cavalry Division were to return to Kuwait several times to conduct major desert exercises as a deterrent to further Iraqi aggression. Operation 'Vigilant Warrior' in 1994 was followed by Operation 'Vigilant Sentinel' in 1995 and Operation 'Intrinsic Action' in 1996 and 1997.

BOSNIAN PEACEKEEPERS

On its return from Kuwait to Fort Hood after the Gulf War, the 1st Cavalry Division was enlarged with the addition of the 3rd 'Greywolf' Battle Team and the Engineer Brigade to become the largest formation in the US Army. In November and December 1992, several of these new units were redesignated with famous historical titles of the 8th, 9th and 12th Cavalry Regiments. In its new configuration, the 1st Cavalry Division became the US Army's largest division and acted as a heavy armoured contingency force ready to deploy worldwide at short notice. It now comprised some 17,000 men and women with three manoeuvre brigades (Ironhorse, Blackjack, Greywolf), an aviation brigade (Warriors), an engineer brigade (Sappers), division artillery (Red Team) and division support command (Wagonmasters) plus an air defence battalion, a signal battalion, a military intelligence battalion and a military police company (Maverick).

Below: Among its many 'firsts', the First Team was the first division to field the M-2 Bradley Fighting Vehicle, the AH-64 Apache attack helicopter, the MLRS Multiple Launch Rocket System and the HMMWV Hummer. This model of the Bradley is the uparmoured M-2A2 that equipped the division just prior to the Gulf War of 1990/91.

On 16 April 1998, the 1st Cavalry Division was selected for peace support operations in Bosnia-Herzegovina to undertake the mission of 'Task Force Eagle'. After several months of intensive training, the 1st Cavalry Division under the command of Maj Gen Kevin P. Byrnes assumed authority of the Multi-National Division North from the 1st Armored Division – 'Old Ironsides'. The 1st Cavalry Division was the first to be deployed from the continental United States in a massive logistical operation as all previous units had come from Germany. The mission was to enforce the military provisions put forward by the Dayton Accords as part of Stabilization Force or SFOR 4 and 5. These were conducted by extensive patrolling in HUMVEEs and, occasionally, Bradley IFVs. At the same time, the Division Engineers cleared 80,000sq m of explosive ordnance and supervised the construction of $41m worth of base camp improvements. On 4 August 1999, the mission of Task Force Eagle was passed to the 10th Mountain Division with the last units of the 1st Cavalry Division returning to Fort Hood by 18 October.

Above: The UH-60 Black Hawk is the successor to the famous UH-1 Huey. In Bosnia, the Black Hawk was flown in support of the 1st Cavalry Division by the 3rd Battalion of the 229th Aviation Regiment, continuing a tradition that was forged over the jungles of South Vietnam, where the helicopter formation had its origins as Co C, the 'Widow Makers', of the 229th Assault Helicopter Bn. In Bosnia, the air assets of Task Force Eagle flew over 17,000 flying hours without mishap which represents one flying hour for every member of the 1st Cavalry Division.

OPERATION 'IRAQI FREEDOM'

The unfinished business of the First Gulf War was comprehensively rectified in March and April 2003 with the destruction of Saddam Hussein's odious regime. Between January and May 2004, the 1st Cavalry Division deployed to Iraq by air and sea to assume control of the Baghdad area with bases at Camp Victory North near the international airport as well as Camp Cooke, Camp Dragoon, Camp War Eagle, Camp Muleskinner and inside the 'Green Zone' headquarters enclave of the Coalition Forces. After leaving its Abrams MBTs at Fort Hood, it was now classified as a Light Motorized, Task Oriented, Cavalry Division and equipped with M-2 Bradley Fighting Vehicles, M-1114 armoured HUMVEEs and the M-1117 Guardian Armored Security Vehicle (ASV-150) to undertake its security mission in the capital and its environs.

With attached units from the Army National Guard, the 1st Cavalry Division assumed responsibility for the Baghdad area from the 1st Armored Division on 15 April 2004. From the outset, operations have been conducted against the al-Mahdi army militia based in the Shiite slums of Sadr City, formerly Saddam City. Repeated and relentless attacks against the 1st Cavalry Division have continued since its arrival in theatre resulting in a steady stream of casualties. Up to the time of the transfer of sovereignty to the interim Iraqi government on 28 June 2004, 49 members of the 1st Cavalry Division had been killed in action undertaking Operation 'Iraqi Freedom'. The price of freedom remains high.

REFERENCE

WEBSITES

www.rolling-thunder.org.uk

The premier UK reenactment group for the era (see above photograph).

www.first-team.us

This official website of the 1st Cavalry Division (Airmobile) is an outstanding source of information on the division from its earliest lineage to current operations in Iraq. It has extensive coverage of all aspects of the division's history from the order of battle to the words of the traditional marching song of the 7th Cavalry – the Garry Owen. This 'Spearhead' volume has drawn extensively from this website with the kind permission of the divisional historian, William Harry Boudreau, and Cavalry Outpost Publications.

Wm. Harry Boudreau is also the author of the current divisional history:

1st Cavalry Division – A Spur Ride Through The 20th Century, From Horses To The Digital Battlefield; Turner Publishing Company, Paducah K, 2002.

BIBLIOGRAPHY

The 1st Air Cavalry Division Vietnam Volume 1
August 1965 to December 1969
This highly illustrated 296-page volume was published by the division in 1970. It provides a general history of the division's activities during the time period stated but its real worth is in the accounts of the various units and sub-units within the division interspersed with some excellent photographs and illustrations.

The Vietnam Experience
Multi-part series by Boston Publishing Company.
This series of almost 40 volumes published during the 1980s is a comprehensive and authoritative history of the conflict covering virtually every aspect of the war. It is an outstanding source of reference.

Brennan, Matthew: *Brennan's War – Vietnam 1965-1969*; Presidio, 1985.
Matthew Brennan was one of those elite helicopter pilots that enlisted at an early age and had an extraordinary flying career in Vietnam where he made over 400 combat air assaults with the 'Headhunters' of the 9th Cavalry. This searing first-hand account gives a vivid impression of the war from the helicopter pilot's seat.
So does Matthew Brennan's subsequent volume *Hunter Killer Squadron – Vietnam 1965-1972* that is a collection of personal stories of the men that made up the elite formation – the 1st Squadron, 9th Cavalry.

Johnson, Lawrence H., III: *Winged Sabers – The Air Cavalry in Vietnam*; Stackpole Books, 1990.
This excellent book gives a comprehensive overview of the development and operations of the Air Cavalry in Vietnam, together with the aircraft, equipment, unit histories and uniforms as well as their distinctive insignia. It is profusely illustrated throughout with remarkable photographs drawn from many sources, particularly those of veterans.

Mertel, Col Kenneth D., US Army (Ret): *Year of the Horse: Vietnam – 1st Air Cavalry in the Highlands 1965-1967*; Schiffer Military History, 1997.
Colonel Kenneth Mertel was the commander of the 1st Battalion, 8th Cavalry and the *Year of the Horse: Vietnam* is a day-by-day account of the exploits of the 'Jumping Mustangs' during the initial years of the Vietnam War. The book has some especially useful appendices on the airmobility in Vietnam and on the air assault into Cambodia in 1970.

Moore, Lt Gen (Ret.) Harold G. and Galloway, Joseph L.: *We Were Soldiers Once…And Young Ia Drang: The Battle That Changed The War In Vietnam*; Random House, 1992.
This book is the definitive account of the battle of the Ia Drang Valley written by the commander of the 1st Battalion, 7th Cavalry, Hal Moore, and by the UPI journalist Joseph Galloway who accompanied the Sky Soldiers into the battle zone as a first-hand witness. The book includes interesting coverage from the

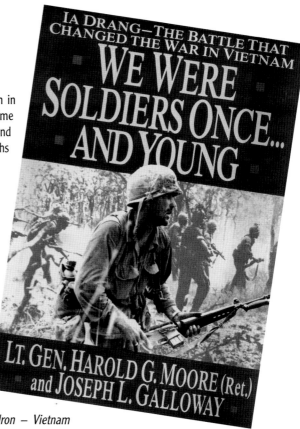

North Vietnamese point of view as well and it formed the basis of the film *We Were Soldiers Once* with Mel Gibson portraying Lt Col Hal Moore at the battle of the Ia Drang Valley.

Shelby L. Stanton: *Anatomy of a Division – 1st Cav in Vietnam*; Presidio, 1987.
Shelby L. Stanton is one of the foremost military historians of the Vietnam War with numerous works on the conflict to his credit. His *Anatomy of a Division* remains an exemplary concise history of the 1st Cavalry Division (Airmobile) from its inception to its return from South East Asia and its reconfiguration as an armoured division.

Shelby L. Stanton: *The Rise and Fall of an American Army – US Ground Forces in Vietnam, 1965-1973*; Presidio, 1985.
As a combat veteran of the Vietnam War, Shelby Stanton is highly qualified to recount the achievements of the US Army on the battlefields of South Vietnam from the initial optimism of the early years to the times of disillusion as the process of withdrawal took place. This important book sets the essential background to the overall conduct of the ground war with numerous references to the 1st Cavalry Division (Airmobile).

Shelby L. Stanton: *Vietnam Order of Battle*; US News Books, 1981.
Any serious student of the Vietnam War must have Shelby Stanton's magisterial and encyclopedic reference work *Vietnam Order of Battle* on his bookshelves. Recently republished, this 416-page compendium covers the entire organisation, structure and operations of US and Allied ground units in Vietnam from 1961 to 1973.

DVD

We Were Heroes – 1st Cavalry Division (Airmobile) Vietnam
DVD 9313 Madacy Entertainment Group Inc 2002
This three-DVD boxed set features archival footage of the arrival of the 1st Cavalry Division (Airmobile) in South Vietnam and the early battles including the Ia Drang and the A Shau Valley. Other features include helicopter operations in Vietnam, air mobility as well as a piece on Know Your Enemy about the Viet Cong.

1st CAVALRY DIVISION (AIRMOBILE) IN VIETNAM TIMELINE

1965

14 August: First 1st Cavalry Division combat troops sent to Vietnam.

27 August: 1st Cavalry Division advance party landed at An Khe, Vietnam.

18 September: First combat of Vietnam War for 1st Cavalry Troopers in Op 'Shiny Bayonet'.

19 October: Op 'Pleiku' begins.

1 November: 1-9 Cavalry fights hospital battle.

3 November: 1-9 Cavalry ambushes 66th NVA Regiment at LZ Betty.

14 November: 7th Cavalry air assaults into LZ X-Ray; 2nd Lt Walter J. Marm, A-1/7 Cavalry earns the Medal of Honor; Capt Edward W. Freeman, A-229th AHB, earns the Medal of Honor.

17 November: 2-7 Cavalry, Company A, 1-5 Cavalry battle at LZ Albany.

19 November: Op 'Silver Bayonet' begins.

26 November: Op 'Pleiku' ends.

17 December: Op 'Clean House' begins.

31 December: Op 'Clean House' ends.

1966

25 January: Op 'Masher/White Wing' begins.

6 March: Op 'Masher/White Wing' ends.

25 March: Op 'Lincoln House' begins.

8 April: Op 'Lincoln House' ends.

4 May: Op 'Davy Crockett' begins.

10 May: Op 'Davy Crockett' ends.

16 May: Op 'Crazy Horse' begins.

18 May: SSgt Jimmy G. Stewart, B-2/12 Cavalry earns the Medal of Honor.

21 May: Sgt David C. Dolby, B-1/8 Cavalry earns the Medal of Honor.

5 June: Op 'Crazy Horse' ends.

19 June: Op 'Nathan Hale' begins.

1 July: Op 'Nathan Hale' ends.

2 August: Op 'Paul Revere II' begins.

15 August: Op 'Paul Revere II' ends at the battle of Hill 534.

25 July: Op 'Byrd' begins.

13 September: Op 'Thayer I' begins.

21 September: PFC Billy L. Lauffer, C-2/5 Cavalry earns the Medal of Honor.

1 October: Op 'Thayer I' ends.

2 October: Op 'Irving' begins, over 2,000 enemy prisoners of war captured.

24 October: Op 'Irving' ends.

26 October: Op 'Thayer II' begins. 31 October: Op 'Paul Revere IV' begins.

1 December: PFC Lewis Albanese, B-5/7 Cavalry earns the Medal of Honor.

27 December: Op 'Paul Revere IV' ends; SSG Delbert O. Jennings, C-1/12 Cavalry earns The Medal of Honor.

1967

30 January: Op 'Byrd' ends.

12 February: Op 'Thayer II' ends; Op 'Pershing' begins.

16 February: PFC James H. Monroe, C-1/8 Cavalry earns the Medal of Honor.

20 March: Sp5 Charles C. Hagemeister, A-1/5 earns the Medal of Honor.

7 April: Op 'LeJeune' begins.

16 April: Sp4 George A. Ingalls, A-2/5 Cavalry earns the Medal of Honor.

22 April: Op 'LeJeune' ends.

21 June: Sp5 Edgal L. McWethy Jr., B-1/5 Cavalry earns the Medal of Honor; Sp4 Carmel B. Harvey Jr., B-1/5 Cavalry earns the Medal of Honor.

1 August: Op 'Song Re' begins.

20 August: Op 'Song Re' ends.

2 October: Op 'Wheller/Wallowa' begins.

15 December: Sgt Allen James Lynch, D-1/12 Cavalry earns the Medal of Honor.

1968

12 January: Sgt William D. Port, C-5/7 earns the Medal of Honor.

21 January: Op 'Pershing' ends.

22 January: Op 'Pershing II' begins; Op 'Jeb Stuart' begins.

25 January: Op 'Wheller/Wallowa' ends.

31 January: CW2 Fredrick Ferguson, C-227 Aviation Battalion earns the Medal of Honor; North Vietnamese and Viet Cong launch 'Tet Offensive' at Hue.

18 February: Op 'Pershing II' ends.

22 February: North Vietnamese and Viet Cong driven from the city of Hue.

31 March: Op 'Jeb Stuart' ends.

1 April: Op 'Pegasus/Lamson 207' begins.

15 April: Op 'Pegasus/Lamson 207' ends.

19 April: Op 'Delaware/Lamson 216' begins.

25 April: Capt James M. Sprayberry, D-5/7 Cavalry earns the Medal of Honor.

4 May: 1st Lt Douglas B. Fournet, B-1/7 Cavalry earns the Medal of Honor.

8 May; Op 'Concordia Square' begins.

17 May: Op 'Delaware/Lamson 217' ends; Op 'Jeb Stuart III' begins; Op 'Concordia Square' ends.

28 June: Sp4 Hector Santiago Colon, B-5/7 Cavalry earns Medal of Honor.

11 September: Op 'Comanche Falls' begins.

3 November: Op 'Jeb Stuart III' ends.

7 November: Op 'Comanche Falls' ends.

12 November: Op 'Toan Thang' begins.

15 November: Op 'Liberty Canyon' ends.

3 December: Sgt John N. Holcomb, D-2/7 Cavalry earns the Medal of Honor.

1969

23 January: Op 'Montana Scout/Raider' begins.

16 February: Op 'Toan Thang' ends.

21 March: Sp4 Donald R. Johnston, D-1/8 Cavalry earns the Medal of Honor.

2 June: 1st Lt Robert L. Poxon, B-1/9 Cavalry earns the Medal of Honor.

18 July: Sgt Rodney J. Evans, D-1/12 earns the Medal of Honor.

14 September: Sgt Donald S. Skidgel, D-1/9 Cavalry earns the Medal of Honor.

2 December: 2nd Lt Robert R. Leisy, B-1/8 Cavalry earns the Medal of Honor.

1970

10 February: Sp4 John P. Baca, D-1/12 Cavalry earns the Medal of Honor.

1 April: Sgt Peter C. Lemon, E-2/8 Cavalry earns the Medal of Honor.

1 May: Op 'Thon Thang Fish Hook' begins; First Team enters Cambodia.

29 June: Op 'Thon Thang Fish Hook' ends.

1971

26 February: Cpt Jon Edward Swanson, B-1/9 Cavalry earns the Medal of Honor.

26 March: 1st Team stands down in Vietnam.

5 May: 1st Cavalry Division assigned to Fort Hood, Texas.

1972

26 June: Op 'Keystone Pheasant' begins.

29 June: 3rd Brigade departs Vietnam.

1973

28 January: Cease-fire in Vietnam begins.

28 March: US ground troops leave Vietnam.

Above: Men of the 1st Cavalry Division (Airmobile) jump from a UH-1D during Operation Oregon, a search and destroy mission, April 1967.

Right: Classic airmobility–an 81mm mortar crew of Company D, 1st Battalion, 501st Infantry (Airmobile), 2nd Brigade, 101st Airborne Division (Airmobile), disembarks from a UH-1H during an operation west of Tam Ky, 1 June, 1969.

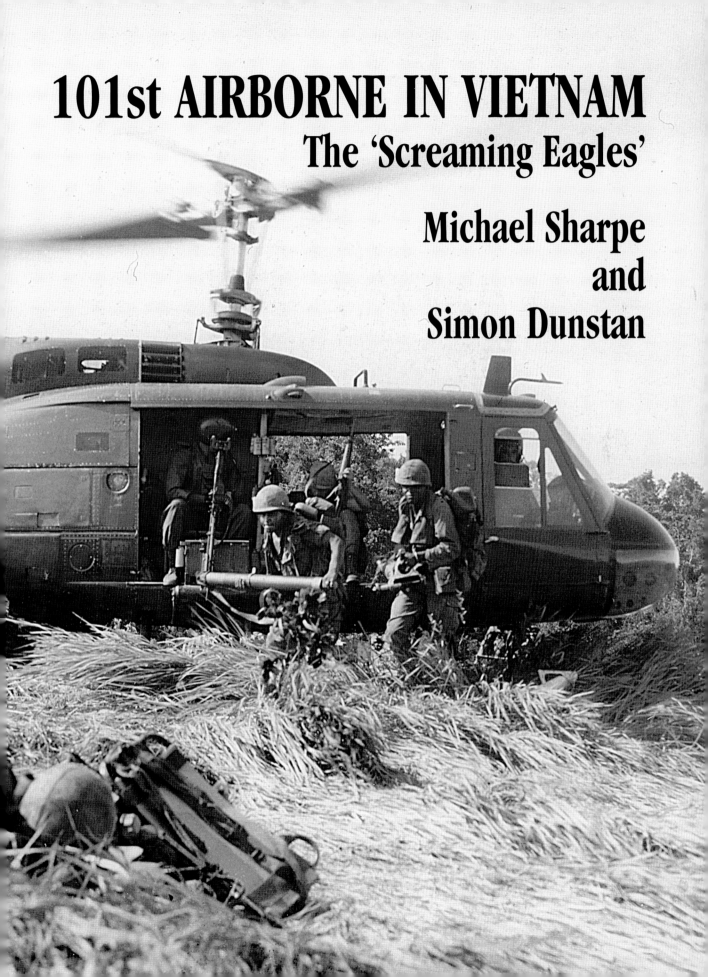

101st AIRBORNE IN VIETNAM
The 'Screaming Eagles'

Michael Sharpe
and
Simon Dunstan

ORIGINS & HISTORY

The story of the 101st Airborne Division – the celebrated 'Screaming Eagles' – stretches back over more than half a century of war and peace. Since its inception at Fort Bragg in 1942, through the tough battles on the Western Front, in Vietnam, and most recently Iraq, the division has earned a reputation as one of the pre-eminent combat units of the US Army. This book covers the 101st Airborne Division in the Vietnam War, in which it was engaged from 1965 to 1971 as one of two designated airborne divisions (alongside the 1st Air Cavalry).

This was a war unlike any the US Army had been sent to fight before. In places the landscape bore some similarities to certain islands of the Pacific, but it was a very different set of circumstances and a different enemy the soldiers faced. Although superbly equipped and trained, the troops on the ground were hobbled by stringent rules of engagement, often indifferent leadership and the difficulties in fighting an experienced enemy on their own ground. The first US Army advisors sent to Vietnam were soon apprised of the difficulties of transporting men and equipment in Vietnam, with its poorly developed infrastructure and vast swathes of jungle. This in turn prompted the army to develop the airmobile doctrine that was so important to US operations in the theatre. As a pioneer and leading proponent in the field of airborne tactics, the 101st Airborne ultimately made a major contribution.

AIRBORNE ORIGINS

In the early 1900s the inventors of the parachute envisaged it as a means of escaping from stricken aircraft, and in this role it achieved some success in the First World War. In 1918 the US Army planned to use parachutists to break the deadlock on the Western Front, but the end of hostilities curtailed this. It was left to leading US aviation pioneer General 'Billy' Mitchell to take up the banner of dedicated parachute forces, specially trained and equipped to be dropped by aircraft into combat. At a demonstration of his concept at Kelly Field at San Antonio, Texas, six soldiers parachuted from a Martin Bomber, landed safely, and less than three minutes after exiting the aircraft had their weapons assembled and were ready for action. However, US observers quickly dismissed Mitchell's revolutionary idea (and later, his theories on strategic bombing) and the US Army was robbed of an opportunity to take an early lead in the development of airborne forces.

Some of those present on that day were less hasty to arrive at the same conclusion. Among others, senior Soviet and German representatives were favourably impressed with the demonstration, and in succeeding years in the USSR, static line parachuting was introduced as a national sport and the population encouraged to join the fledgling Russian Airborne Corps. In 1927 the Red Army carried out the first experiments with airborne troops and in August 1930, at Voronezh, Russia, its paratroops participated for the first time in the annual military manoeuvres. Their actions proved so effective that a

Below: Elements of Company A, 2nd Battalion, 502nd Infantry (Airborne), 1st Brigade, 101st Airborne Division (Separate) move out on patrol from a helicopter landing zone during Operation 'Cook' on 8 September 1967. The beautiful but hostile terrain of Vietnam is well illustrated in this photograph.

repeat performance was given in Moscow a month later. However, the programme lapsed following the execution of its leading proponent, Tukhachevsky, in 1937, and although at the start of the Second World War there were some 100,000 paratroops in the Red Army, these were hardly used at all in their dedicated role.

The German observers also eagerly grasped the idea and planners worked quickly to develop an effective military parachute organisation, leading to the establishment in 1935 of an experimental airborne staff under Kurt Student. Airborne forces were also quickly integrated into the blitzkrieg strategy that was being formalised by German military planners in the interwar years. Under the rapid expansion of the armed forces that accompanied the Nazis' consolidation of power, considerable resources were earmarked for these formations. At the start of the Second World War, Germany's parachute branch undoubtedly led the field, and in the early 'lightning' campaigns in the West her airborne troops spearheaded the assaults on key positions in the enemy rear. One of their most notable feats was the attack on the fortress of Eben Emael on the Albert Canal in Belgium. Here, two of the key assets of the paratrooper – speed and surprise – played a major role in the Belgian defeat.

UNITED STATES

In the United States things got off to a rather slower start. Despite his demonstrations, few of America's military men shared Mitchell's enthusiasm for the potential of aircraft and airborne forces, and little attention was paid to their development. However, the successful employment of airborne troops by the Germans in their invasion of the Low Countries exposed such short-sightedness and provided the much needed spur. US military branches began an all-out effort to develop this new form of warfare, but considerable opposition remained.

In April 1940 the Department of War approved plans for the formation of a test platoon of Airborne Infantry to form, equip, and train under the direction and control of the Army's Infantry Board. In June, the Commandant of the Infantry School was directed to organise a test platoon of volunteers from Fort Benning's 29th Infantry Regiment. Later that year, the 2nd Infantry Division was directed to conduct the necessary tests to develop reference data and operational procedures for air-transported troops.

In July 1940, the task of organising the platoon began. First Lieutenant William T. Ryder of the 29th Infantry Regiment volunteered and was designated the test platoon's Platoon Leader, with Lieutenant James A. Bassett as Assistant Platoon Leader. On the criteria of high standards of health and rugged physical characteristics, 48 enlisted men were selected from a pool of 200 volunteers. Quickly thereafter, the platoon moved into tents near Lawson Field, and an abandoned hangar was obtained for use as a training hall and for parachute packing.

Lieutenant Colonel William C. Lee, a staff officer for the Chief of Infantry, arranged for the men to be moved to the Safe Parachute Company at Hightstown, New Jersey, for training on the parachute drop towers used during the New York World's Fair. Eighteen days after organisation, the platoon was moved to New Jersey and trained for one week on the 250-foot towers.

The army was so impressed with the tower drops that two were purchased and erected at Fort Benning, on what is now Eubanks Field. Later, two more were added. Three of the original four towers are still in use training paratroopers at the base.

Less than 45 days after organisation, the first jump from an aircraft in flight by members of the test platoon was made from a Douglas B-18 over Lawson Field on 16 August 1940. Thirteen days later, also at Lawson Field, the platoon made the first mass jump held in the United States.

Above: Troopers of the 1st Battalion, 327th Infantry (Airborne), 1st Brigade, 101st Airborne Division (Separate) return fire from old Viet Cong trenches as the enemy mounts an attack during Operation 'Hawthorne' on 7 June 1966. Following on from Operation 'Paul Revere', the 1st Brigade accounted for 531 enemy casualties during Operation 'Hawthorne' through massive firepower including 27,000 artillery rounds and 473 US Air Force close air support sorties. US losses were high with 48 dead and 239 wounded but the 1st Brigade was awarded the Presidential Unit Citation (see box on pages 28–9) for what the brigade commander, Brig Gen Willard Pearson, declaimed was 'our biggest and best fight, our greatest battle.'

The first parachute combat unit to be organised was the 501st Parachute Battalion. It was commanded by Major William M. Miley, later a major general and commander of the 17th Airborne Division, and the original test platoon members formed the battalion cadre. The Civilian Conservation Corps cleared new jump areas and three new training buildings were erected. Several B-18 and C-39 aircraft were provided for training.

The 502nd Parachute Infantry Battalion, commanded by Lieutenant Colonel William C. Lee with men from the 501st as a cadre, was activated on 1 July 1941. However, the 502nd was far below its approved strength, and Lieutenant Colonel Lee petitioned the 9th Infantry Division at Fort Bragg, North Carolina, for 172 volunteers. The response was very favourable: more than 400 men volunteered, including many non-commissioned officers who were willing to take a reduction in rank to transfer to the new battalion.

In December 1941 the path of history took another turn, when Japan attacked the US Naval Base at Pearl Harbour. The British Army had by this time successfully used parachute infantry in combat, prompting the US Army to authorise the raising of two Airborne Infantry Divisions: 82nd and 101st Airborne. On 15 August, the 101st Airborne Division (Air Assault) was activated at Camp Claiborne, Louisiana. The 101st Division had originally been activated on 23 July 1918 as part of the mobilisation for the First World War. However, because weapons, ammunition and other supplies were scarce for training, it was never fully organised or manned. After the war was over, the unit was demobilised, but it was reconstituted as the 101st Infantry Division in 1921, as part of a build-up of reserves, and made its headquarters in Milwaukee, Wisconsin. For the most part it was a paper division with little in the way of real units, and it remained that way until the United States entered the Second World War.

At the activation ceremony on 19 August 1942, the first commander, Major General William C. Lee, issued the following now-famous order to his new recruits. It reads: 'The 101st Airborne Division, activated at Camp Claiborne, Louisiana, has no history, but it has a rendezvous with destiny. Like the early American pioneers whose invincible courage was the foundation stone of this nation, we have broken with the past and its traditions in order to establish our claim to the future.

'Due to the nature of our armament, and the tactics in which we shall perfect ourselves, we shall be called upon to carry out operations of far-reaching military importance and we shall habitually go into action when the need is immediate and extreme.

'Let me call your attention to the fact that our badge is the great American eagle. This is a fitting emblem for a division that will crush its enemies by falling upon them like a thunderbolt from the skies.

'The history we shall make, the record of high achievement we hope to write in the annals of the American Army and the American people, depends wholly and completely on the men of this division. Each individual, each officer and each enlisted man, must therefore regard himself as a necessary part of a complex and powerful instrument for the overcoming of the enemies of the nation. Each, in his own job, must realise that he is not only a means, but an indispensable means for obtaining the goal of victory. It is, therefore, not too much to say that the future itself, in whose molding we expect to have our share, is in the hands of the soldiers of the 101st Airborne Division.'

TRAINING

With the expansion of the airborne force, it became apparent that a centralised training facility should be established. Consequently, a facility was organised at Fort Benning, Georgia, on 15 May 1942. In October, the 101st Airborne reported there to begin parachute and combat training. The programme was intense, and unforgiving. As well as being required to master basic infantry skills, the troops had to learn entirely new ways of fighting a war. A significant number of the men entering the programme 'washed out' in the first few days. According to statistics given in Stephen Ambrose's book, *Band of Brothers*, only 148 out of 500 officer volunteers were accepted into the airborne forces; only 1,800 graduated from the training out of every 5,300 enlisted men.

At first the parachute troops and the glider troops trained separately, but from early 1943 as a division. With this training completed by June, 506th Parachute Infantry Regiment was added to the ranks of the 101st Airborne just in time for the Second Army manoeuvres, in which the division was given the opportunity to prove itself fully prepared for battle. In July 1943, the unit was certified as combat ready and began to move to embarkation points in New York, from where on 5 September, it set sail for England.

PREPARING FOR WAR

The passage across the grey, U-boat infested waters of the North Atlantic, though cramped and tedious, passed without incident. Safely conveyed to England, the 101st was quartered in Wiltshire and Berkshire to wait until all the personnel and equipment could be transported across the Atlantic. The division then commenced advanced training in night fighting, urban warfare, German equipment familiarisation, land navigation and many other skills. In addition, a jump school was established to certify the new units then being added to the divisional roster.

The early months of 1944 were a time of change. In January the 101st received its third parachute regiment, the 501st Parachute Infantry. On 5 February General Lee, who had championed the airborne cause from the beginning, suffered a heart attack. Although he had brought the division from its initial organisation through training for the fight in Europe, General Lee was not to be part of the 101st's baptism of fire. He was relieved of his command and returned to the United States. Brigadier General Maxwell D. Taylor, former commander of the 82nd Airborne Division Artillery who went on to become one of America's most famous generals, assumed command on 14 March.

The division underwent another organisational change that month, when 2nd Battalion, 401st Glider Infantry, was permanently transferred to the 82nd Airborne Division. The 1st Battalion was attached to the 327th Glider Infantry to operate under that regiment as a third battalion. (1st Battalion, 401st Glider Infantry Regiment, was made an official element of 327th Glider Infantry Regiment in April 1945.)

In March, a demonstration of American military prowess was staged for the British Prime Minister Winston Churchill, Supreme Allied Commander General Dwight D. Eisenhower, and dozens of high ranking civilian and military officials. The 101st was tasked with demonstrating airborne operations, and so successful was this, and Division Artillery Commander McAuliffe's briefing to Churchill and Eisenhower on the capabilities of the 101st Airborne Division, that it was chosen to spearhead the assault on Europe.

Shortly after this demonstration, Taylor received his orders for Operation 'Overlord'. Training intensified and culminated with three large-scale operations – 'Beaver', 'Tiger' and 'Eagle' – that were designed to familiarise the soldiers with conditions they would encounter in France.

During Operation 'Beaver', at Slapton Sands on the Devonshire coast, elements of the division jumped from trucks instead of planes with the mission of capturing the causeway bridges that crossed the estuary behind the beach. The division performed much the same mission during the second exercise, Operation 'Tiger'.

Operation 'Eagle', held during the second week of May, was the division's dress rehearsal for its role in the coming Normandy invasion. The 101st, this time jumping from actual planes, was once again assigned to capture the causeways leading away from a

Above: The pathfinder unit of the 101st Airborne Division, dropped by parachute, sets up radar equipment near Bastogne, Belgium, 23 December 1944. It is their job to guide planes with medical supplies and ammunition to the division, besieged by the Germans during the Battle of the Bulge.

H&HC, 101st Airborne Division cited in War Department General Orders 4, 12 January 1945:

The 101st Airborne Division Headquarters and Headquarters Company is cited for extraordinary heroism and outstanding performance of duty in action in the initial assault on the northern coast of Normandy, France. Before daylight on the morning of 6 June 1944, the parachute and glider echelon of this unit landed in the vicinity of St Come-du-Mont, France. They were widely dispersed initially because of a bad drop and encountered heavy enemy fire delivered from strongly fortified positions. Many fierce and vicious battles took place between small detachments of airborne soldiers and strongly emplaced enemy forces as the parachutists and glider men moved to assemble and to their objectives. Innumerable acts of gallantry and self-sacrifice were performed in the determined and successful efforts of the officers and men of the 101st Airborne Division Headquarters and Headquarters Company. Although this unit was chiefly composed of clerks, technicians, and specialists, usually not considered as combat soldiers, they wiped out many enemy pill boxes, artillery positions, and other fortifications. Under extremely difficult conditions they established the division command post at the predesignated location, established contact with the scattered elements of the division and organised them into a unified command which successfully accomplished its mission of insuring the establishment of the beachhead Utah. The second glider echelon landed near Hiesville, France, on the evening of D-Day. Despite heavy enemy resistance encountered at the landing fields, this group successfully reached the division command post and augmented the command group then operating the command post. The combined efforts of

simulated beach. Although a misunderstanding caused most of the division to jump at the wrong coordinates, the mission was accomplished and the exercise was considered a success. The division then returned to its stations to continue preparation for the coming battles on the continent.

INTO EUROPE

In late May, with D-Day imminent, the 101st left their training areas and moved to their staging and jump-off points. The division had been given the mission of landing behind enemy lines in the area designated as Utah beach on the Cherbourg Peninsula. Once on the ground they were to clear the exit points from Utah for the 4th Infantry Division's breakout. In addition they were to prevent any reinforcements from reaching Utah.

On the night of 5–6 June, the pathfinders of the 101st became the first Americans to set foot in occupied France. After they had cleared the way for the 1st and 4th Infantry Divisions behind Utah Beach, a bitter battle developed for the town of Carentan. This and subsequent battles for the bridgehead raged over the following month; the 101st Airborne was fighting almost continuously, until it returned to England in July to prepare for the liberation of Holland – Operation 'Market Garden'.

Under this operation, on 17 September 1944, the division seized and held the Eindhoven–Arnhem corridor for 10 days against heavy odds and spent a total of 72 days in battle. In November the 101st returned to France to rest and re-equip, only to be called to action again in December as Hitler unleashed his offensive through the Ardennes. While guarding the crucial transportation hub of Bastogne, Belgium, the division was surrounded by advancing enemy forces. Called on to surrender by his German adversary, divisional commander Brigadier General Anthony McAuliffe gave the brusque retort 'Nuts!' and the unit fought on until the 8-day-long siege was lifted.

Following the siege of Bastogne, the 101st was ordered into the Ruhr area of Germany, but without 501st Parachute Regiment, which was ordered into reserve and began training for a possible rescue attempt of Allied prisoners of war. However, due to a shortage of transport aircraft and the relatively low priority of the mission, this operation was never mounted.

The other elements of the 101st took part in operations to reduce one of the few remaining cohesive German Army Groups, which was concentrated in the Ruhr River region of Germany. In the beginning of April, the US First and Ninth Armies attacked and by the end of the month, the German forces within the pocket had largely been eliminated; 325,000 prisoners fell into Allied hands.

The final mission for the 101st was an assault on Hitler's retreat at Berchtesgaden in conjunction with 3rd Infantry Division. Here the division accepted the surrender of the German XIII SS and LXXXII Corps, and also took prisoner several key members of the Nazi regime who were later brought before the War Crimes Tribunal at the Hague – Field Marshal Albert Kesselring, Julius Streicher, the anti-Semitic editor of *Der Sturmer*, and Obergruppenführer Karl Oberg, the chief of German SS in occupied France. Colonel General Heinz Guderian, the armour expert, was another of their prisoners.

The 101st remained in Germany on occupation duty until November 1945, when it was deactivated in France and shipped home. During the Second World War, the division spent 214 days in combat. For their deeds during the conflict, the 'The Battered Bastards of Bastogne' were awarded four campaign streamers and two Presidential Unit Citations, in addition to two Medals of Honor. Soldiers of the 101st Airborne Division were awarded 47 Distinguished Service Crosses, 516 Silver Stars and 6,977 Bronze Stars.

POSTWAR

The 101st Airborne was reactivated as a training unit at Camp Breckinridge, Kentucky, in 1948 and again in 1950. Although it did not fight in the Korean War, it was responsible for training the 11th Airborne Division, which served with honour.

It was reactivated once again in 1954 at Fort Jackson, South Carolina, and in March 1956 the 101st was transferred, less personnel and equipment, to Fort Campbell, Kentucky, to be reorganised as a combat division. The division colours were unsheathed and presented there on 21 September 1956, and since that time Fort Campbell has been its home base. In the years to follow, the 101st continued to train paratroopers. Then in 1965 it was informed that it was being shipped to Vietnam to fight the war that was escalating in that country. In the words of Major General B.E. Powell, US Army Division Commander in 1965:

'The history of the 101st Airborne Division was not to end, finally, with the triumph of American arms on the battlefields of WWII. To meet the rising challenge of Communist imperialism, its colors were uncased and the best of a new generation of soldiers was chosen to fill its ranks again. Today, ever ready to keep its "Rendezvous With Destiny," the Division of that new generation does credit to the great heritage of Bastogne. The place of the 101st is secure in the annals of history; its exploits in combat will be remembered for as long as men honor the memory of valor.'

A brief history of the origins of each brigade follows.

1st Brigade

The major organic unit in the 1st Brigade was the 327th Infantry Regiment, composed of the 'Above the Rest', 'No Slack' and 'Battle Force' Battalions. The regiment traces its history to the 164th Infantry Brigade of the 82nd Infantry Division formed on 17 September 1917 at Fort Gordon, Georgia. That unit, too, has a long history of campaigns and honours. The 'Bastogne' Brigade has been involved in three conflicts and one peacekeeping mission: As well as fighting in the First World War, during the Second World War, it participated in the Normandy, Ardennes–Alsace, Rhineland, and Central European campaigns.

2nd Brigade

Headquarters and Headquarters Company, 2nd Brigade, traces its lineage to the 159th Infantry Brigade, an element of the 80th Division, organised in August 1917. During the First World War, the 159th Infantry Brigade participated in the Picardy (1918), Somme (1918), and Meuse–Argonne campaigns against the Imperial German Army.

Reorganised as the 80th Reconnaissance Troop (Mechanized) of the 80th Infantry Division, the unit participated in the Northern France, Rhineland, Ardennes–Alsace and Central European campaigns against Germany in the Second World War.

A major reorganisation took place on 3 February 1964, when the 2nd Brigade of the 101st Airborne Division was activated at Fort Campbell, replacing the 1st Airborne Battle Group 501st Infantry Regiment. The new 2nd Brigade's original organic battalions were the 1st and 2nd Battalions, 501st Infantry, and the 1st Battalion, 502nd Infantry.

3rd Brigade

The 3rd Brigade, 101st Airborne Division (Air Assault), traces its lineage back to the organisation of Headquarters, 160th Infantry Brigade. This was organised in August 1917 as an element of the 80th Division at Camp Lee, Virginia. Through numerous

---

the 101st Airborne Division Headquarters and Headquarters Company in establishing and protecting the division command post in the face of bitter enemy resistance permitted the Commanding General and his staff to formulate and direct the successful execution of the plans for the division.

Presidential Unit Citation (Army), Streamer embroidered BASTOGNE

101st Airborne Division (less 2d Battalion, 401st Glider Infantry Regiment) cited in War Department General Orders 17, 13 March 1945 (along with other attached units):

These units distinguished themselves in combat against powerful and aggressive enemy forces composed of elements of eight German divisions during the period from 18 to 27 December 1944 by extraordinary heroism and gallantry in defense of the key communications center of Bastogne, Belgium. Essential to a large-scale exploitation of his break-through into Belgium and northern Luxembourg, the enemy attempted to seize Bastogne by attacking constantly and savagely with the best of his armor and infantry. Without benefit of prepared defenses, facing almost overwhelming odds and with very limited and fast-dwindling supplies, these units maintained a high combat morale and an impenetrable defense despite extremely heavy bombing, intense artillery fire, and constant attacks from infantry and armor on all sides of their completely cut-off and encircled position. This masterful and grimly determined defense denied the enemy even momentary success in an operation for which he paid dearly in men materiel and eventually morale. The outstanding courage, resourcefulness, and undaunted determination of this gallant force are in keeping with the highest traditions of the service.

reorganisations and redesignations, Headquarters and Headquarters Company, 3rd Brigade, evolved into its modern configuration in February 1964. In Vietnam, the Brigade comprised three infantry battalions, 3rd Battalion, 187th Infantry Regiment, and the 1st and 2nd Battalions of the 506th Infantry Regiment. Between 1964 and 1967 these units conducted operations in various locations ranging from the Mojave Desert to Norway, where it prepared for both conventional and unconventional war contingencies.

101st Aviation Brigade

On 1 July 1968, at Camp Eagle in the Republic of Vietnam, the 160th Aviation Group was constituted. On 25 June 1969, the 160th was redesignated as the 101st Aviation Group. With the air mobility concept added to the organic capabilities of the 101st Airborne Division, 101st Aviation Group was attached to it. The 101st Aviation Group served from the Delta to the DMZ, and from the east coast to Cambodia and Laos, and in 1972 returned to Fort Campbell, Kentucky with the other units of the 101st.

159th Aviation Battalion

The 159th Aviation was originally formed as the 159th Aviation Battalion in Vietnam on 1 July 1968, from the dissolved 308th Combat Aviation Battalion. Organised as the medium and heavy lift Assault Support Helicopter Battalion (ASHB) of the 101st Airborne Division, the unit was composed of three CH-47 companies and one CH-54 company. In February 1972, the 159th ASHB returned to Fort Campbell.

In July of 1965, the first element of the 101st Airborne Division was deployed to the Republic of South Vietnam. The remainder of the division arrived in South Vietnam in October and November of 1967.

In 1965, the 101st Airborne consisted of three brigades, each consisting of three battalions. The 1st 'Bastogne' Brigade deployed to Vietnam in 1965, and was joined in 1967 by the other two.

Below: Brigadier General Anthony C. McAuliffe, artillery commander of the 101st Airborne Division, gives his men last-minute instructions before the take-off from England during Operation 'Market Garden', September 1944.

READY FOR WAR

RECRUITMENT AND TRAINING

The level of professionalism that distinguished the rank and file troops of the 101st Airborne Division from their peers can largely be attributed to thorough and exacting training and to the way in which they were recruited.

Although the division drew from the same pool of manpower as other units, recruitment into the airborne/airmobile units of the US Army has always been on a volunteer basis. No man was or is ever drafted in 'off the street' so to speak. However, there were many conscripts who, having been drafted into the military, volunteered for service in the airborne.

Men came from all backgrounds and walks of life and from every corner of the Union, ensuring that there was no regional bias in the unit. Typically, recruits enlisted, or were drafted into the US Army, after a year or two of college, or else straight from school, at the age of 18–20.

Those wishing to join the Airborne Infantry first had to pass the induction exams that qualified them to begin basic training. After completing Basic Training recruits embarked on Advanced Infantry Training. With these two stages successfully completed they moved on to Airborne School at Fort Benning, Georgia.

Army basic training, a rite of passage for generations of soldiers, is designed to transform civilians into fighters by teaching them to march, shoot rifles and kill the enemy. However, a fundamental problem existed in the mid-1960s in the fact that most of the US armed forces training programme was based on the likelihood of a war on the central European plain against regular forces. Their equipment in many ways reflected this, with much of it was badly suited to conditions in Vietnam. The US Army thus made changes to the programme to accommodate the peculiarities of the war in Southeast Asia. Starting in the 1960s, recruits were also taught how to detect and avoid booby traps, how to search suspected Viet Cong bolt holes, and personal health and hygiene guidelines for tropical climes.

Every 101st Airborne recruit attended basic training in these skills for a minimum of eight weeks, at any one of a number of designated training centres, including among others Fort Bliss, Texas, and Fort Ord, California. During basic training, the recruit was taught how to march in close order, clean, press, shine, salute and all the rest of those military staples. There was also instruction in how to fight using rifle, bayonet, hand grenade and hand to hand combat techniques, and procedures for dealing with tear gas. Those old enough might also receive training in how to drive military trucks and jeeps.

The recruits were tested and graded in each of these skills, and those who qualified with high marks might be rewarded with a weekend pass. Those who attained sufficiently high marks in the military entry exams might have qualified to go to Officer Candidate School.

Above: There is an old military adage – 'There is nothing more dangerous than a young officer with a map'. With the high turnover of officers who did six-month tours of duty in the field to 12 months for the other ranks, the knowledge and experience of the NCOs were vital for unit cohesion and success or survival in the field. Here, with their RTOs close to hand, the company commander and platoon leaders of Company C, 2nd Battalion, 327th Infantry (Airborne), 1st Brigade, 101st Airborne Division (Separate), confer during Operation 'Geronimo I' near Tuy Hoa on 22 November 1966.

After basic training recruits were promoted to Private E-2 and sent to advanced infantry training (AIT) school, typically at Fort Dix in New Jersey, or Fort Gordon, Georgia, where they learned more about how to survive on the battlefield. There was more training with the M-14 rifle or the new M-16 rifle (depending on the period), M-60 machine gun and other infantry weapons. Recruits learnt small unit tactics, and how to fire and move as teams in combat. There was further practice in musketry on the ranges, and a much feared Survival, Evasion and Escape course. Those trainees who were captured while trying to evade their pursuers on this course were usually left with a lasting mental and physical impression of the experience.

On graduation from AIT, airborne hopefuls were promoted to Private First Class (Pfc. E-3), and sent to the Basic Airborne Course (BAC) at Fort Benning, Georgia, home of the US Army Airborne School. However, after the 101st Airborne became an airmobile unit, troopers were no longer required to qualify as parachutists. Prospective officers reported to Officer Candidate School, also located at Fort Benning.

In Vietnam the 101st Airborne established its own Replacement Training School at Camp Ray.

AIRBORNE TRAINING

Things began to get a lot tougher when the recruit embarked on the BAC. The first aim of this course was to qualify the recruit in the use of the parachute as a means of combat deployment, by building up his confidence to jump from an aircraft while in flight.

The second goal was to develop leadership, self-confidence and an aggressive spirit through mental and physical conditioning.

The third was to maintain the level of physical fitness required of a military parachutist through daily physical training. It was, however, assumed that any recruit who started the physically gruelling course at Fort Benning had thus far attained a high level of personal physical fitness. The physically weak were more likely either not to complete the course because of an injury, or to fail due to an inability to qualify on the training apparatuses. PT sessions were on the menu for the first and last period each day, and in between there were seven hours of demanding, vigorous training. The physical training programme placed great emphasis on squad runs, in either gym gear or Full Battle Order, with as many as five of these in one day. Failure to complete two of these in any one week resulted in disqualification from the course.

Running concurrently with this PT programme, the airborne instruction undertaken at Fort Benning was divided into three phases: a ground training phase, tower training phase and jump training phase.

During the ground phase, recruits were subject to an intensive programme of instruction to build individual airborne skills, and prepare them to make a parachute jump and land safely. This included training on a mock aircraft door, a 34-foot tower, and an apparatus that replicated the sensation of lateral drift (LDA). To go forward to tower training week, they had to qualify on the 34-foot tower and the LDA, and pass all PT requirements.

The individual skills learned during the ground phase were refined during a week during which the recruits trained on the 34-foot towers, swing landing trainer (SLT), a mock aircraft door for mass-exit training, and suspended harness. All these were intended to build individual and team skills. To go forward to jump training week, recruits had to qualify on the SLT, master the mass-exit procedures from the 34-foot tower, and pass all PT requirements. Following on from this, there was another week of training, this time using real aircraft, at the end of which the coveted 'wings' were awarded at a special graduation ceremony.

Above: Personnel of the 1st Brigade, 101st Airborne Division (Separate), jump from a CV2 Caribou during a demonstration at Dong Ba Thien on 29 July 1965 to mark the arrival of the 3,700 men of the 1st Brigade at Cam Ranh Bay where they disembarked from the World War II Liberty ship, USNS *General Leroy Eltinge* after a three-week ocean voyage. They were met by two former commanders of the 101st Airborne Division, Maxwell D. Taylor, US Ambassador to South Vietnam, and General William W. Westmoreland, commander of MACV.

It should be noted however that from the late 1960s, as the 101st moved from an Airborne to an Airmobile Division, the Airborne School switched its focus away from parachute operations and was used to teach rappelling skills.

After completing the BAC, or rappelling instruction, recruits moved to Fort Campbell, Kentucky, to embark on a course of jungle training.

The US Army Jumpmaster School, also at Fort Benning, trained select personnel in the skills necessary to lead a combat-equipped jump. The Pathfinder School course taught procedures for establishing and operating day/night helicopter landing zones and parachute drop zones, slingload operations, and air traffic control.

DEPLOYMENT OF 1ST BRIGADE

In the wake of the Gulf of Tonkin incident, US intervention in Vietnam was escalated dramatically. Late in the winter of 1965 President Lyndon B. Johnson announced that US forces in Vietnam would be raised from 75,000 to 125,000 and that additional forces would be sent as requested.

The Marines were first to deploy, around Da Nang, followed by 173rd Airborne Brigade. In the spring the 101st Airborne Division was alerted that it was to send a brigade of infantry plus support troops to Vietnam in the summer. Clearly, this gave the division staff little time to carry out the myriad of necessary preparations. Furthermore, it was unclear for how long the unit was expected to deploy, adding to the administrative headaches.

Prior to the movement by sea of the main body, an advance party flew to Nha Trang in two ageing C-124 aircraft; because of mechanical and administrative difficulties, the journey took a week. The main body of over 3,600 troops was flown from Fort Campbell on the evening of 6 July to San Francisco, where they took buses to Oakland Army Terminal. Here they were greeted by an Army band, Red Cross 'Donut Dollies', and saw for the first time the grey ship that was to ferry them to war on the other side of the world.

The USNS *General Leroy Eltinge* was 510 feet long, every inch painted grey. The ship departed Alameda Navy Yard on 9 July. It was not a happy passage. Into the *Eltinge,* which had a normal capacity of 2,200, were crammed 3,600 men, the bulk of the brigade's manpower. Furthermore, during the voyage there were problems with the electricity, plumbing and a lack of ventilation below decks, which added to the men's misery at being cooped up. The *Eltinge* also broke down while crossing the Pacific, bobbing around without power for about a day and then limping into Subic Bay for repairs.

Finally, on 29 July, the ship arrived at Cam Ranh Bay, where two former, distinguished commanders of the 101st Airborne Division, Maxwell D. Taylor, Ambassador to South Vietnam, and General William C. Westmoreland, commander of MACV, were there to officially welcome the men of the 1st Brigade to Vietnam.

Until 21 August, the brigade manned a defensive perimeter in the Cam Ranh Bay area. During this initial deployment and on subsequent operations, the troops familiarised themselves with new equipment and brigade structure, and conducted exercises in airmobile operations. However, they found that many of the items that they had brought into the country, such as camouflage nets, were completely extraneous and many things they had not brought, such as additional water trucks, were absolutely essential.

Three weeks after arriving in Vietnam the brigade moved to Binh Dinh Province in II Corps to commence combat operations under Operation 'Highland'.

Above: Pfc. Rodger Lyle of the 1st Brigade, 101st Airborne Division (Separate), wields a chainsaw as he clears trees and scrub to create a landing zone for resupply helicopters during Operation 'Austin VI', a search and destroy mission against the VC/NVA operating in Phuoc Long and Quang Duc Provinces near the Cambodian border on 15 May 1966. Operation 'Austin VI' was conducted to block NVA infiltration routes from Cambodia.

DEPLOYMENT OF 2ND AND 3RD BRIGADES

Nearly two years after the 1st Brigade was sent to Southeast Asia, in the late spring of 1967 the 2nd and 3rd Brigades were ordered to make ready for a move to Vietnam, scheduled for February of the next year.

Preparations began immediately. Between 22 May and 3 June, the two brigades conducted a war game, Operation 'Goblin Hunt I', in Stewart County, Tennessee. The 3rd Battalion of the 506th Infantry teamed with Special Forces teams to provide the aggressor force for this exercise, which was designed to familiarise the men with the kind of tactics employed by the Viet Cong (VC). Then in mid-July Operation 'Crocigator' was staged in the swamps surrounding Fort Stewart, Georgia, to demonstrate to the men the problems of fighting in such an environment.

In the last week of the month there was a slight interruption to the training schedule when the 101st Airborne Division received an Executive Order from President Johnson to help restore order in Detroit, where serious race riots had broken out. After training in riot control techniques some 4,700 paratroopers were airlifted to the city, where they helped to restore order.

In August, after the units returned to Fort Campbell, operation-readiness tests were conducted. There was also a spell of mountain training in the Cherokee National Forest in Tennessee, to train the men and leaders in small unit tactics in mountainous terrain.

Preparation for overseas movement began on 24 August. This was a huge administrative task, requiring every individual's health, dental and ID records to be checked. There was more training and unit photographs, and training on Viet Cong mines, booby traps, and mine warfare techniques at Viet Cong village at Fort Campbell. Battalion Officers and NCOs attended Combat Intelligence Training,

On 2 October the 3rd Battalion of the 506th Infantry departed from Fort Campbell, travelled via commercial airlines to San Francisco, California, and boarded the USNS *General William Weigel* at Oakland Naval Base. Next day, the ship steamed out of San Francisco for South Vietnam. After a 19-day passage, it docked on the west coast of Vietnam at Qui Nhon to let off the 3rd Battalion; the 173rd Airborne Brigade, disembarked at Vung Tau the following day and finally arrived at Cam Ranh Bay on 26 October. After barely two weeks of training the battalion was thrust into its first combat assault on 11 November 1967.

The remaining units of 2nd and 3rd Brigades were airlifted to Vietnam in December during Operation 'Eagle Lift', which is detailed in the next chapter.

TACTICS

From the perspective of most ground commanders, the primary purpose of tactical ground operations in Vietnam was to defeat enemy forces. Consequently, 'find, fix, fight, and finish' the enemy became a much-repeated slogan during the Vietnam War.

In jungle operations, small-unit tactics were essential, since heavy vegetation and broken terrain provided ideal concealment for the enemy. One former battalion commander stated: 'As I saw the war in Vietnam, it belonged to the company commander. He was the key to success – a planner, a doer, an independent operator, and a leader of men.'

The key aspect of the Vietnam War was the very widespread use of helicopters by the US and its allies, which emerged as one of the most important innovations of the conflict. From the initial phases of US participation, the helicopter's great mobility and carrying capacity provided the essential ingredient for operations against the enemy's light infantry in the diverse terrain of Southeast Asia. As a means of transporting supplies,

Below: UH-1D helicopters loaded with personnel of 2nd Battalion, 502nd Infantry, fly over a small Vietnamese village on way to combat area during Operation 'Harrison' near Tuy Hoa.

ammunition, equipment and wounded personnel, its functions ranged far beyond being simply a combat vehicle. Only the helicopter could accomplish such a variety of tactical tasks, ranging from the insertion of a long-range patrol to the vertical assault of an entire division.

Employment of the helicopter enabled allied forces to mass men and equipment in a fashion that affected tactical methods fundamentally. They could transport units to a battle area and could enable them to manoeuvre or to reinforce, displace or withdraw combat power during the battle. They could also be used to concentrate forces quickly. The dominant characteristic of the development of infantry organisations and tactics during the war was the increasing application of airmobile concepts and tactics.

Armed helicopter and aerial rocket artillery (ARA) also provided important support to ground units. Helicopters armed with machine guns, rockets and grenade launchers provided light fire support, which was particularly effective against enemy troops in the open or without fortifications. ARA units provided heavier fire support, often in areas beyond the range of a unit's direct support artillery. Highly mobile, the ARA units could answer calls for fire over extremely large areas, and along with armed helicopters provided especially important support in air assault operations.

OPERATIONS

Search-and-destroy operations
Three basic types of operations were conducted in Vietnam. The first type aimed to 'search and destroy'. Operations of this type sought to locate the enemy and destroy him, and variations could be conducted from company to multidivisional level, though the norm was a multi-battalion operation. In April 1968, the Army dropped the term 'search and destroy' since it was, as General Westmoreland noted, 'equated in the (American) public mind with aimless searches in the jungle and destruction of property'. Other terms, such as combat sweep, reconnaissance in force and spoiling attack, replaced the phrase 'search and destroy'.

Clearing operations
Although 'clearing' operations resembled search-and-destroy operations, they usually placed a greater emphasis on pacification. While search-and-destroy operations chased enemy forces from an area or destroyed them, clearing operations kept them off balance and allowed the South Vietnamese government to extend its influence into the area.

Reconnaissances in force, combat sweeps or other offensive operations continued to be conducted, but the greatest emphasis in clearing operations was placed on eliminating local or main force enemy resistance and destroying his support base. Local commanders and political authorities, for example, often used cordon-and-search operations to 'clear' a village or area. Thus, clearing operations usually lasted longer than search-and-destroy operations.

Securing operations
The final activity was the 'securing' operation. These operations protected pacification accomplishments, but concentrated on eliminating local guerrilla units and the enemy's political infrastructure and support base. Although multi-battalion offensive sweeps could be used to secure an area, the norm was probably saturation patrolling and cordon and searches of hamlets.

Theoretically, the proper sequence of operations was, first, search and destroy, and second, clear and secure, with the final phase being dominated by the South Vietnamese Regional and Popular Forces and the police. While search-and-destroy operations

AIRMOBILITY

Airmobility was a tactical doctrine that began to be developed by the US Army in the early 1960s, entailing the use of helicopters to find the enemy, carry troops into battle, provide them with gunship support, position artillery, and provide communications and resupply. In Vietnam, although the Allied ground forces made extensive use of helicopters, 1st Cavalry and 101st Airborne were the only divisions with their own dedicated aircraft, and during that time, these pioneering airborne units helped further the development of airmobile concepts.

Studies on the viability of airmobility were initiated by the Army Concept Team in 1962 for Army of the Republic of Vietnam (ARVN) and entailed the uplift into combat of fighting troops by H-21 Shawnee helicopters. The trials proved successful and led to the raising of the first dedicated airmobile division, 1st Cavalry. In 1968, 101st Airborne became the second such unit when it was redesignated as 101st Airborne Division (Airmobile). Between 1965 and 1971 the 'Screaming Eagles' employed airmobile tactics in seven of the 15 major ground offensives in which they were engaged, out of a total of 17 launched by US forces in the Vietnam War.

engaged the enemy's main force and provincial battalions, the remaining smaller elements were rooted out in clearing and securing operations.

The tactics employed by American ground troops in South Vietnam were heavily influenced by the enemy's organisation and tactics. Because of their detailed knowledge of local terrain, extensive combat experience in guerrilla warfare and often intense dedication to their cause, VC soldiers were formidable opponents throughout the war. People's Army of Vietnam (PAVN) units were better equipped than the VC units and usually operated as battalions, regiments or even divisions. Except for their greater firepower and usually larger units, PAVN methods of operation resembled those of main force Vietcong.

The VC and PAVN used essentially infantry tactics, and mobility was the key to all their operations, from the small actions of the local forces to the larger actions of the regular forces. The enemy rarely accepted battle in unfavourable situations and only

accepted decisive contact under exceptional circumstances. Their operations were usually ruled by Sun Tzu's maxim, 'When the enemy advances, withdraw; when he defends, harass; when he is tired, attack; when he withdraws, pursue'.

VC and PAVN units used several techniques to weaken the effects of the allied firepower. One of the most important of these was night fighting. Their ability to operate at night under the concealment of darkness often served to nullify the overwhelming firepower advantage of an American unit.

If the Vietcong or North Vietnamese Army were forced to defend or were to remain immobile for a period, as at Dong Ap Bia (see next chapter), they built elaborate networks of trenches, bunkers and tunnels that provided protection against the firepower of attacking allied units. The enemy also engaged allied units at very close distances, especially in jungle fighting, thereby limiting the allied use of artillery, air strikes and helicopter support. Their stress on surprise and mobility also enabled them to strike and escape before allied firepower could be concentrated against them.

Some of the most successful techniques for finding the enemy involved the helicopter. Air assaults struck suspected enemy locations, and a series of successive assaults often checked a number of areas for possible enemy presence. A variation on this emphasised the insertion of small assault forces into a number of potential areas where the enemy might be located. The helicopter also provided an easy method for reconnoitring large areas. Decoy helicopters could be used to draw enemy fire, and 'Eagle Flights' consisting of approximately one heliborne infantry platoon could develop the situation. The helicopter's mobility permitted commanders to extend their influence over areas vastly greater than they could otherwise have done.

After enemy contact was established, mobile US troops reinforced the unit in contact and encircled the enemy's position. These were the first steps in what came to be called 'pile-on' tactics. If there was any manoeuvre, it usually occurred before contact was made or during the 'pile on' of additional troops and equipment.

Using the great mobility of heliborne or mechanized forces, units occupied blocking or ambush positions in order to destroy fleeing enemy forces. According to the size of forces and area involved, such encircling methods were sometimes called 'rat-hole' or 'bull's-eye' tactics.

During and following the concentration of US forces, attacks were usually conducted by fire rather than by ground assault. Under normal circumstances, an infantry assault was avoided or was delayed until after the enemy had been virtually destroyed by supporting fire. The high proportion of automatic weapons among the enemy caused heavy loss rates in assaulting and exposed allied troops. The function of ground forces (especially the infantry) thus became the 'finding' and 'fixing' of the enemy, but the 'fighting' and 'finishing' were most often accomplished by massive artillery and air firepower. Such tactics minimised American casualties and made maximum use of the overwhelming US advantage in firepower. The standing operating procedure for most units became, 'Save lives, not ammunition'.

Thus, the need to provide adequate fire support clearly affected the conduct of ground operations. The establishing of fire support bases often became the first step in major operations. While this sometimes revealed an upcoming operation to the enemy, the deceptive emplacement of fire support bases tended to keep the enemy guessing about allied intentions. The emphasis on operating from and defending these bases, however, led to what General Westmoreland described as a 'fire base psychosis'. American commanders were reluctant to operate beyond the support of their artillery and to risk fighting on near-equal terms with VC or PAVN units. While this excessive caution detracted from the manoeuvre and offensive capabilities of US units, it minimised American casualties.

Left: Troopers of 2nd Battalion, 502nd Infantry (Airborne), 1st Brigade, 101st Airborne Division (Separate), congregate at the pick-up zone for a combat air assault by UH-1D helicopters during Operation 'Harrison' on 27 February 1966. During its service in Vietnam as the 1st Brigade, 101st Airborne Division (Separate) until the arrival of the complete division in November 1967, the troopers of the 'Screaming Eagles' undertook 31 tactical deployments covering more than 2,500 miles together with 25 major operations. Acting as a 'fire brigade' formation across the country, the 1st Brigade, 101st Airborne Division (Separate), dubbed themselves as the 'Nomads of Vietnam'.

Below: The long-range recon team of the 1st Brigade, 101st Airborne, prepares for Operation 'Harrison' near Tuy Hoa, February 1966.

IN ACTION

VIETNAM

For the duration of the war Vietnam was divided into three military zones – I, II and III Corps. Although 101st Airborne conducted military operations in all three Corps, it was primarily engaged in the northern five provinces of South Vietnam, which made up I Corps, and throughout most of the war shared responsibility for this zone with III Marine Amphibious Force and the Americal Division. The Demilitarized Zone formed the northern border and Laos was to its west. The A Shau Valley in western I Corps was a major terminus of the Ho Chi Minh Trail and a logistical staging area for the North Vietnamese. The major cities in this area were Quang Tri, Hue, Da Nang, Tam Ky and Quang Ngai. Unlike the rest of Vietnam, from the outset the war in I Corps was essentially against North Vietnamese regulars, organised as regiments and divisions, and suported by artillery. More than half of all US casualties occurred in I Corps.

Prefacing more specific information on the actions of the 101st Airborne Division, a brief overview of policy and overall strategy for each phase of US involvement in Vietnam is given, in chronological sequence beginning in 1965 and ending in 1971. This it is hoped will give the reader a clearer overall picture of the war.

DEFENCE

8 March–24 December 1965

Beginning in 1964, PAVN and VC forces infiltrating via the Ho Chi Minh Trail attempted to cut South Vietnam in two from the Central Highlands to the coast. US Army adopted a defensive strategy, which had the objective of containing the enemy while gaining time needed to build base camps and logistical facilities. Operations as a part of this defensive strategy, which characterised US involvement until mid-1965, ultimately frustrated the efforts of the North Vietnamese and enabled the US military to consolidate positions from which to launch counteroffensives. Commensurate with the arrival of large numbers of US troops from mid-1965, General Westmoreland adopted a new strategy based on the belief that US forces, with their vastly superior weaponry and training, could defeat the enemy through the incremental attrition of their forces.

During this time, the United States also attempted to consolidate its ground operations more efficiently. For this purpose, it organised the US Army Vietnam (USARV). The I Corps tactical zone, composed of the five northernmost provinces, was to be primarily a Marine Corps responsibility; the US Army was to operate mainly in the II and III Corps tactical zones, which comprised the Central Highlands, adjacent coastal regions, and the area around Saigon; and formations of the Army of the Republic of Vietnam (ARVN) troops were to retain primary responsibility for the Delta region of the IV Corps.

Operation 'Highland'

After deploying to Vietnam at the end of July, the 1st Brigade of 101st Airborne was given precious little time to adjust to their new surroundings before commencing operations. The brigade was still without a home, as it had had no opportunity to establish a base camp, and was well on its way to earning the nick-name 'Nomads of Vietnam' that would endure throughout the war.

From 10 to 21 August the brigade conducted operations southwest of Nha Trang, and on 22 August moved north by sea and air to Binh Dinh Province, where it was to fight its first major action as part of Operation 'Highland'. The objective of 'Highland' was to secure a base at An Khe for the arrival of the 1st Air Cavalry Division (Airmobile). To allow the cavalry to debark safely, deploy to An Khe, and achieve a combat configuration, it was also essential to secure first Qui Nhon, second, Highway 19 connecting Qui Nhon and An Khe, and finally, An Khe itself.

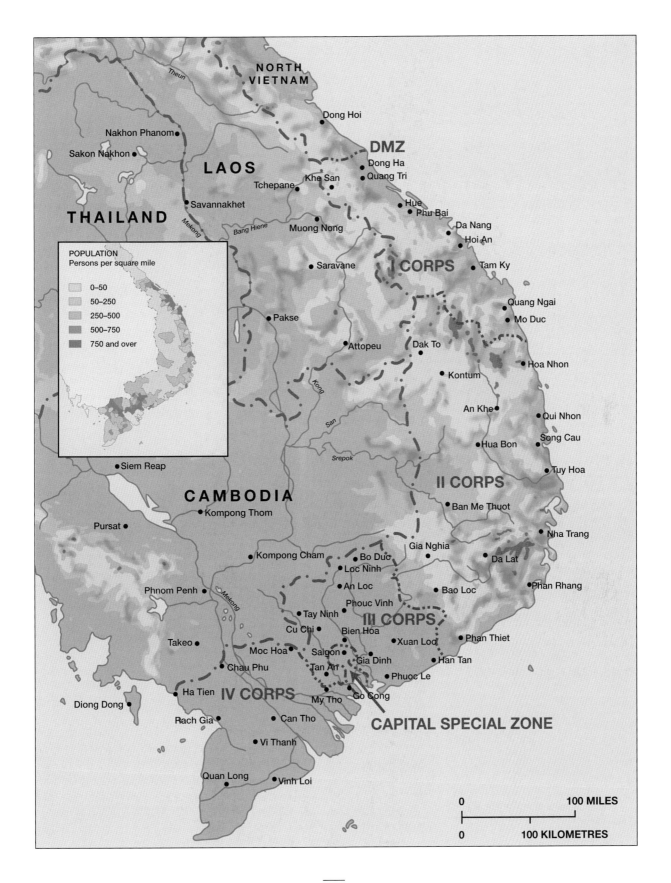

NORTH
VIETNAM

Dong Hoi

DMZ

Nakhon Phanom ●

Sakon Nakhon ●

LAOS

Dong Ha
Khe San ● Quang Tri
Tchepane ●

THAILAND

Savannakhet

Hue
Phu Bai

Bang Hiene

Muong Nong

Da Nang
Hoi An

Mekong

POPULATION
Persons per square mile

☐ 0–50
☐ 50–250
☐ 250–500
☐ 500–750
☐ 750 and over

Saravane ●

I CORPS

Tam Ky

Quang Ngai
Mo Duc

Pakse ●

Attopeu ●

Dak To

Hoa Nhon

Kong

Kontum ●

An Khe ●

Qui Nhon

Song Cau

San

Hua Bon ●

Srepok

Tuy Hoa

II CORPS

● Siem Reap

Ban Me Thuot ●

CAMBODIA

● Kompong Thom

Nha Trang

Pursat ●

Gia Nghia ●

Bo Duc ●
Loc Ninh ●

Da Lat ●

Kompong Cham ●

An Loc ●

Bao Loc ●

Phan Rhang

Phnom Penh ●

Phouc Vinh ●

Mekong

● Tay Ninh

III CORPS

Cu Chi ●

Bien Hoa ●

Xuan Loc ●

Phan Thiet

Takeo ●

Moc Hoa ●

Saigon ●

Gia Dinh

Han Tan ●

Tan An ●

Phuoc Le ●

Chau Phu ●

Ha Tien

IV CORPS

My Tho
Go Cong

Diong Dong ●

CAPITAL SPECIAL ZONE

Rach Gia ●

● Can Tho

● Vi Thanh

Quan Long ●
● Vinh Loi

0   100 MILES

0   100 KILOMETRES

MAJOR OPERATIONS 1965–71

Operation	Location	Date
'Highland	Binh Dinh	Aug–Oct 1965
'Gibraltar	An Khe	Sept 1965
'Van Buren'	Tuy Hoa	Jan 1966
'Hawthorne'	Kontum	June 1966
'Paul Revere IV'	Chu Pong–Ia Drang	May–Dec 1966
'Wheeler'	Quang Nam–Quang Tri	Sept–Nov 1967
'Rose'	Phan Rang	Oct 1967
'Klamath Falls'	Song Mao/Bao Loc	Nov–Dec 1967
'Jeb Stuart'	Quang Tri	Jan–Mar 1968
'Carentan I'	Hue	March 1968
'Carentan II' (Lam Son 216)	Hue	Apr–May 1968
'Delaware'	A Shau Valley	Apr–May 1968
'Nevada Eagle' (Lam Son 224)	Thua Thien Province	May–Aug 1968
'Somerset Plain'	A Shau Valley	August 1968
'Kentucky Jumper'	Thua Thien Province	Mar–Aug 1969
'Massachusetts Striker'	A Shau Valley	Mar–May 1969
'Apache Snow'	A Shau Valley	May–June 1969
'Lamar Plain'	Tam Ky	May–Aug 1969
'Montgomery Rendezvous'	A Shau Valley	June–July 1969
'Saturate'	Thua Thien Province	Oct–Dec 1969
'Randolph Glen'	Thua Thien Province	Dec 1969–Mar 1970
'Texas Star'	Thua Thien Province	Apr 1969–Aug 1970
'Jefferson Glen'	Thua Thien Province	Sept 1970–Oct 1971
'Lam Son 719'	A Shau Valley/Laos	Mar–May 1971
'Lam Son 720'	A Shau Valley	Apr–Aug 1971

A task force designated 'Collins', consisting of the 2nd Battalion, 327th Infantry, moved overland from Cam Ranh Bay to Nha Trang and from there was airlifted to An Khe on the 24th of August. Between 22 and 25 August, all other elements of the brigade moved by truck from Cam Ranh Bay to Nha Trang, then by landing ship to Qui Nhon.

The initial landing at Qui Nhon was made by elements of the 1st Battalion, 327th Infantry, who along with 2nd Battalion, 502nd Infantry, assaulted west to clear Highway 19. This phase of Operation 'Highland' was successfully completed when a heliborne assault (Operation 'Talon') by the 1st Battalion, 327th Infantry, secured the critical An Khe pass – the same pass where previously the French Mobile Group 100 had been virtually annihilated.

Operation 'Gibraltar': Battle of Ah Ninh

Subsequently, a special task force was organised to secure convoy movement along Route 19 and establish strong points along the critical terrain bordering the route from Qui Nhon to the An Khe Pass. Tactical air cover was provided for all convoy traffic. While elements of the brigade guarded the 1st Cavalry Division's lifeline from Qui Nhon to An Khe, it also conducted eight airmobile assaults and many large ground operations to secure the division base area, utilising company-size or larger forces. These used a system of overlapping patrols and a series of sweeping operations designed to find, fix and destroy the enemy. Remarkably, there was no major loss of life or equipment due to enemy action in this period.

In mid-September one of these sweeps, dubbed Operation 'Gibraltar' and involving the 2nd Battalion, 502nd Infantry, and 1st Cavalry and 2nd Battalion, 320th Artillery, turned into the first major contact for the brigade and the first major battle for the US Army in Vietnam.

At 0700 hrs on 18 September, 26 Army UH-1 and Marine UH-34D helicopters landed all of C and part of B Companies of 2nd Battalion, 502nd Infantry, (some 224 men) near the village of An Ninh, almost nine miles north of Route 19. Upon landing, in what was later identified as a Viet Cong battalion command post, the troopers found themselves completely surrounded and outnumbered. Two of their 'slicks' were shot down. In the second wave, only half the choppers were able to set down on the landing zone (LZ). Most of the third wave was waved out of the area by a captain on the ground who was later killed, and even so it lost three helicopters to ground fire.

Below: Pfc Jack Concannon, the chaplain's assistant, sets up an improvised altar during Operation 'Van Buren' on 23 January 1966. Note the M7 bayonet in its M8A1 scabbard attached to the shoulder of his M1956 load carrying equipment harness – obviously useful for dispensing communion wafers.

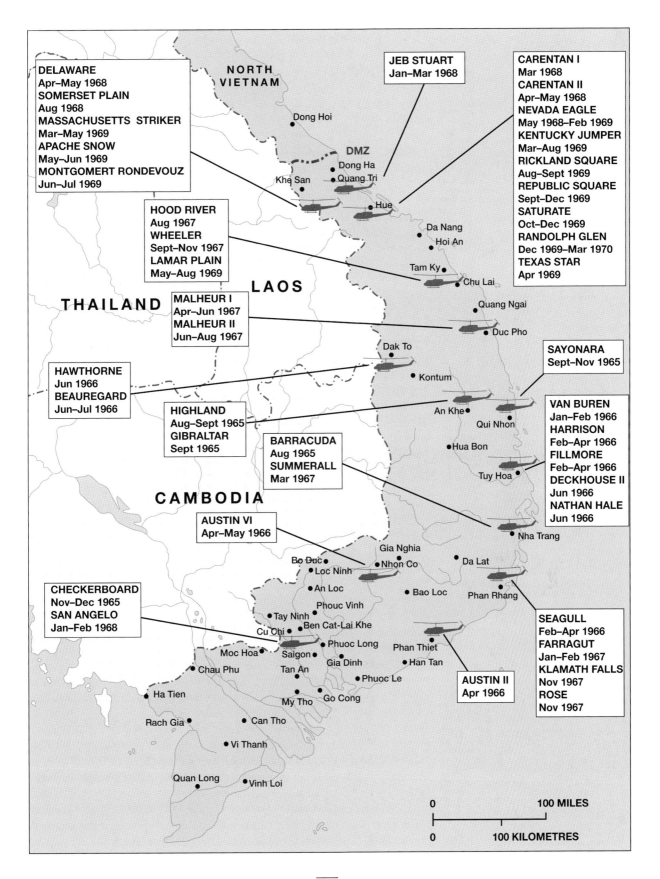

DELAWARE
Apr–May 1968
SOMERSET PLAIN
Aug 1968
MASSACHUSETTS STRIKER
Mar–May 1969
APACHE SNOW
May–Jun 1969
MONTGOMERT RONDEVOUZ
Jun–Jul 1969

JEB STUART
Jan–Mar 1968

CARENTAN I
Mar 1968
CARENTAN II
Apr–May 1968
NEVADA EAGLE
May 1968–Feb 1969
KENTUCKY JUMPER
Mar–Aug 1969
RICKLAND SQUARE
Aug–Sept 1969
REPUBLIC SQUARE
Sept–Dec 1969
SATURATE
Oct–Dec 1969
RANDOLPH GLEN
Dec 1969–Mar 1970
TEXAS STAR
Apr 1969

HOOD RIVER
Aug 1967
WHEELER
Sept–Nov 1967
LAMAR PLAIN
May–Aug 1969

MALHEUR I
Apr–Jun 1967
MALHEUR II
Jun–Aug 1967

SAYONARA
Sept–Nov 1965

HAWTHORNE
Jun 1966
BEAUREGARD
Jun–Jul 1966

HIGHLAND
Aug–Sept 1965
GIBRALTAR
Sept 1965

VAN BUREN
Jan–Feb 1966
HARRISON
Feb–Apr 1966
FILLMORE
Feb–Apr 1966
DECKHOUSE II
Jun 1966
NATHAN HALE
Jun 1966

BARRACUDA
Aug 1965
SUMMERALL
Mar 1967

AUSTIN VI
Apr–May 1966

CHECKERBOARD
Nov–Dec 1965
SAN ANGELO
Jan–Feb 1968

SEAGULL
Feb–Apr 1966
FARRAGUT
Jan–Feb 1967
KLAMATH FALLS
Nov 1967
ROSE
Nov 1967

AUSTIN II
Apr 1966

NORTH
VIETNAM

LAOS

THAILAND

CAMBODIA

DMZ

Dong Hoi
Khe San
Dong Ha
Quang Tri
Hue
Da Nang
Hoi An
Tam Ky
Chu Lai
Quang Ngai
Duc Pho
Dak To
Kontum
An Khe
Qui Nhon
Hua Bon
Tuy Hoa
Nha Trang
Gia Nghia
Nhon Co
Da Lat
Bo Duc
Loc Ninh
An Loc
Bao Loc
Phuoc Vinh
Phan Rhang
Tay Ninh
Ben Cat-Lai Khe
Cu Chi
Phuoc Long
Phan Thiet
Moc Hoa
Saigon
Gia Dinh
Han Tan
Chau Phu
Tan An
Phuoc Le
Ha Tien
My Tho
Go Cong
Rach Gia
Can Tho
Vi Thanh
Quan Long
Vinh Loi

0   100 MILES
0   100 KILOMETRES

**101st AIRBORNE DIVISION
ORDER OF BATTLE
VIETNAM (1968)**

1st Brigade
    1st Battalion, 327th Infantry
    2nd Battalion, 327th Infantry
    2nd Battalion, 502nd Infantry

2nd Brigade
    1st Battalion, 501st Infantry
    2nd Battalion, 501st Infantry
    1st Battalion, 502nd Infantry

3rd Brigade
    (3rd Battalion, 506th Infantry)
    3rd Battalion, 187th Infantry
    1st Battalion, 506th Infantry
    2nd Battalion, 506th Infantry

101st Aviation Group
    101st Aviation Battalion
    158th Aviation Battalion
    159th Aviation Battalion
    163rd Aviation Company

    2nd Squadron, 17th Cavalry

101st Airborne Division Artillery
    4th Battalion, 77th Artillery
    2nd Battalion, 319th Artillery
    2nd Battalion, 320th Artillery
    1st Battalion, 321st Artillery

101st Military Police Company
326th Engineer Battalion
501st Signal Battalion
101st Airborne Division Support
    Command
101st Administration Company
326th Medical Battalion
426th Supply and Service Battalion
801st Maintenance Battalion
5th Transportation Battalion

Note: The 3rd Battalion, 506th Infantry
was detached from the 101st Airborne
Division from January 17th, 1968 to
August 26th, 1970, during which period
it was known as Task Force 3-506.

To compound the problem, 2nd Battalion of the 320th Artillery could not move its 105 mm guns into supporting position because of muddy roads, and had to wait until the evening for the 1st Cavalry's CH-47s Chinooks to airlift them into position.

By early the next morning, the supporting arms were in place and more infantry was inserted. As these reinforcements arrived, it became evident that the original assault had caught the enemy completely by surprise, and they were never able to reorganise their forces. Much of the credit must go to the surrounded troopers, who took the offensive and badly mauled the confused Viet Cong. When the battle ended three days later, 226 VC lay dead on the battlefield, bringing the number of enemy killed to date to 692, as against the 1st Brigade's losses of 21.

By the end of the month the 1st Cavalry had assumed responsibility for the An Khe area and the 101st was uprooted to Qui Nhon to provide security for the incoming Republic of Korea Capital ('Tiger') Division. In early November, the brigade at last established a base camp at Phan Rang, some 175 miles up the coast from Saigon. But except for a few hundred support troops inhabiting a corner of the base, Phan Rang was deserted for all but 21 days in two years, as the brigade moved to support operations around the country.

Battle of Ia Drang

Elsewhere, on 19 October 1965, three VC regiments totalling 6,000 men attacked a Civil Irregular Defense Group (CIDG)/US Special Forces camp at Plei Me, near the entrance to the Ia Drang Valley, in what purported to be the start of a thrust to cut the country in half. With the assistance of massive air strikes, elements of the newly arrived 1st Cavalry Division thwarted the enemy in a battle that lasted nearly a month and included several engagements. The Ia Drang Valley action was the costliest in terms of US casualties to date, yet the successful defence of the region improved security in and around the Central Highlands and raised the morale of the soldiers involved.

COUNTEROFFENSIVE

25 December 1965–30 June 1966

In December 1965 the United States again halted air attacks against North Vietnam, and invited the North Vietnamese government to negotiate an end to the fighting. The offer was refused. Ho Chi Minh's conditions for peace were clear cut. He demanded an end to the bombing and a complete American withdrawal. But withdrawal would mean almost certain defeat for the Republic of Vietnam, and its fall to Communism. President Johnson would not accept Ho's terms, and instead offered his own proposals, the most important of which was an immediate ceasefire between the belligerents. Neither side would compromise, however, and the fighting went on. In 1966 Johnson renewed the bombing attacks in North Vietnam, and also increased the number of US troops committed in the south.

Following the US victory in the Ia Drang Valley, American forces for the remainder of 1965 and well into 1966 sought to keep the enemy off balance while building base camps and logistical installations. This policy involved the use of search-and-destroy operations to protect the logistical bases under construction along the coast and the base camps for incoming US units in the provinces near Saigon.

Also of particular concern to the American military mission was the protection of the government and the people of South Vietnam. To these ends US efforts were concentrated in the most vital and heavily populated regions. The III Marine Amphibious Force supported the South Vietnamese I Corps in the northern provinces; I Field Force supported the Vietnamese II Corps in the central region; and II Field Force supported the South Vietnamese III Corps around Saigon. Consequently, the major battles of the year occurred in these critical areas.

Operation 'Van Buren'

Early in the new year, on 19 January, the 1st Brigade, 101st Airborne Division, the Korean 2nd Marine Brigade and the ARVN 47th Regiment began Operation 'Van Buren' to locate and destroy the PAVN 95th Regiment, which intelligence believed to be in the Tuy Hoa Valley. A second objective was to protect the rice harvest produced in the coastal region from seizure by the enemy.

Upon arriving at Tuy Hoa, the 1st Brigade moved straight into its operational areas. In the ensuing operation, 679 enemy casualties were verified. The 1st Brigade accounted for 282 enemy killed in action (KIA) plus 66 killed by artillery (KBA), 33 captured and 238 suspects detained. (The term killed-by-artillery was introduced a means of classifying enemy casualties for the statistics hungry Department of Defence.) Over 100 weapons, and several caches of ammo and supplies were also taken. The brigade's own casualties were 55 KIA and 221 WIA. During 20–23rd January, a temporary ceasefire was proclaimed in respect of the lunar new year (Tet), although minor clashes continued throughout this period.

Operation 'Hawthorne'

With the seasonal monsoon hampering air operations, spring 1966 passed relatively peacefully for the 1st Brigade. Then, in June, under the cover of rain and fog shrouding the Central Highlands, came a major PAVN offensive in Kontum Province. During this was fought the first battle of Dak To, a strategically important outpost in northern Kontum, which had been surrounded by units of the 24th PAVN Regiment. Against this a counterstrike – Operation 'Hawthorne' – was launched, to which the 1st Brigade was committed. While this succeeded in blunting the PAVN offensive in Kontum Province, it was to be a costly and hard-won victory.

Operation 'Hawthorne' began with a mission to rescue Vietnamese irregulars at the Tou Morong Special Forces Camp, near Dak To. The 1st Battalion of the 327th Infantry, commanded by Lt. Col. David H. Hackworth, and 1st Battalion of the ARVN's 42nd Regiment, were ordered to relieve it, and fought through moderate resistance to reach the hilltop garrison and evacuate the 150 inhabitants.

Hackworth then detached the 1st Battalion, 327th Infantry Regiment, to pursue the PAVN forces into the surrounding valleys. At 0230 hrs on the night of 6– 7 June, a battalion of the PAVN 24th Regiment counterattacked and partially overran the position held by Battery B, 2nd Howitzer Battalion (Airborne), 2nd Battalion of the 502nd Infantry, and Company A of the 226th Engineer Battalion in a valley west of Tou Morong. A major firefight broke out and raged until dawn, at which point the assaults halted. In a sweep of the area 86 enemy bodies were counted, 13 of them within the perimeter of the artillery position.

During the day, attacking north out of Tou Morong, one of the companies of the 1st Battalion, 327th Infantry, was badly mauled when it wandered into a PAVN base camp, and was saved only by artillery barrages and the insertion of additional infantry. It was now readily apparent to the officers directing the operation that a major PAVN force was present, and they sought an opportunity to destroy it. Companies of the 101st's 2nd battalion, 502nd Infantry, were quickly airlifted in to Dak To by C-130, from where they were to sweep south to aid the beleaguered force on the ground.

Dak To, in the heart of verdant jungle of the Central Highlands, is ringed on all sides by mountains, and behind those are yet taller ranges. 'I've never seen Dien Bien Phu,' one trooper remarked at the time, 'but this sure looks like the description.'

His apprehensions proved well founded; the ensuing battle (the first of a series that would be fought for control of the area) rapidly developed into one of the most viciously

---

Unit Headquarters (from 1967)

Bien Hoa Nov 67 - Feb 68
Bien Hoa/Phu Bai Mar 68 - Apr 69
Bien Hoa/Gia Le May 69 - Sept 69
Bien Hoa/Hue/Phu Bai Oct 69 - Nov 69
Hue/Phu Bai Dec 69 - Mar 72

1st 'Bastogne' Brigade - consisting of 1st and 2nd Battalion, 327th Infantry Regiment and 2nd Battalion, 502nd Infantry Regiment deployed to Vietnam from July 1965 to December 1971. Initially, the brigade operated out of Phan Rang, Ninh Thuan province, in II Corps Tactical Area of Responsibility (TAOR).

2nd 'Ready to Go' Brigade deployed to Vietnam between December 1967 and was originally based in the III Corps area, while the 1st Brigade continued operations in II Corps.

The 3rd Brigade was sent to the Dak To Highlands in mid-1968 and elements of that unit were later sent down to reinforce the 25th Infantry Division around Saigon. In September 1968, 3rd Brigade redeployed to I Corps at Phong Diem (just north of Camp Evans and south of Quang Tri). Although nominally a part of the brigade, 3rd Battalion, 506th Infantry operated out of Phan Thiet for most of the war and did not participate in any joint operations with any other elements of the 101st during the entire war. In May 1970, it was the only unit of the 101st to participate in the invasion of Cambodia.

On November 20th, 1971, 3rd Brigade redeployed to the United States and returned to its home at Fort Campbell.

6666

VALOROUS UNIT AWARD, STREAMER EMBROIDERED TUY HOA

Headquarters and Headquarters Company, 1st Brigade, 101st Airborne Division cited in Department of the Army General Orders 17, 23 April 1968, as amended by Department of the Army General Orders 1, 8 January 1969 (along with other attached units):

While participating in military operations: The 1st Brigade, 101st Airborne Division distinguished itself by extraordinary heroism from 17 January 1966 to 25 March 1966 while conducting Operations VAN BUREN and HARRISON against armed hostile forces in the vicinity of Tuy Hoa, Republic of Vietnam. After commencing Operation VAN BUREN on 17 January, the 1st Brigade deployed in the Tuy Hoa area to locate, fix, and destroy Viet Cong forces, while simultaneously protecting the local rice harvest from hostile seizure. The 1st Brigade not only defeated the insurgents decisively in four major battles, but also enabled the Vietnamese people to harvest a rice crop triple that of the previous year, when Viet Cong interference was unchecked. At Canh Tinh on 6 February, the 2d Battalion (Airborne), 502d Infantry killed 64 Viet Cong and completely routed a numerically superior force from heavily fortified emplacements. On the following day the 1st Battalion (Airborne), 327th Infantry took a toll of 66 insurgents in a savage conflict. During Operation HARRISON, that began on 21 February, the 1st Battalion (Airborne), 502d Infantry continued maneuvers in the Tuy Hoa area by searching out and destroying 118 of the enemy in a 5-hour pitched battle in the rice paddies around My Phu. After three days of difficult marching through mountainous jungle, the 2d Battalion (Airborne), 327th Infantry discovered a

contested actions of the Vietnam War. On the night of 7 June, human waves of the PAVN 24th Infantry Regiment surrounded and nearly overran the night laager of one of the companies. The company commander, an All-American football player at West Point named Captain William S. Carpenter, called in napalm strikes on his own position to repel the attack. While this earned him a citation for the Medal of Honor from General Westmoreland, some of his surviving men threatened to kill him.

Moving slowly from bunker to trench line, spider hole, bamboo thicket and stream bed the operation was nearing termination when tragedy struck. On 17 June a company of the 1st Battalion, 327th Infantry, engaged a small PAVN force in dense terrain. Responding to a call for support, 1st Cavalry helicopter gunships hit the company position itself.

But by the end of 'Hawthorne', the 24th PAVN Regiment had been all but destroyed. Hit by over 27,000 artillery rounds and 473 Air Force sorties, it suffered more than 1,200 dead and wounded, and the North Vietnamese offensive in Kontum was stopped dead in its tracks. US losses were more than 50 dead and 200 wounded.

As the 101st Airborne buried its dead, General Stanley R. Larsen, then commanding general of I Field Force, was moved to state publicly that the 1st Brigade was the 'best fighting unit in Vietnam'.

Battle of Truong Long

Even as Operation 'Hawthorne' was approaching its conclusion, another lesser-known but equally vicious action was about to be fought by the 101st Airborne in the Central Highlands. In early June, US Intelligence officers had identified a North Vietnamese unit of unknown size and location concentrated in the vicinity of Trung Luong. Fearing that these troops would attempt to take the US Special Forces base at nearby Dong Tre, II Corps called in the 1st Battalion, 5th Infantry (1st Cavalry Division), from An Khe and 2nd Battalion, 327th Infantry, from Tuy Hoah.

For these men, the remote hamlet of Truong Long was to become a name indelibly imprinted on their minds, and the battle fought there is acknowledged as one of the most brutal of the entire Vietnam War.

At the time the 2nd Battalion of 327th Infantry was commanded by Lt. Col. Joseph 'Wild Gypsy' Wasco, a 44-year-old veteran of the Second World War and the Korean War. At Trung Luong, working with the available intelligence, Wasco estimated he was faced by a battalion-strength unit in the order of 300 men. In fact, elements of three hardened North Vietnamese regiments were dug in around the hamlet – a force of some 3,000 to 4,000 men. Aerial reconnaissance missions did not detect the troops hidden in one of the most elaborate tunnel networks of the war, the fortified bunkers beneath ricestacks or the bunkers carved into the banks of winding creeks.

On the afternoon of 19 June 1966, A Company of the 2nd Battalion air-assaulted down toward the valley of Trung Luong. Just minutes after the 'slicks' touched down at the LZ, the company began taking casualties. Several paratroopers collapsed with heatstroke, overcome by stifling 100° temperatures and the smoke from burning bush grass, which had been set alight by artillery and helicopter gunships.

To make matters worse, the men were loaded like mules, typically carrying three days' worth of canned C rations, bandoliers of M-60 ammunition, their own M-16 rifles, extra ammo clips, claymore mines, grenades, clean socks, sleeping bags, ponchos, entrenching tools and two canteens of water per man.

The 139 men of A Company marched north with this load through the midday heat for almost three hours in the direction of Trung Luong. At nightfall, they halted and ambush patrols were sent out. Then at 0830 hrs the following morning, the company commander, Captain Tom Furgeson, got an urgent radio call from Wasco. The battalion's

C Company was pinned down by heavy enemy fire. Alpha Company was ordered to move west through Trung Luong to reinforce its sister company two miles away.

Furgeson led his company about a mile to a ridge finger known as Hill 48. He then sent a platoon, led by Lt. Walter Eddy, into the hamlet. As they approached, the air suddenly came alive with automatic fire and men began to drop wounded or dead to the ground. For 90 minutes A Company lay pinned down, before Furgeson was compelled to radio for permission to pull back to the ridge and call in air strikes. The survivors marched back up the ridge, exhausted, and watched as Navy aircraft laced the hamlet with napalm. From his command post on the ridge finger, Furgeson radioed Wasco again. C Company still desperately needed help. Both officers agreed: A Company had to go back into Trung Luong.

Early that same afternoon, 20 June, B Company was preparing to assault into a LZ atop Hill 258, just northwest of Trung Luong. The company had been yanked from another battle and ordered to take the hill, then link up with A and C Companies. As the Hueys touched down on Hill 258, they came down slightly off the intended landing zone, into a swarm of enemy fire. By the time the last chopper landed, at about 1500 hrs, dead and wounded littered the ridge top, but by daybreak on 21 June, the position was taken.

Back at Hill 48, Furgeson had taken A Company back down into Trung Luong shortly after 1400 hrs on 20 June. As the men approached down a dry creek bed the PAVN troops opened fire from bunkers set in the creek bank. The firefight was still raging when a helicopter brought in Colonel Hal Moore, a brigade commander with the First Cavalry, who now assumed command of the situation.

A Company's wounded were loaded onto choppers. The remainder – tired, thirsty, some sick with dysentery and all of them scared – went back into the hamlet on the morning of 21 June. This time, as they approached the hedgerow where they had been ambushed the day before, most were certain they going to die. Another fierce firefight erupted, but in the face of fresh reinforcements, during the night the enemy began to melt away. By the next morning, they had evacuated. There was only scattered resistance as A and C Companies came within sight of one another in Trung Luong, now deserted. A Company pulled back for the final time, bringing out its casualties.

In the aftermath of the battle, some 371 enemy dead were counted on the battlefield. US commanders estimated the full figure to be nearer 400. Although the remainder of 24th PAVN Regiment managed to escape into Laos, North Vietnamese battle reports reveal that it had been seriously mauled. In them, PAVN officers speak of hunger, malaria, desertions, sleep deprivation and shell-shock (118 tons of napalm, 107 tons of bombs and 26,000 artillery rounds had been directed at them) among their men.

A Company had also suffered grievously. In truth, it had been virtually annihilated. Of the 139 men who had gone in on 19 June, plus two dozen reinforcements, only 42 were still standing. More than 70 had been killed or wounded, and dozens more had been felled by heat stroke. (The PAVN claimed it had killed 144 Americans.)

The Fields of Bamboo, an account of Trung Luong and two other battles by US Army historian S.L.A. Marshall has this to say. 'Few, if any, United States rifle companies in the Vietnam War were more sorely tried.'

Other operations

During 1966 there were 18 major operations, the most successful of these being Operation 'White Wing' (originally named 'Masher' and sometimes referred to as the 'Bong Son Campaign'). Launched on 24 January, 'Masher' was the first major search-and-destroy operation of the Vietnam War. It entailed a 42-day sweep over 2,000 square miles of forested mountains and rugged valleys by the 1st Cavalry Division, Korean Capitol Division and ARVN 22nd Division in northern Binh Dinh Province in II Corps

Viet Cong regimental headquarters. The men fiercely broke the hostile defenses that were in a nearly impregnable cave complex and uncovered one of the largest caches captured in the counterinsurgency efforts. While suffering only light casualties in both operations, the 1st Brigade killed more than 500 Viet Cong, wounded hundreds more and captured nearly 500 insurgents and suspects. Not content with merely defeating the enemy, the men of this exceptional unit strengthened the safety and health of the local Vietnamese population by tireless efforts in medical treatment, road building and protection of the valuable rice crop. Their extensive military and civic accomplishments deeply depressed enemy morale and struck an irreparable blow to insurgency efforts in the vicinity of Tuy Hoa. The extraordinary heroism and devotion to duty displayed by the men of the 1st Brigade, 101st Airborne Division, were in keeping with the highest traditions of the military service and reflect distinct credit upon themselves and the Armed Forces of the United States.

Tactical Zone. In the process they decimated a division, later established as the North Vietnamese 3rd Division. The operation ended on 6 March.

Running concurrent with 'Masher', Marine Corps and ARVN units working with the 1st Cavalry Division (Airmobile) made an unsuccessful attempt to trap PAVN and VC units in the Tam Quan region of Quang Ngai Province in a pincer envelopment: Operation 'Double Eagle'.

Also during February and March, US intelligence reported heavy North Vietnamese Army infiltration from Laos and across the demilitarised zone into Quang Tri Province. The US 3rd Marine Division was moved into the area of the two northern provinces to operate in concert with the ARVN 1st Division and 173rd Airborne Brigade. On 12 April, US B-52s based on Guam bombed infiltration routes near the Laos border, in the first use of these bombers against PAVN troops. These actions succeeded in driving the PAVN back, forcing it to take refuge in Laos, Cambodia and North Vietnam; they temporarily removed the threat of harassment to the populace by North Vietnamese regular forces and curbed local guerrilla activity.

COUNTEROFFENSIVE, PHASE II

1 July 1966–31 May 1967

During this period the American military establishment in Vietnam grew ever larger. The elaborate system of base camps continued to be developed, ports and airports were built or improved, and massive logistical support was provided. By 3 December 1966 US military personnel in South Vietnam numbered 385,300, and by 30 June 1967 this number had risen to 448,800.

Allied operations after 1 July 1966 were by and large a continuation of the earlier counteroffensive campaign. The Joint Chiefs of Staff declared that American military objectives should be to cause North Vietnam to cease its control and support of the insurgency in South Vietnam and Laos, to assist South Vietnam in defeating Viet Cong and North Vietnamese forces in the country, and to assist South Vietnam in pacification and extending governmental control over its territory.

However, the essence of Communist control over the populace – the VC infrastructure in the hamlets and villages – remained essentially unaffected as the pacification programme failed to make significant headway. At the same time, North Vietnam continued to build its own forces inside South Vietnam; their total strength was in excess of 282,000 in addition to an estimated 80,000 political cadres.

Infiltration was first routed by sea and along the Ho Chi Minh trail and then, in early 1967, through the demilitarised zone (DMZ). US air elements received permission to conduct reconnaissance bombing raids and tactical air strikes into North Vietnam just north of the DMZ, but ground forces were denied authority to conduct reconnaissance patrols in the northern portion of the zone or inside North Vietnam. Confined to South Vietnamese territory, US ground forces were forced to fight a war of attrition, relying for a time on body counts as one standard indicator for measuring successful progress in the conduct of the war.

Operation 'Paul Revere IV'

From May to December 1966, Allied units were heavily engaged in screening operations along the Cambodian border in the northeastern sector of II Corps, under the operational designation 'Paul Revere'. 'Paul Revere IV' (18 October–30 December) was a major search-and-destroy operation along the border, conducted primarily by the newly arrived 4th Infantry Division in conjunction with the 1st Cavalry Division. It was centred on the Chu Pong–Ia Drang area. When it became clear that the enemy was attempting to withdraw into Laos, a massive helicopter airlift of the 1st Brigade, 101st Airborne Division, was staged, but the brigade was landed just as the enemy was crossing into Laos and safety. 'Paul Revere IV' was declared officially concluded on 30th December, and the brigade was subsequently ordered into reserve in Phu Yen Province.

During the early part of 1967, the brigade was used as a rapid reaction force, reinforcing American and South Vietnamese forces when necessary and responding to enemy attacks. In April, the brigade was attached to Task Force Oregon, placed under operational control of the III Marine Amphibious Force and moved to Chu Lai on the eastern coast. Task Force Oregon was a multi-brigade army force, organised by Major General William Rosson, and composed of the 196th Light Infantry Brigade, 1st Brigade of 101st Airborne, and the 3rd Brigade of 25th Infantry Division. At Chu Lai, it assisted in operations to blunt an offensive by the PAVN 2nd Division and to enable units of the 3rd Marine Task Force to relocate to Quang Tri province. Later, it was called in to assist a Marine battalion in beating off an enemy attack around Khe Sanh, to where it would return in the long, bloody siege of 1968. Also in April, the 3rd Battalion (Airborne), 506th Infantry, was reactivated at Fort Campbell under Lt. Col. John P. Geraci.

Other operations

In November 1966 a major sweep – Operation 'Attleboro' – was undertaken in the so-called 'Iron Triangle' area (War Zone C) about 25 miles northwest of Saigon. For years this area had been under development as a VC logistics base and headquarters to control enemy activity in and around Saigon. Some 22,000 US and ARVN troops were pitted against the VC 9th Division and a PAVN regiment. Several pitched battles occurred between the opposing forces, the most significant at Ap Cha Do, before the PAVN/VC fled over the border to safe havens in Cambodia or Laos. Generally, 'Attleboro' was a success, destroying the 9th VC Division's extensive base area and reducing its effectiveness for about six months. Furthermore, it demonstrated that large numbers of battalions could arrive quickly in an operational area and bring the enemy to battle, thus setting the scene for subsequent large scale operations: 'Cedar Falls' and 'Junction City'.

On 8 January 1967, US and South Vietnamese troops launched further drives against two major VC strongholds in the Iron Triangle, under Operation 'Cedar Falls'. The Allies captured caches of rice and other foodstuffs, destroyed an elaborate system of tunnels, and seized documents of major intelligence value.

Following a little over a month after 'Cedar Falls', on 22 February these same US forces were committed with other units in the largest allied operation of the war to date: Operation 'Junction City'. The primary objective of this corps-sized action was the elimination of the Viet Cong 9th Division in War Zone C. Some 22 US and four ARVN battalions engaged the enemy, but by the time 'Junction City' terminated on 14 May they had not been unable to decisively neutralise the area. The operation did, however, convince the Communists to move their headquarters into Cambodia and out of reach of Allied forces.

COUNTEROFFENSIVE, PHASE III

1 June 1967–29 January 1968

From midway through 1967 until early in the new year, efforts aimed at 'Vietnamisation' of the conflict, so that the armed forces of the Republic of Vietnam could assume greater responsibility for operations against North Vietnam, were

companies of the Battalion at one time, each in a separate fire fight. As the battle raged, the Battalion's elite Tiger Force was hard hit and almost overrun by an estimated two companies of heavily armed, well trained North Vietnamese Army Regulars. On 7 June 1966, the 2d Battalion (Airborne), 502d Infantry, was helilifted into a blocking position where it began a sweep south to link up with its heavily engaged sister Battalion. Throughout the battle, the enemy strength was fixed as a well trained North Vietnamese Army Regiment. Their heavy weapons were strategically placed in sturdy bunkers which were spread out along the fingers and draws of mountainside. As the battered but courageous 2d Battalion (Airborne), 502d Infantry companies regrouped and the 1st Battalion (Airborne), 327th Infantry, continued their relentless attack from the south, a decision was made to have B-52 Bombers strike Dak Tan Kan Valley before the Brigade moved in for the final kill. 'Hawthorne' was one of the most viciously contested battles of the Vietnam War. Day and Night the battle raged, moving from bunker to trench line, to spider hole, to bamboo thicket, to stream bed, and finally to victory. At the conclusion of 'Hawthorne' the 24th North Vietnamese Army Regiment was rendered ineffective as a fighting unit, suffering 1200 casualties by body count and estimate. By comparison, friendly casualties were 48 dead and 239 wounded. A major North Vietnamese offensive to seize the North Central Highlands was blunted. Throughout 'Hawthorne' the extraordinary heroism, dogged determination, gallantry, and indomitable spirit with which the 1st Brigade, 101st Airborne Division, successfully accomplished all assigned missions were in keeping with the finest traditions of the United States Army and reflect great credit upon all members of the Brigade who participated in this remarkable combat action.

Above: Lt Daniel Hill of Company B, 2nd Battalion, 327th Infantry (Airborne), 1st Brigade, 101st Airborne Division (Separate), sets fire to a village hut during Operation 'Van Buren' on 23 January 1966. Operation 'Van Buren' was conducted in Phu Yen Province to deny the local rice harvest to the VC/NVA. Such acts did much to alienate US forces from the rural population who were caught between the fear of intimidation from the communists and the lack of security provided by the Saigon government. For the average peasant farmer, it was a no-win situation.

increasingly realised. Vietnamese Special Forces assumed responsibility for several Special Forces camps and for the CIDG companies manning them. In each case all of the US advisors withdrew, leaving the Vietnamese in full command. With an increased delegation of responsibility to them, the South Vietnamese conducted major operations during 1967 and, in spite of VC attempts to avoid battle, achieved a number of contacts.

The number of US troops in Vietnam continued to increase. In August 1967, the remainder of the 101st Airborne Division was alerted for deployment to Vietnam from Fort Campbell, two years and 27 days after the departure of the 1st Brigade.

Throughout this period the nature of operations in South Vietnam remained basically unchanged. In II Corps, as Operation 'Junction City' ended, elements of the US 1st and 25th Infantry Divisions, the 11th Armored Cavalry Regiment and the forces of the Army of the Republic of Vietnam swung back toward Saigon to conduct another clearing operation – 'Manhattan' – conducted in the Long Nguyen base area just north of Iron Triangle.

Operation 'Wheeler'

In I Corps TAOR, following on from Task Force Oregon, Operation 'Wheeler' was launched in Quang Nam and Quang Tin Provinces on 11 September 1967. During this operation the 1st Brigade encountered elements of the 2nd PAVN Division west of Tam Ky, and used surprise airmobile assaults into the Song Tranh Valley to flush them out. The fleeing PAVN were killed in droves. After three weeks close to 400 had been killed, and by early November this had more than doubled, making 'Wheeler' the largest single operation conducted by the brigade in Vietnam to date. By the time it was concluded after 75 days, the 1st Brigade troopers had killed 1,105 enemy. With 'Wheeler' successfully concluded, the 1st Brigade was detached from the Americal Division to prepare for the arrival of 2nd and 3rd Brigades and support elements. (The Americal or 23rd Infantry Division had been formed from the former Task Force Oregon, to which the 1st Brigade was still seconded, Shortly after the operation commenced.)

On 26 October, the USNS *General Weigel* arrived at Cam Ranh Bay carrying the 3rd Battalion (Airborne), 506th Infantry. The troops disembarked at 1030 hrs and then moved to Phan Rang base camp in II Corps: the 'Eagle's Roost'. Soon after arrival they began 'P-training' (Proficiency School), while two groups of battalion officers and NCOs went to Chu Lai (I Corps) for 'on-the-job' training with their counterparts in the 1st Brigade.

Between 11 and 30 November the battalion engaged in Operation 'Rose', its first combat operation. 'Rose', a combination search-and-destroy and reconnaissance-in-force mission was conducted southwest of Phan Rang. Although the primary mission was to find, fix, and destroy Viet Cong/NVA forces and to neutralise their base camps, especially Secret Base 35, it was also designed to provide security for engineers working on Highway QL 1 (Route 1). Assaulting into a hot LZ the battalion's B Company, under Captain Landgraf, made the first contact with the enemy, the Viet Cong's 112th and C-270 Local Force Companies. Over the ensuing two weeks the battalion skirmished with enemy units on almost a daily basis. By the time the operation ended on 30 November (Thanksgiving Day), eight NVA/Viet Cong were confirmed KIA. US casualties were nine WIA.

Late in November, the 1st Brigade moved back to the divisional base camp at Phan Rang after an eight-month deployment to I Corps. In the two and a half years since arriving, the unit had made 31 tactical deployments, travelling more than 2,500 miles to conduct 25 major operations in three of the four tactical zones. The troopers accounted for 6,000 enemy killed, captured enough weapons to equip eight enemy battalions, and took 2,000 tons of rice. Medical treatment was provided for more than 25,000 Vietnamese, and more than 15,000 refugees were relocated. Four thousand miles of road were cleared of enemy control.

Operation 'Klamath Falls'

After refitting at Phan Rang, an advance party of the 3rd Battalion, 506th Infantry, moved by helicopter to Song Mao in preparation for a new operation: 'Klamath Falls'. Following the current pattern of US Army operations, 'Klamath Falls' was a combination search-and-destroy and reconnaissance-in-force mission. The primary objective was to seek out and destroy the headquarters of the enemy's MR-6 (Military Region 6) and all enemy forces in the area of operations – Binh Thuan and Lam Dong Provinces – including the PAVN/Viet Cong 146th, 186th, 482nd, and 840th Main Force Viet Cong Battalions. Another operational objective was to open and keep open Highway QL-1 from the II Corps boundary to the Binh Thuan–Ninh Thuan Province boundary.

Below: Capt. Dennis Anderson, the Intelligence Officer of the 2nd Battalion, 502nd Infantry (Airmobile), 101st Airborne Division (Separate), listens as an ARVN officer interrogates a VC suspect during Operation 'Cook', a search and destroy mission in the mountains of Quang Ngai Province on 7 September 1967. At this time, the 1st Brigade was part of Task Force Oregon, a division-sized US Army formation that was created from several different units to allow the US Marines in Quang Ngai Provinve to redeploy to the DMZ area in strength. Task Force Oregon operated between April and September 1967 when it was superseded by the 23rd Infantry Division (Americal).

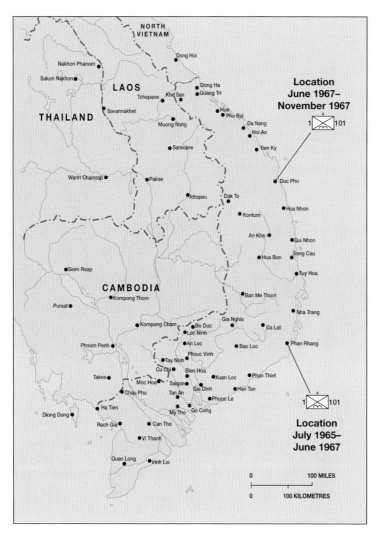

Above: The location of the 1st Brigade of 101st
Airborne during the period July 1965–June 1967..

Under 'Klamath Falls', 3rd Battalion operated for the first time with its parent unit: the 1st Brigade, 101st Airborne Division. Also involved were elements of the 2nd Battalion of the 7th Cavalry, 1st Cavalry Division, based at Phan Thiet, the 23rd ARVN Division and Company B of the 5th Special Forces Group. The 'Currahees' (the 'Stand Alone' 3rd Battalion of the 506th Infantry) joined the battle on 3 December and were soon in the thick of the fighting. During the night of the 8th the three Montagnard Popular Forces (PF) platoons guarding the hamlet of Tahine were overrun and destroyed by the 186th Main Force VC Battalion armed with mortars, machine guns, and rocket launchers. A relief force from 3rd Battalion, 506th Infantry, was ordered in, but met with heavy opposition.

After more than two weeks of heavy fighting, at 1800 hrs on Christmas Eve, a temporary ceasefire became effective, allowing the men to make the best of their Christmas away from home. Although all Battalions of the 1st Brigade ceased search-and-destroy operations, rifle companies continued to conduct security patrolling activities in their immediate areas. All too briefly, at 1800 hrs on Christmas Day, the ceasefire agreement ended and normal operations resumed. Over the New Year, there was another brief hiatus in respect of the new year.

Other operations

In the autumn of 1967 there were indications of another enemy build-up, particularly in areas close to Laos and Cambodia. In late October, the VC struck again at the Special Forces Camp at Loc Ninh, but the timely intervention of South Vietnamese reinforcements saved the position. At the same time, approximately 12,000 VC troops converged on the Special Forces camp at Dak To, in northern Kontum Province. In response to these threats, the US and South Vietnam committed a total of 16 battalions to the region.

Operation 'Eagle Lift'

As the year drew to an end, the 2nd and 3rd Brigades of the 101st Airborne Division arrived in Vietnam to bring the division up to its full strength and enable it to convert to a full airmobile division. Originally, the deployment was scheduled for 10 February 1968, but this movement was brought forward to December. The culmination of the division's preparations was Operation 'Eagle Thrust' – the largest and longest military airlift ever attempted into a combat zone. Ending on 18 December, it brought 10,024 troops and over 5,300 tons of the division's essential equipment to Bien Hoa Air Base in 369 C-141 Starlifter missions and 22 C-133 Cargomaster missions.

Once in country, division headquarters was set up at Bien Hoa; the 2nd Brigade established an area of operation (AO) around Cu Chi. Next they moved to Phuoc Vinh to prepare a base camp for the 3rd Brigade. Prior to commencing operations the troopers went through a 30-day in-country training programme designed by the 25th Infantry, receiving daily instruction on booby traps, reconnaissance and explosives. Small-unit leaders who lacked combat experience accompanied elements of the 25th Infantry on search and destroy missions.

With the temporary cease fire ended on 1 January, 3rd Battalion, 506th Infantry, continued its operations in Bao Loc. On 2nd, a platoon of the battalion ran into a large, dug-in Viet Cong force at the knoll on Di Linh Plateau southeast of Bao Loc. The ensuing 'Battle of the Knoll' raged into the night, resulting in the loss of six men KIA and another 20 wounded. On the following day reinforcements in the form of the battalion's Alpha Company arrived, and over the next five days the platoon skirmished with the enemy and uncovered numerous enemy sites, bunker complexes, base camps, weapons, medical supply caches, hospitals, mess halls and graves. These finds were significant enough to have I Field Force commander, General William B. Rosson, and 1st Brigade commander, Brigadier General S.H. Matheson, visit the field sites.

On 8th 'Klamath Falls' was terminated. Task force elements were extracted from the area of operations to the battalion LZ along Highway QL-20 to prepare for a motor convoy move to Phan Rang on 9 January. Battalion losses for the operation were 10 KIA and 34 WIA.

In the middle of the month, the battalion received an unexpected order to make ready for a combat jump into an NVA Division Headquarters northwest of Song Be, scheduled for 1000 hrs, 17 January 1968. The men dutifully began preparations for this mission. It was all in vain; at the last moment, word came from General Westmoreland that due to a security violation the jump was cancelled.

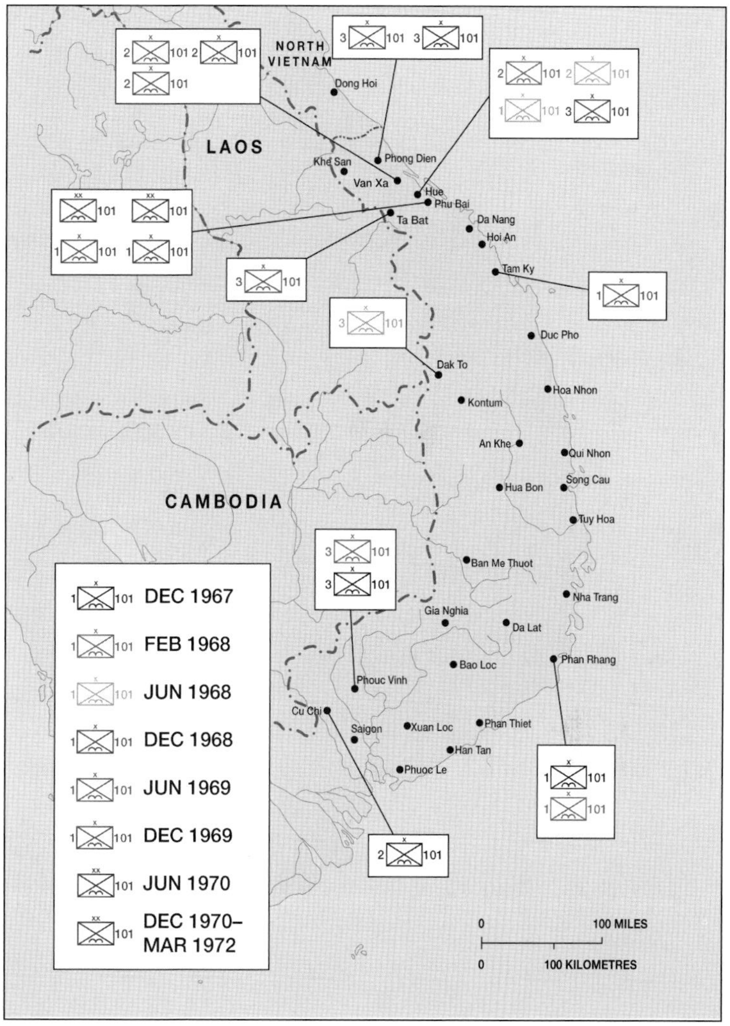

Map legend dates:
DEC 1967
FEB 1968
JUN 1968
DEC 1968
JUN 1969
DEC 1969
JUN 1970
DEC 1970–MAR 1972

Above: 101st Airborne deployments in Vietnam December 1967–March 1972.

They moved instead to Phan Thiet in Binh Thuan Province, located in II Corps area, and assumed responsibility for AO Byrd – covering the four southern provinces of Ninh Thuan, Binh Thuan, Tuyen Duc and Dam Dong – from the departing 1st Cavalry Division (Airmobile). At Phan Thiet the 3rd Battalion, 506th Infantry, became the nucleus of an airborne-airmobile task force under the operational control of the commander, First Field Force Vietnam (I FFORCEV). On 20th Task Force 3/506 initiated Operation 'McLain', an open-end search-and-destroy operation that ran for a little over a year in AO Byrd, as well as in portions of Binh Tuy Province in III Corps. As with all other US offensive operations, this was halted on 29 January for the upcoming three-day celebration of the Vietnamese lunar New Year (Tet) for 1968 beginning on 30 January.

TET/TET COUNTEROFFENSIVE

30 January 1968–1 April 1968

In 1968, however, Tet did not pass in its customary peace. In fact it was marked by the biggest PAVN/VC offensive of the war thus far. Between 30 January and the end of

February 1968, some 84,000 VC and North Vietnamese attacked or fired upon 36 of 44 provincial capitals, five of six autonomous cities, 64 of 242 district capitals and 50 hamlets, extending from Khe Sanh in the north to Ca Mau on the country's southern tip. In addition, the enemy raided a number of military installations, including almost every airfield. Perhaps most daring though was the attack at the very heart of the US administration: its embassy in Saigon.

Now known as the Tet Offensive, this operation was timed to coincide with the beginning of Tet, an annual celebration of the lunar New Year, and the most festive of Vietnamese holidays. Planned by PAVN General Vo Nguyen Giap, the objective was to stimulate an popular uprising (*khoi nghia*), a means that the Vietnamese had previously employed to overthrow oppressors.

Determined enemy assaults began in the northern and Central provinces before daylight on 30 January, and in Saigon and the Mekong Delta regions that night. The first wave of assaults lasted three days, and Saigon and Hue came under the most intense and sustained attack. Although most incursions were crushed in a few days, fighting continued in some areas for up to two months. Collectively, it was the bloodiest phase of the entire war. North Vietnam lost 50,000 soldiers killed, South Vietnam 14,000 and the US 2,000. In addition, an estimated 12,500 civilians were killed, and Tet created as many as a million new refugees.

As it turned out, the PAVN suffered a heavy military defeat, but Tet is widely seen as an enormous psychological and propaganda victory for North Vietnam. It came as a profound shock to the US public, which up to that time had been fed greatly exaggerated claims by the military establishment about the efficacy of the US-led campaign, and led to believe that the North Vietnamese were a largely spent force. Tet did irreparable damage to public confidence in the politicians and soldiers running the Vietnam War.

It was no less of a shock to the troops, as previously both sides had observed a ceasefire during Tet. Hence the American forces and their South Vietnamese allies, relaxing and celebrating as in years past, were caught completely off guard. At the time all eyes were focused instead on an isolated Marine Corps outpost strategically sited near the Laotian border and DMZ in the far northwestern corner of South Vietnam: Khe Sanh.

Khe Sanh

Ten days prior to the opening attacks, three PAVN divisions had begun probing attacks on the perimeter of Khe Sanh, part of a network of interconnected bases along the DMZ, envisaged by General Westmoreland as a barrier to enemy

Below: Men of the 4th Platoon, Company C, 1st Battalion, 327th Infantry (Airmobile), 1st Brigade, 101st Airborne Division (Airmobile), cross a river by means of a rope strung from bank to bank during Operation 'San Angelo' on 20 January 1968. The numerous waterways and paddy fields of Vietnam often made progress across the countryside a slow and painful process with the constant fear of ambush or bobby traps.

infiltration. US staff officers had been predicting a major assault on Khe Sanh for some time, and recent intelligence seemed to confirm this. General Giap, the North Vietnamese commander, had in fact gathered close to 30,000 experienced troops in the area, and beginning on 20 January they laid siege to Khe Sanh for over six weeks. With memories of the French debacle at Dien Bien Phu not far from their thoughts, President Johnson and Westmoreland ordered massive resources to be funnelled into the effort to save the base. It was held at huge cost in men and materiel, only to be abandoned in the summer.

Above: Men of the 327th Infantry (Airborne), 1st Brigade, 101st Airborne Division (Separate), come ashore from an LST – Tank Landing Ship – as part of a search and destroy operation conducted by Task Force Oregon in May 1967 in the Duc Pho district of Quang Ngai Province. Although qualified paratroopers, the troopers of the 101st Airborne Division deployed into battle by any means during the long and frustrating war in Vietnam in their attempts to find and eliminate the elusive enemy.

Whether the attack on Khe Sanh was intended to act as a decoy for the main offensive is still debated, but there is no question that the US forces were caught off guard.

This was certainly true at Bien Hoa, headquarters of the 101st Airborne, where one of the biggest attacks fell. Although the divisional intelligence had known of the enemy build-up at the Bien Hoa–Saigon area prior to the beginning of Tet, they had no idea of when or where an attack might come, and like other units the 101st Airborne was observing the 36-hour ceasefire. At around 0300 hrs on 31 January an assault began at the main gate of the installation, within sight of the headquarters building itself. The 2nd Battalion, 506th Airborne Infantry, was quickly flown in by helicopter from Phuoc Vinh and within a half hour was fighting a pitched battle. In the next seven hours, more than 100 enemy fell, and another 58 the next day, 1 February.

Battle of the Embassy

Also on 31 January, a dramatic battle was fought by troopers of C Company, 3rd Platoon, 1st Battalion, 502nd Airborne Infantry, at the US Embassy in Saigon.

In the early hours of the morning the division commander, Major General O.M. Barsanti, received a message requesting a reinforcing element for the forces under attack at the US Embassy in Saigon. A 35-man reaction force, led by Major Hillel Schwartz, assistant division intelligence officer, was quickly assembled. Schwartz gave a quick appraisal of the situation to his men; Marines were barricaded in the Embassy; military police units were on the outside perimeter of the courtyard and Viet Cong armed with automatic weapons and rocket-propelled grenade (RPG) launchers were inside the embassy itself.

At 0633 hrs, Schwartz, Captain Speedy and two sergeants boarded a helicopter and flew to Saigon. Flying over the city, they observed gun battles all over, and particularly in the area of the embassy. As it came into land on the embassy roof, the helicopter began to take hits from small arms, wounding the door gunner in the hand and shoulder. The chopper was forced to pull away, with Schwartz returning fire at the muzzle flashes below with the M-16 rifle he had hastily poked out the door.

The pilot, Lt. Col. John McGregor, commander of the 101st Aviation Battalion, noted that the aircraft was overheating and recommended they divert to Long Binh, where the wounded gunner could be hospitalised and another chopper could be obtained. With this accomplished they took off again for the embassy, and this time got in without taking any hits. After searching the roof, the team moved to the ground floor using the elevator.

Everywhere the walls were peppered with bullet holes, and out in the courtyard MPs were pursuing Viet Cong dressed in civilian clothes and carrying AK-47 assault rifles.

Schwartz ordered the area to be methodically swept, and when this had been done 19 bodies littered the ground, some lying sprawled among the big flower planters. While the paratrooper platoon secured the area, the bodies were searched for captured documents and weapons.

With the embassy compound restored to US control, General Westmoreland arrived and was accompanied by Schwartz on an inspection of the courtyard. As the two looked at the big hole blown in the embassy wall, the general was called to the phone. It was a call from the President in Washington, anxious to know what was happening.

Battle for Hue: Operation 'JEB Stuart'

But it was in and around Hue, the ancient former Imperial capital of Vietnam, that the bitterest and bloodiest battle of the Tet Offensive was fought. In the early hours of 31 January, the 6th PAVN Regiment and 12th VC Sapper Battalion stormed the old Imperial Citadel on the northern bank of the Perfume River, while the 4th PAVN Regiment attacked the Military Assistance Command Vietnam (MACV) compound on the south bank. By dawn most of the city, and large parts of the Quang Tri/Thua Thien area north of Hue was in communist hands. Although ARVN and Marine units launched immediate counterattacks to recapture the city, the citadel was only retaken on 24 February.

Shortly after the opening attacks on Hue, C-130 transport aircraft carried the 2nd Brigade 500 miles north to I Corps. En route, it stopped first at Phu Bai Airport then bivouacked briefly at nearby LZ El Paso (later to become Camp Eagle), a 1st Cavalry Division firebase, before joining operations with the Cavalry in the vicinity of Quang Tri. On 2 February, anticipating that the Viet Cong and North Vietnamese would attempt to withdraw to the west, and in order to prevent reinforcements from reaching those PAVN units already inside the city, the 3rd Brigade, 1st Cavalry, and 1st Battalion of the 501st Infantry established blocking positions to the west. Units of the 1st Cavalry and elements of the 101st Division also attacked south along QL-1 (Highway 1) and toward the northern quadrants of Hue City.

Initial contact with the enemy in the Battle for Hue occurred near the village of Van Xa/PK 17, which was part of an area known generally as the 'Street Without Joy' (and which later became the site of LZ Sally, adjacent to the village of Van Xa) a little over six miles northwest of Hue. At about the time these elements fought through to the northern outskirts of Hue City itself, the enemy broke contact and fled north, west and east to avoid annihilation.

By 9 February, Marines had fought from house to house to clear the south bank of the Perfume River. On the north bank the action was similarly intense, but movement was slower and it wasn't until the 21st that a combined Marine/ARVN force managed to link up with the 1st Cavalry moving from the west. On 9 March, after completing their phase of the operation, 2nd Brigade rejoined the division.

Although the battles on the outskirts of Hue are largely ignored, former airborne troopers are quick to point out that during Operation 'JEB Stuart' the army took more casualties in one week than the Marines lost in their very famous and well-publicised month-long fight to liberate Hue (attacking from the south).

COUNTEROFFENSIVE, PHASE IV

2 April–30 June 1968

Although the fight for Hue was over, much fighting remained to be done in the area to eliminate the large number of enemy units that had filtered in amongst the populated areas in the coastal lowland paddies, hedgerows and sand dunes surrounding the coastal village of Quang Dien, northeast of Hue. In the late spring these efforts were focused on a major counteroffensive conducted in Quang Tri and Thua Thien Provinces, which encompassed three major operations; 'Carentan', 'Carentan II/Lam Son 216', and 'Nevada Eagle' ('Lam Son 224').

In advance of the counteroffensive, it was decided to move the division to I Corps. Division headquarters and support battalions were airlifted north in late February and March; the division base camp (Camp Eagle) was established on 8 March off Highway 1 north of Phu Bai.

Operation 'Carentan'
8 March–31 March 1968

That same day Operation 'Carentan I' – named for the Normandy victory of June 1944 – was launched with 3rd Brigade of the 82nd Airborne Division on secondment. The initial assault was led by elements of 82nd Airborne, together with members of B Troop, 2nd Squadron (Airborne), 17th Cavalry Division and F Company, 58th Infantry Long-Range Reconnaissance Patrol (LRRP).

On 10 March, in a pattern that would be repeated on an almost daily basis over the coming two weeks, large weapons caches and rice stocks were uncovered. While clearing the area 501st and 502nd Infantry engaged regular and irregular forces north of Hue, along Route 547 leading out of Hue toward Fire Support Base (FSB) Bastogne. On 21 March, late in the evening, the North Vietnamese made a daring attack on the night defensive perimeter of the 2nd Battalion, 501st Infantry, using B-40 rockets as covering fire. Responding with small arms, automatic weapons and direct artillery fire, the paratroopers drove the enemy force off, killing 22. The following day, five miles west of Hue, gunships of B Company, 101st Aviation Battalion, caught a company of NVA in an open field, killing 34. Later three sampans were destroyed by a light fire team (LFT) from the battalion, resulting in nine more enemy deaths. Sweeping north of Hue, the 1st Battalion, 501st Infantry, met with stiff enemy resistance, indicating a sizeable force in

Below: Lt Steven Page of the 326th Engineer Battalion supervises the positioning of fuel bladders by an M578 Vehicle Tracked Recovery at Fire Support Base Bastogne on 16 April 1968. Fuel was the lifeblood of the airmobile divisions and their fleets of helicopters consumed it in vast quantities.

the area, later discovered to be the 803rd PAVN Regiment. A 48-hour battle ensued, in which more than 50 enemy were killed and more weapons recovered.

31 March – the last day of Operation 'Carentan' – saw no let-up in the relentless search for enemy soldiers and Viet Cong around Hue. Fifteen miles northwest of the city, the 1st Battalion (Airborne), 321st Artillery, trapped 85–100 NVA soldiers in an open field with accurate fire. Thirty of the NVA were killed. Six and a half miles west of Hue, members of the 1st Battalion (Airborne) 501st Infantry encountered a well-positioned enemy company. Air strikes were called in, resulting in 18 more enemy dead.

For the statisticians in Washington the operation was a great success. 861 enemy were killed. The total weapons and munitions captured included 186 individual and crew-served weapons, along with 1,027 rocket, mortar and artillery rounds. More than 41,000 rounds of small arms ammunition and 45 hand grenades were captured, along with nearly 17 tons of rice and grain.

On 5 April, Operation 'Pegasus/Lam Son 207' finally relieved Khe Sanh and thereby opened Route 9 for the first time since August 1967. This operation not only severely restricted PAVN movements in western Quang Tri Province but also inflicted casualties on the remnants of two North Vietnamese divisions withdrawing from the area. Preparations were by this time already underway at 1st Cavalry HQ for a major strike into the A Shau valley.

'Carentan II/Lam Son 216'
1 April–17 May 1968, Quang Tri Province, I Corps, South Vietnam

On the first day of April, with 'Carentan' only recently concluded, the 1st and 2nd Brigades, together with the 3rd Brigade, 82nd Airborne Division, launched Operation 'Carantan II', a continuation of Operation 'Carentan' in the same area of operations.

On 5 April a platoon of NVA was spotted in an open field north of Hue by a forward observation post of the 1st Battalion, 501st Infantry, and blasted by the guns of the 1st Battalion, 321st Artillery. Twenty-two enemy soldiers were killed. The same day, C Company of the 1st Battalion, 501st Infantry, engaged the enemy in two successful ambush attempts and fought a two-hour battle north of Hue that resulted in 21 enemy killed.

On 6 April, at a village 10 miles southwest of Hue, members of A Company, 2nd Battalion, 502nd Infantry, engaged a PAVN company in a network of bunkers. After the supporting barrage was lifted, paratroopers from the 1st Brigade's B Company, 2nd Battalion, 502nd Infantry, moved in to ring the village with a night perimeter. An attempt to break through the small cordon proved unsuccessful and resulted in two enemy killed. At first light, A Company paratroopers swept

Below: A soldier from Company A, 326th Engineer Battalion (Airborne) uses his AN/PRS 3 metallic mine detector to search for enemy weapons or booby traps in a pile of rice stalks.

through the village, uncovering 27 NVA bodies, and capturing six weapons. That same day, members of B Company, 1st Battalion, 501st Infantry, claimed 27 enemy kills and captured eight weapons in a battle 10 miles southwest of Hue. In another action, riflemen from A Company, 2nd Battalion, 501st Infantry, accounted for 17 dead PAVN 35 miles northwest of Hue.

Between 11 and 13 April A, B and D Companies of 2nd Battalion, 501st Infantry, cordoned A Phong Dien, a village 10 miles northeast of Hue along the 'Street Without Joy', which had been occupied by PAVN. A sweep of the village following a night of constant bombardment found 66 enemy dead and 26 weapons. Meanwhile paratroopers of A and C Companies, 1st Battalion, 501st Infantry, and A, B and C Companies of the 82nd Airborne's 1st Battalion, 505th Infantry, ended a week-long search and destroy mission along the Song Bo, three miles northwest of Hue. Army aviation, artillery, tactical air and the airborne troopers combined to kill 200 enemy and capture 44 weapons.

Eighteen miles north of Hue, elements from the 2nd Battalion, 501st Infantry discovered an enemy base camp on 16 April containing 20 underground tunnels and bunkers. Stored in the tunnels were 1,000 AK-47 rounds, 20 rounds for 60 mm mortars and various medical supplies. In the 1st Brigade AO, A and B Companies, 2nd Battalion, 327th Infantry, killed 12 NVA and captured five weapons during a fierce battle 12 miles southwest of Hue.

The following day, 17 April, a battalion-size cordon was established by paratroopers of the 1st Battalion, 501st Infantry, at the fortified village of Dong Xuyen three miles north of Hue. Following Army aviation, artillery and tactical air strikes, the troopers entered the village, and in three days had accounted for 53 enemy dead. Eight more kills were recorded by B Company, 2nd Battalion, 327th Infantry.

Above: As an airmobile division, the 101st was supported by considerable aviation assets that came under the 101st Aviation Group, formerly the 160th Aviation Group. The latter was formed on 1 July 1968 to convert the 101st Airborne Division to its new airmobile configuration. It was redesignated as the 101st Aviation Group on 25 June 1969 and comprised the 101st, 158th and 159th Aviation Battalions, the 163rd Aviation Company (General Support) and the 478th Aviation Company (Heavy Helicopter) as well as the 2nd Squadron, 17th Cavalry (Air) in the divisional reconnaissance role.

Casualties for both operations were US 193 KIA, 1,190 WIA, 11 MIA; enemy 1,892 KIA and 69 POWs.

The A Shau Valley: Operation 'Delaware'
19 April–17 May 1968

At this point, mid-way through 'Carentan II', the 1st Brigade of 101st Airborne Division was seconded to the 1st Air Cavalry. During the following month, together with elements of the 196th Infantry Brigade of ARVN 1st Division and an ARVN airborne task force, it undertook the first strike in two years into the A Shau Valley: Operation 'Delaware/Lam Son 216'. Though tentative plans had been made for a singular allied spoiling operation against this enemy redoubt sometime before, final preparations were only concluded in the last days of Operation 'Pegasus'. The 1st Brigade of 101st Airborne committed three infantry battalions; 196th Infantry Brigade committed three more and 1st Cavalry Division committed seven infantry battalions plus the 1st, 9th Cavalry.

The A Shau Valley

The A Shau Valley runs 35 miles along the Vietnam–Laos border, between two high mountain ranges. Its tactical value as a main supply and infiltration route from Laos into Thua Thien and Quang Nam Provinces rendered it an area of contest for many years. In late April 1968 it was the target of one of the 101st's toughest missions.

Not least of the problems was the terrain, for the thickly-wooded mountains flanking the sides of the valley climb to over 3,000 feet with the angle of slope varying from 20–45°. Also, the Laotian border is barely six miles away, and at that time within easy access of PAVN/VC safe havens and logistical bases. The North Vietnamese forces had been in control of the valley since March 1966 when they overran the Special Forces camp at the southern end. Since that time they had built a major base for the infiltration of personnel and supplies from North Vietnam through Laos along Route 547 into Thua Thien Province and the northern I Corps Tactical Zone. Furthermore, the PAVN had concentrated a very large amount of its anti-aircraft resources in the valley, meaning that the pilots flying into it would face what was undoubtedly the heaviest and most sophisticated enemy air defence encountered in airmobile operations up to that time.

Operation 'Delaware' envisaged a move through the valley to pre-empt enemy preparations for an attack on the Hue area, block off their communication routes leading out of the A Shau valley toward Hue, and take advantage of the damage done to the enemy by 'Pegasus'.

This was to be achieved by a coordinated airmobile and ground attack on two axes, using elements of three divisions: the 1st Cavalry, 101st Airborne and 1st ARVN Division. The 1st Cavalry, forming the initial prong, was to assault into A Luoi and Ta Bat on the valley floor. The 101st Airborne Division's role, in coordination with the 3rd ARVN Airborne Task Force, was to complement the 1st Cavalry assault by attacking along and astride Routes 547 and 547A, and interdict the enemy's routes of withdrawal and infiltration in the area. The 101st Airborne's FSB Bastogne, far to the east on Route 547, would just be able to reach the north end of the A Shau Valley with its long range 175-mm guns. The ARVN Airborne Task Force was to be responsible for clearing Route 547A.

During the period 14–19 April, over 100 B-52 sorties, 200 Air Force and Marine fighter sorties, and numerous aerial rocket artillery missions were ordered by the commander of the 1st Cavalry Division to identify and neutralise the AA sites concentrated in the valley. Also at this time, the 1st Brigade, 101st Airborne, and the ARVN Airborne Task Force were moved into pre-assault positions ready to make a separate attack on D-day east of the A Shau. Two major fire support bases were built up:

Below: Lt Robert Birch of Company A, 2nd Battalion, 501st Infantry (Airmobile), 2nd Brigade, 101st Airborne fills his one-quart plastic canteen with water from two-gallon cylinders on Hill 549 some 15km southwest of Hue on 28 January 1969. Such vital water containers were readily carried by resupply helicopters or as an underslung load.

Veghel, six miles east of the valley, and Bastogne. These would prove important throughout Operation 'Delaware'.

On the morning of 19 April, 'Delaware' jumped off with assaults by the 1st Cavalry into LZs in the A Shau. Although the initial assaults of the 5th and 1st Battalions of the 7th Cavalry were virtually unopposed by ground action, subsequent assault lifts received intense anti-aircraft fire. In these later assaults, 23 helicopters were hit by ground-to-air fire and 10 aircraft were destroyed.

While the 1st Cavalry Division was operating in the valley, the 1st Brigade, 101st Airborne, began operations to the east together with the 3rd ARVN Airborne Task Force. The 1st Brigade initiated operations out of FSB Bastogne with one battalion attacking to the southwest. Later in the morning of the 19th, another battalion air-assaulted into a landing zone near the junction of Routes 547 and 547-A. Both battalions made light to moderate contact throughout the day and major supply caches were uncovered.

The heroism of the C-130 and helicopter crews deserves special mention here, for the weather during Operation 'Delaware', in the words of the 1st Cavalry CO 'was almost unbelievably bad'. He goes on to say that 'Heavy clouds, fog, thunder storms, and low ceilings made heroic feats of airmanship almost commonplace'.

On D+1, the 3rd Brigade of the 1st Cavalry continued to deploy into the northern A Shau Valley and to spread their area of operations. On the 21st, action was joined near Thon Kim Doi village, five miles north of Hue, when C Company troops from the 2nd Battalion, 501st Infantry, spotted and killed two members of a VC squad. The survivors fled, leading the pursuing troopers into the village, whence an enemy company had decamped. Early that evening, A and B Companies air-assaulted into blocking positions, to effect a cordon of the village. An intense firefight broke out as PAVN brought down a barrage of fire on the attackers, trying to break out the trapped unit from within the tightening noose. It raged all night, and at dawn the paratroopers called down artillery fire and air strikes on the beleaguered VC unit. When it had all died down, 47 of the enemy were counted dead, and when the cordon of Thon Kim Doi was completed on 23 April, another 27.

In the 1st Brigade area of operations, the 1st Battalion, 327th Infantry, continued clearing operations at landing zone Veghel, meeting scattered resistance as the LZ was prepared for the insertion of heavy engineer equipment and artillery pieces.

On the afternoon of 25 April, C Company of 2nd Battalion, 327th Infantry, engaged two PAVN companies along Route 547, 15 miles southwest of Hue. The battalion's A Company then moved in while C Company maintained contact, forcing the enemy from their positions. At the same time paratroopers from B Company, 2nd Battalion (Airborne),

Above: A CH-47A Chinook comes to the hover as it delivers an M102 105mm howitzer as a Fire Support Base is created during a 101st Airborne Division (Airmobile) operation in February 1966. If the Huey was the workhorse of the airmobile divisions, then the Chinook was the packhorse with early models capable of carrying 33 fully equipped troops or 10,000lb of cargo. In Vietnam Chinooks commonly incorporated almost a ton of combat equipment such as armoured seats for the pilots, body armour for the flight crew, M60D suppressive fire weapons at the doors and often an extra crewman – so a typical load in the hot and humid conditions of Vietnam was between 7,000 and 8,000lb although safety margins were often exceeded. (See also photo and caption page 43.)

502nd Infantry, who were patrolling the southern ridges along the highway, were suddenly confronted by an company of North Vietnamese regulars occupying well-fortified bunker positions. As B Company riflemen engaged the enemy with heavy volumes of small arms and automatic weapons fire, the battalion's C Company moved in from the north. The two units linked up and overran the enemy positions, killing 16 of the regulars and capturing 12 weapons. Later that afternoon, airborne infantry from B Company, 2nd Battalion, 327th Infantry, assaulted an enemy-held heavy machine gun position that was harassing division helicopters heading to FSB Bastogne from Veghel.

Beginning on 28 April, a five-day battle was fought by the men of A Company, 1st Battalion, 327th Infantry, at Phuoc Yen, an enemy base camp deep in the jungles east of Veghel, where intelligence had reported the 8th Battalion, 90th PAVN Regiment. Reconnaissance-in-force missions near Veghel continued over the following days, during which contact was made with the enemy three times. Five companies, drawn from the 'First Strike' battalion and the two 'Geronimo' units, killed 429 enemy soldiers and captured 107 prisoners – and lost only five killed and 31 wounded.

At 0425 hrs on 30 April, one mile east of FB Bastogne, the commanding general's command and control helicopter received hits from ground automatic weapons fire, slightly wounding Major General Barsanti in the left leg. After directing artillery onto the enemy location, Barsanti was evacuated to the 22nd Surgical Hospital, treated and returned to duty at 1715 hrs the same day. Ironically, during the five-day Phuoc Yen cordon, General Barsanti spent most of his time on the ground, moving from position to position, advising subordinate commanders and bolstering morale.

In the next few days, all units engaged in Operation 'Delaware' would continue to uncover major enemy supply depots. The week's total munitions captured by the 1st Brigade paratroopers alone included: 442 rounds of 75 mm shells, 415 rounds of 76 mm tank ammunition, 112 B-40 rockets, 29 rockets of 122 mm, 30,000 rounds of 23 mm anti-aircraft shells, 100 rounds of 85 mm shells, and 225 rounds of 12.7 mm anti-aircraft shells. However, early in the morning of 5 May, division headquarters at Camp Eagle was hit by a barrage of nearly 50 enemy mortar rounds, proving that their stocks were far from depleted. Counter-battery fire from Division Artillery units was immediately placed on the suspected mortar positions.

Meanwhile action around Hue continued as Operation 'Carentan II' entered its second month. On 8 May, a three-day cordon of La Chu village, three miles northwest of the city, was completed by four companies of the 1st Battalion, 501st Infantry, with elements of 17th Cavalry and 34th Armored Cavalry. Fifty-five PAVN were killed, five prisoners were taken and 30 weapons were captured in the action.

During this time, paratroopers from B Company, 1st Battalion, 502nd Infantry had established an ambush position in the jungle four miles north of Hue. Early in the morning on 8 May, two squads of PAVN soldiers walked right into the position and in the ensuing firefight 17 were killed. There were no casualties among the paratroopers.

Six miles northwest of Hue, the cordon tactics that had been proving so successful with the 1st Battalion,

Below: An M30 4.2-inch (120-mm) mortar crew watches the impact of a 'Willie Peter' (White Phosphorous) round on an enemy position during Operation 'Harrison' conducted by the 1st Brigade, 101st Airborne Division (Separate), in the Rice Bowl area near Tuy Hoa. The M30 mortar weighed 672lb and had a maximum range of 5,650m.

501st Infantry, were used once again to trap a reinforced NVA company in Phu Luong A village. Fifteen enemy were killed in the initial contact.

In the A Shau Valley, also on 8 May, the paratroopers of C Company, 1st Battalion, 327th Infantry, captured the ninth enemy ammunition cache of the operation. Less than two miles east of Veghel, they found more than 2,000 rounds of 76 mm high explosive ammunition, and 6,300 rounds of 23 mm anti-aircraft shells. The cache was stored in bunkers built into a hillside and protected from aerial observation by triple canopy jungle.

With all missions nearing completion, a difficult extraction now had to be initiated before the monsoon rains became too intense. Beginning on 10 May, all units and their equipment were airlifted out of the A Shau Valley. Extraction in many ways proved more difficult than the assault. Rain had already washed out a major portion of the A Luoi dirt airstrip, and consequently all men and supplies had to be lifted out by helicopter.

First out was the 3rd Brigade, 1st Cavalry Division, followed by the 3rd ARVN Regiment. The 101st Airborne units continued offensive operations in their AOs, meeting scattered, sporadic resistance. The division also assisted the small Department of Defense team of electronic experts sent from Washington to emplace the then-new acoustic sensors in the valley, to monitor enemy activity after allied forces left the area. Finally, they too bade farewell to the A Shau; few of the men were sorry to be leaving.

By the time Operation 'Delaware/Lam Son 216' was officially terminated on 17 May there was little doubt that the enemy had been severely mauled, with 739 PAVN/VC killed and vital supply lines cut. The volume of captured materiel was staggering. In one days search, for example, Company C, 1st Battalion, 327th Infantry, uncovered 6,300 rounds of anti-aircraft ammunition. Two days later the company found 582 mortar

Above: A CH-47C Chinook of the 159th Aviation Battalion (ASH) – the 'Liftmasters' – of the 101st Airborne Division (Airmobile) deposits an M101A1 105mm howitzer and an underslung load of ammunition at a Fire Support Base. As an airmobile division, the 101st was equipped with the lighter M102 105mm howitzer so this weapon was probably being delivered for another formation. In the last years of the war, the division's aviation assets were employed extensively by the ARVN as the 101st adopted a more defensive posture. A complete six-gun battery of M102 howitzers with crews inside the Chinooks and 105mm ammunition underslung could be moved by air in just seven Chinook sorties with the seventh aircraft carrying the men and equipment of the Fire Direction Center as well as more ammunition.

rounds, 200 recoilless rifle rounds and 50 grenades. The loss of these munitions further limited enemy capabilities in providing fire support for large scale operations; the interdiction of Route 547 had also been also achieved during this operation, completely cutting off its use by enemy forces as a resupply route. From another perspective, the enemy had been prevented from further attacking I Corps Tactical Zone population centres and forced to shift attention to the III Corps Tactical Zone.

But the battles had in no way been completely one-sided. While engaged in these operations, the 101st Airborne was exposed to some of the heaviest ground fire received in Vietnam up to that time. Furthermore, although the enemy had been temporarily driven from the A Shau, they returned to haunt it within weeks. As it transpired, the 101st Airborne had not seen the last of the valley.

In the sixth week of Operation 'Carentan II', there was no abatement in the fighting around Hue. In an action centred five miles north of Hue along the Pha Tam Giang inlet, C Company, 1st Battalion, 502nd Infantry, trapped an PAVN platoon inside a horseshoe cordon and drove the enemy from their position toward the water, leaving 21 of their number behind. On 11 May, 10 miles southwest of Hue, a division reconnaissance unit observed the enemy preparing a rocket launching site. The gunships of 308th Aviation Battalion were despatched to the scene and quickly scattered the enemy with 2.75-inch rocket and mini-gun fire. Secondary explosions were observed by the pilots as they made passes over the target area.

Eight miles to the northwest of Hue, paratroopers of A Company, 2nd Battalion, 501st Infantry, and D Company of the regiment's 1st Battalion, with members of 17th Cavalry in support, fought a two-day battle at Co Thap village, beginning on 13 May. The infantrymen had cordoned a PAVN battalion suspected of protecting a nearby enemy regimental headquarters.

Operations under 'Carentan II' were finally terminated at midday on 17 May. During

Below: Brigadier General Salve H. Matheson confers with Lt Ralph Puckett Jr, the commanding officer of the 2nd Battalion, 502nd Infantry (Airborne), 1st Brigade, 101st Airborne Division (Separate), during Operation 'Cook' in Quang Ngai Province on 6 September 1967. Brig Gen Salve H. Matheson was the commander of the 1st Brigade from February 1967 and while it rejoined the complete division in November when the Division Headquarters was established at Bien Hoa.

the 47-day operational period the combined force had killed 2,100 PAVN troops, captured 157 prisoners and 581 weapons. Most importantly, it had to a large extent fulfilled the mission goal of relieving the pressure on the area around Hue.

Operation 'Nevada Eagle'

Also on 17 May, Operation 'Nevada Eagle', the most protracted of all the operations to which the 101st Airborne was committed, was initiated by the 1st and 2nd Brigades and the 3rd Brigade of the 82nd Airborne Division in Thua Thien Province, in the I Corps AO. The operation, which ran for 288 days from May 1968 to February 1969, was designed to deny the enemy the rice crop soon to be harvested in the lowlands of Thua Thien. Its larger purpose was to drive the enemy out of the plains and into the mountains where they could be tracked down and destroyed. During the operation allied forces carried out numerous sweeps through the valley, but there were few contacts of any size. Those of note are detailed below.

The first real contact occurred on 20 May when, exploiting intelligence information, members of B Company, 1st Battalion, 501st Infantry, trapped an enemy force in Dong Gi Tay village northeast of Hue. Three more rifle companies and one Popular Forces (PF) platoon were rushed in to cordon the village, and heavy casualties were inflicted on the enemy. A second minor action was touched off when airborne infantrymen from A Company, 2nd Battalion, 327th Infantry, were subjected to a mortar attack and an attempt to infiltrate their night defensive perimeter. The enemy was driven off with artillery and small arms fire, and a sweep of the area the next morning revealed 31 dead.

The only major action of 'Nevada Eagle' was fought on the night of on 21–22 May. Just after midnight, while most of the division was engaged on sweeps along the mountains in Thua Thien, a PAVN battalion, augmented by personnel from a sapper demolition team, launched a daring ground attack against Camp Eagle. Following a

Below: Marked by a purple smoke grenade, a UH-1D Command and Control helicopter carrying the brigade commander comes into land at the command post of the 2nd Battalion, 502nd Infantry (Airborne), 1st Brigade, 101st Airborne Division (Separate) during Operation 'Cook' in the mountains of Quang Ngai Province on 6 September 1967.

preparatory barrage in which more than 400 rounds of 122 mm rockets, 82 mm mortars, B-40 and B-41 ammunition were targeted on the division headquarters area, sappers attacked the 1st Brigade's positions at Gia Le on the southwest edge of the perimeter.

One 10-man sapper team managed to penetrate through the barbed wire as far as the brigade helipad, nearly half a mile inside the perimeter, before being chased off by a lone trooper. The attack was finally beaten back by the 1st Brigade's H&HC troops, members of the 2nd Battalion, 502nd Infantry, and swarms of helicopter gunships. Fast-thinking gunners from the 320th Artillery rolled in a 105 mm howitzer without sighting devices and killed 12 enemy at the edge of the wire with four 'Beehive' anti-personnel rounds.

At first dawn, a sweep of the area revealed 54 enemy bodies and 16 individual weapons. Additional ordinance uncovered included 40 satchel charges, 30 bangalore torpedoes, and 50 RPG rounds. Damage to the base area was minimal, but the action proved that the enemy had lost none of their audacity and daring.

In the following days, 327th Infantry units sweeping the mountains of Thua Thien made some spectacular discoveries. North of FSB Veghel, the 1st Battalion captured three light artillery pieces, two anti-aircraft guns and one truck, together with 23 mm and 85 mm ammunition and fuses. Yet better was to come. The largest haul of 'Nevada Eagle' was uncovered by members of A Company, 2nd Battalion along Route 547, 12 miles southwest of Hue nestled in the triple canopy jungle. Hidden in several 5 by 8 ft bunkers under three feet of overhead cover they found a cache of 238 individual and crew-served enemy weapons. The cache included 167 SKS rifles and 32 cases of new AK-47s. The same unit found a second major arms cache in a bunkered enemy base camp four miles east of the A Shau valley, this one containing 12 complete 60 mm mortars, 150 bolt-action Chicom rifles (K-44), four light machine guns, 80 rifle grenades and 40 B-40 rockets. And at the end of the month 49 enemy trucks and four 23 mm anti-aircraft guns with 2,100 rounds of ammunition were captured along a road 15 miles southwest of Hue by elements of the 1st Battalion. The trucks were intact but minus their engines; closer investigation of the scene unearthed the missing engines buried 5–10 yards alongside them!

A third major discovery was made on 29 May, by riflemen from A Company, 2nd Battalion. The haul included 107 SKS rifles, 59 K-44 rifles, four AK-47s, 102 rounds of 75 mm shells, 5,660 rounds of small arms ammunition, 3,300 grenade fuses, 26 B-41 rockets and 24 rounds of 60 mm mortar ammunition. Rounding out actions in May, a two-day cordon operation seven miles east of Hue near Le Xa Dong hamlet was conducted by B Company, 1st Battalion, 501st Infantry, with the 2nd Squadron of the 17th Cavalry and elements of the 1st ARVN Division. Some 91 PAVN were killed, 19 prisoners taken and 34 weapons captured.

On 3 June another major weapons cache was seized by A Company, 2nd Battalion, 327th Infantry, in the coastal plains area. The same day marked the end of a two-day cordon around Trung Phuong hamlet, three miles southeast of Hue, where a multi-company airborne task force composed of 17th Cavalry, the 2nd Brigade of the 101st Airborne and ARVN airborne troopers killed 66 enemy, took 51 prisoners and captured 55 weapons. On the fourth, paratroopers of A Company, 2nd Battalion, 327th Infantry, continued to uncover large quantities of weapons as they conducted an extensive search of the complex found on 3 June. Added to the previous total were 87 AK-47s, 174 AK-47 magazines with 1,500 rounds of ammunition, and more than 300 82 mm mortar rounds.

From early June the rice denial programme also began to yield some spectacular successes. In the first two weeks of the month, allied forces seized rice in large quantities from caches scattered throughout the 'Nevada Eagle' AO. Added to the weight of rice already captured, the haul now amounted to more than 156 tons, all of which was distributed to various district chiefs throughout Thua Thien province.

Below: SP4 David Weeks of Company L, 75th (Ranger) Infantry, 101st Airborne Division (Airmobile), sets up an M18A1 Claymore mine as part of a training exercise at the MACV Recondo School, operated by the 5th Special Forces Group (Airborne), 1st Special Forces, on Hon Tre Island in the Bay of Nha Trang, one of the most beautiful areas of South Vietnam and a Special Forces adventure playground throughout the war. The Claymore Anti-Personnel Mine was a fearsome weapon that spewed out 700 steel balls with a killing range of 50m and was fired either by a trip wire or a hand-held initiator.

And this is the way it went on, week after week. Two months into the operation, more than 1,100 of the enemy had been killed, 235 taken prisoner, nearly 2,000 weapons taken, and the rice haul stood at 280 tons. However, Communist units had thus far refused to be drawn into major conflict and successfully used mines and booby traps to inflict US casualties. 'Nevada Eagle' also revealed the North Vietnamese ability to entice US helicopter pilots into ambushes by using small groups as bait and then, as the helicopters came in to engage, opening fire with concealed weapons.

Above: Two 'redlegs' of the 2nd Battalion, 320th Artillery (105mm) (Airborne), 1st Brigade, 101st Airborne Division (Separate), plot a fire mission for their 105mm howitzers at Fire Support Base Berchtesgaden during August 1968. The standard towed 105mm howitzer was the fundamental artillery weapon of the Vietnam war and provided the majority of the fire support to the infantry operating in the hostile countryside. However the limited HE charge of the 105mm shell was often ineffective in the dense jungles of Vietnam.

Other operations

In III Corps area during the period 5–12 May 1968, the Viet Cong launched an offensive with Saigon as the primary objective. Small Viet Cong cells did manage to get into the outskirts but these were easily fragmented and driven out, and at no point was the city in danger of being overrun as had nearly been the case in January.

COUNTEROFFENSIVE, PHASE V

1 July–1 November 1968

Beginning in the summer of 1968 a countrywide effort was begun to restore government control of territory lost to the enemy since the Tet offensive. The enemy attempted another such offensive on 17–18 August, but again their efforts were comparatively disjointed and were quickly overwhelmed by Allied forces. In the autumn the South Vietnamese government, with major US support, launched an accelerated pacification campaign. All friendly forces were coordinated and brought to bear on the enemy in every tactical area of operation. In these intensified operations, friendly units first secured a target area, and then Vietnamese government units, regional/popular forces, police and civil authorities screened the inhabitants, seeking members of the Viet Cong infrastructure. This technique was deemed so successful against the communist political apparatus that it became the basis for subsequent friendly operations. Government influence expanded into areas of the countryside previously dominated by the Viet Cong to such an extent that two years later at least some measure of government control was evident in all but a few remote regions.

Above: A CH-54A Tarhe towers over a diminutive OH6A Cayuse at a refueling point in the field. US Army helicopters were named after native American tribes such as the UH-1 Iroquois but most acquired unofficial nicknames. The Tarhe was commonly known as the 'Skycrane' or 'Flying Crane' as that was on of its principal roles. The markings on the tail boom of this Skycrane indicate the 478th Aviation Company (Heavy Helicopter). With the callsign Hurricane, the four Skycranes were attached to the 159th Aviation Battalion (Assault Support Helicopter) as the heavy lift capability the 101st Airborne Division (Airmobile) in the latter years of the war.

The second airmobile division

On 28 June 1968 US Army, Pacific, published General Order 325, which initiated reorganisation of the 101st Airborne Division into the Army's second airmobile division. This order called for the division to be redesignated the 101st Air Cavalry Division, effective 1 July 1968. However, the term 'air cavalry division' was revoked by the Department of the Army on 26 August 1968, and the designation was re-established as the 101st Airborne Division (Airmobile).

Conversion of the 101st to an airmobile configuration had been considered by the Department of the Army prior to the deployment of the 2nd and 3rd Brigades in December 1967. However, the continued deficit in aviation assets during the build-up of forces in Vietnam had made such conversion impractical. The division developed a three-phase plan to accomplish the conversion from the airborne to the airmobile configuration, under which it would swap its 15,000 or so parachutes for more than 400 helicopters.

The first phase (1 July to 1 December 1968) would involve the activation and organisation of the 160th Aviation Group and a reorganisation of the division base. The second phase, which would not be completed until June 1969, involved the conversion of the armoured cavalry squadron to an air cavalry squadron. The last phase involved the activation of an aerial rocket artillery battalion. It was predicted that the whole process would take a full year, given the need to procure aviation assets and the fact that the division would continue to conduct combat operations throughout the conversion period. As it turned out, the reorganisation progressed smoothly with a few exceptions, one of these being in the aircraft maintenance area.

On 19 July 1968, command of the 101st Airborne Division officially passed from Major General O.M. Barsanti, to Major General Melvin Zais. During his seven months in the field, Barsanti had won the respect of his men with a lead-from-the-front approach, for which he received the Distinguished Service Cross, two Silver Stars and five Purple Hearts.

Back to the A Shau: Operation 'Somerset Plain'

In August 1968, the 101st Airborne began preparing for a move back into the A Shau, where a task force composed of units of 101st Airborne, 3rd Brigade of 82nd Airborne and ARVN 1st Infantry was to conduct a search-and-destroy operation to clear the enemy from the valley and attempt to bring them to a decisive battle – something the MACV had long craved.

Operation 'Somerset Plain' started on 3 August with the 2nd Battalion, 502nd Infantry, and the 2nd Battalion, 327th Infantry, combat-assaulting the valley floor near the old A Luoi and Tabat airstrips. The assault did not go well. One F-4 fighter-bomber and no less than 17 helicopters were felled by the intense anti-aircraft fire. Two battalions of the ARVN 1st Division and the 1st Battalion, 327th Infantry, joined the battle later that day.

The main objective of the initial phase was to disrupt enemy movements that might lead to an assault toward the lowlands. However, once the landing zones had been secured and the ARVN and US units had linked up, the PAVN broke contact and began to move towards the safety of Laos. Things took another wrong turn when on 10 August, a F-100 Super Sabre accidentally strafed the 101st Airborne troops, killing seven and

Above: An M102 105mm howitzer of the 2nd Section, Battery C, 2nd Battalion, 320th (105mm) (Airborne), 1st Brigade, 101st Airborne, fires in support of ground troops during Operation 'Somerset Plain' in the A Shau Valley in August 1968. During the 17-day operation, 170 NVA were killed with four POWs and 58 weapons captured. The M102 had an effective range of 11,500m and a battery of six guns could saturate a target with 48 33lb HE shells in one minute. A well-drilled battery could have 36 rounds in the air before the first one landed.

wounding 54 others. The operation rapidly degenerated into a small series of patrolling actions, with no real contact with the enemy. Allied losses were 34 killed and 161 wounded; 171 PAVN were killed, four were taken prisoner and 58 weapons captured. Although claimed as a victory in the aftermath by MACV, which stated that the enemy 'had been driven out of the A Shau', this was clearly not true. All told, it would be difficult to label 'Somerset Plain' a success, although this should not be attributed to any fault in the performance of the 101st Airborne Division.

Meanwhile operations continued in Thua Thien Province under 'Nevada Eagle'. September saw a rather more successful sweep than that recently undertaken in the A Shau, in which 'classic' cordon tactics were utilised to trap and eliminate PAVN troop concentrations instead of trying to draw them into the kind of set-piece battles that they knew well to avoid.

In this operation, the 1st Battalion, 501st Infantry, participated in the 11-day combined-force cordon of Vinh Loc Island, a 15-mile-long peninsula lying in the South China Sea. The VC had moved in after the Tet Offensive, and had since used the district as a recuperation area and supply base. In the early morning of 11 September the 101st Airborne men, together with the 1st Battalion, ARVN 54th Regiment, air-assaulted to landing zones on the eastern coast while armoured personnel carriers of the 3rd Squadron, ARVN 7th Cavalry, moved in from the north. The US Navy's Swift Boats and the Hue River Security Group sealed off the island on the seaward side. During the following 11 days, the airborne troopers and ARVN soldiers made a systematic search of the southern half of the island, rounding up VC suspects. When the operation was over, 154 enemy had been killed, 178 weapons captured and 126 members of the VC infrastructure on the island captured. In addition, 53 enemy had rallied to the government.

In the late autumn 'Nevada Eagle' was focused inland of Thua Thien Province; the same pattern of sweeps in the mountains and continual ambushes and patrols in the coastal plains continued. Also in September 1968, the 3rd Brigade redeployed to I Corps at Phong Diem, just to the south of Quang Tri.

COUNTEROFFENSIVE, PHASE VI

2 November 1968–22 February 1969

By late 1968 the unshakeable confidence on which had been built the colossal United States military apparatus in Vietnam was showing signs of cracking. The unsatisfactory results in Vietnam, growing domestic opposition to the war and a changing international political climate were leading some of those in Washington to ask serious questions about America's future role in Vietnamese – and global – politics.

In the autumn of 1968, Richard M. Nixon was elected president, and concurrent with his taking office a change of policy was brought about. In January 1969 Nixon announced a coming end to US combat operations in Southeast Asia and a simultaneous strengthening of South Vietnam's ability to defend itself. Already, in November 1968, the South Vietnam government with American support had began a concentrated effort to expand security in the countryside, known as the 'Accelerated Pacification Campaign'. Perhaps most significant of all, formal truce negotiations began in Paris on 25 January 1969.

Away from the negotiating tables it was business as usual, with no less than 47 ground combat operations recorded during this period. Operation 'Nevada Eagle' was still proving successful in severely limiting enemy activity in Thua Thien Province, if not in bringing them to battle. The sweeps and rice collection programme continued to score results; From 7 May, when 'Nevada Eagle' started, to the beginning of December, 2,759 enemy were killed and 803 prisoners captured, along with enormous quantities of arms,

Left: A Huey mechanic grabs some much needed rest in a hammock improvised beneath the tail stinger of a UH-1H at Camp Evans. The many helicopters of the 101st Airborne Division (Airmobile) came under the control of the 101st Aviation Group – in the words of the divisional commander, Major General John M Wright – 'The 101st lived by helicopters. Other divisions had to ask for helicopter support but in the 101st the helicopters stayed in the field. We had over 400 helicopters organic to the division, able to react immediately to calls from commanders. We had the lift plus weapons helicopters for support. It just replaced the jeep. It was that common in the 101st.'

Below Left: Another day, another drop as a Huey comes into land on a resupply run for men of Company A, 2nd Battalion 501st Infantry (Airmobile), 1st Brigade, 101st Airborne Division (Airmobile), at Fire Support Base Birmingham located on Hill 549, some 15kms southwest of Hue on 28 January 1969. The majority of helicopter sorties in Vietnam were simple administrative 'ash and trash' runs such as this but the provision of fresh provisions and mail in the field was vital for troop morale.

Above: A gaggle of Huey 'slicks' of the 158th Aviation Battalion (Assault Helicopter) lands at Camp Evans on 30 May 1969 to pick up more supplies for the 3rd Brigade, 101st Airborne Division (Airmobile), during Operation 'Apache Snow' in the A Shau Valley following the battle of Hamburger Hill that proved to be a turning point of the division's operations in Vietnam.

ammunition, equipment and rice. A rather morbid statistic from this war of numbers is given in a routine report written early in the month. From this it was learned that the milestone of 10,000 enemy killed by the 101st was reached late in November.

During early December, activity in the AO was confined to some minor skirmishes. Of more interest is the two-phase action of 11–14 December, when the 1st Battalion, 501st Infantry, combined with ARVN troops, the Hue River Security Group and National Police, assaulted by air and sea to cordon the northern part of Vinh Loc Island. This was a reprise of the tactics that had earlier proved so successful. On the first day, 500 persons were screened, with five classified as VC.

14 December marked the start of the fourth in the series of combined forces operations around Phu Vang. The 1st Battalion of the 506th Infantry, and 3rd Battalion of the187th Infantry (with the ARVN 54th Regiment) conducted multi-battalion air assaults into landing zones near Fire Base (FB) Maureen, which then directed a major effort against a PAVN 6th Regiment base area near Phu Vang. The 1st Battalion, 501st Infantry, teamed with the 54th ARVN Regiment to conduct further cordon and search missions aimed at preventing PAVN and VC units from regrouping in the area east and southeast of Hue.

On Christmas Eve the traditional ceasefire was observed and was mostly peaceful. On Christmas Day however, at FB Anzio, Company C, 2nd Battalion, 502nd Infantry fought off an attack on their perimeter. Early the following day, the battalion's A Company fought a running battle with a platoon of enemy soldiers who were moving out of a nearby village.

As the year came to its close, the division initiated a year-round offensive, a combined forces operation in Nam Hoa District aimed at PAVN battalions in the area. It was initiated with multiple air assaults by the 1st Battalion of the 506th Infantry and ARVN troops along the Song Thao Ma. Elsewhere, elements of 3rd Battalion, 506th Infantry, in the southern part of II Corps area killed two VC in two contacts and captured large quantities of food and medical supplies.

TET 69/COUNTEROFFENSIVE

23 February 1969–8 June 1969

By late 1969, US forces operating within South Vietnam had radically changed their tactics. They began to base their operations on the heavily gunned 'fire-bases', from where they sent out sorties and launched sweeping manoeuvres into known enemy territory. With increased support from aircraft and artillery, infantry platoons or company-sized units would frequently set out to ambush, reconnoitre or destroy the enemy.

Although Tet 1969 was largely peaceful, soon after the three-day holiday through the month of June, PAVN/VC units again tried to sustain an offensive. These efforts were by and large thwarted by aggressive allied ground operations; in this period a total of 70 significant named ground operations were terminated country wide.

Operation 'Nevada Eagle' continued in the new year with the same objectives as before: to defeat enemy personnel in small-scale actions, and to capture rice caches, materiel and installations within its AO. As before, offensive sweeps were undertaken along Route 547 and around Song Bo. It was not until three weeks into the post-Tet offensive that the divisional HQ at Hue was attacked by some rockets, which caused little damage. This was cited by some as evidence that Thua Thien Province was largely pacified. At the end of February, Operation 'Nevada Eagle' ended. Over 4,000 PAVN/Viet Cong soldiers – the equivalent of eight 400-man battalions – had been killed, another two battalions captured, and yet two more had changed allegiance under the Chieu Hoi programme. At the same time enough weapons (3,702) were captured to arm nine enemy battalions. Perhaps most important of all, 668 tons of rice were taken – enough to feed the men of 10 battalions for about a year.

Impressive those these achievements were it should be pointed out that once again the main objective, to draw the enemy to a major battle, was never realised. Another familiar pattern was also repeated, in that that once the allied forces had left the valley, the PAVN/VC returned within a short time.

Operation 'Kentucky Jumper'
1 March–14 August 1969

On 1 March 1969, the 2nd Brigade initiated the first of three separate operations in Thua Thien Province that were known overall as 'Kentucky Jumper'. This was a division-wide effort over a 167-day period that encompassed Operations 'Massachusetts Striker', 'Apache Snow' and 'Montgomery Rendezvous'. In the words of the official operational report, the objectives were 'to interdict enemy base areas and infiltration routes, seek out and destroy PAVN/VC units, detect, capture or destroy local Viet Cong and their infrastructure and their sympathisers, and to disrupt the routes of supply between the rice producing lowlands and population centres, and mountain base areas'.

Unlike previous operations, Operations 'Massachusetts Striker' and 'Apache Snow' attempted to deny the enemy the use of the A Shau for an indefinite period of time, something that thus far had proven beyond the capabilities of US and ARVN forces. 'Striker' was directed against the southern portion of the valley, while 'Apache Snow' followed with the invasion of the northern area. Finally, 'Montgomery Rendezvous' aimed at clearing the eastern slope and the middle of the valley floor.

However, in contrast to their response to many previous operations, the PAVN resolved to stand its ground during Operation 'Kentucky Jumper', resulting in two particularly ferocious battles at 'Bloody Ridge' (Dong A Tay) and Dong Ap Bia – the infamous 'Hamburger Hill'.

Operation 'Massachusetts Striker'
A Shau Valley, 28 February–8 May 1969

Following closely in the wake of the latest withdrawal from the A Shau, MACV intelligence reported a predictable increase in PAVN logistical activity in the valley. Consequently, beginning on 1 March, the 101st Airborne went back to the valley for the third time under Operation 'Massachusetts Striker' to conduct further sweeps.

On the first day, A Company, 326th Engineering Battalion, was inserted onto a hilltop overlooking the valley. Under the protection of troopers of the 2nd Squadron, 17th Cavalry, they began construction of Fire Base Whip, the proposed forward base camp of the brigade.

From Whip the 2nd Brigade was to conduct operations in the southern A Shau and Rao Nai valleys, the success of which depended on bold insertions of the manoeuvre battalions, followed by forced combat marches to the Laotian border to cut off enemy withdrawals. Little intelligence was available regarding the enemy strength and disposition, but it was clear that they were highly trained, well-equipped, hard-core troops.

Almost as soon as the engineer company was on the ground, monsoon rains descended on the mountains. No flying was possible and the engineers had to continue their construction work without adequate food or water supplies. For days they subsisted on rainwater they could catch in their ponchos.

The bad weather persisted until finally, on 12 March, the 1st Battalion of the 502nd Infantry was able to stage forward as far as FB Veghel. However, unbeknown to them, a company of the PAVN 9th Regiment was dug in inside the perimeter of the abandoned position.

VALOROUS UNIT AWARD, STREAMER EMBROIDERED THUA THIEN

H&HC, 3d Brigade, 101st Airborne Division announced in Department of the Army General Orders 2, 18 January 1971, and cited in United States Army, Vietnam, General Orders 4338, 17 September 1970:

The 3d Brigade, 101st Airborne Division (Airmobile) and its assigned and attached units distinguished themselves by extraordinary heroism while engaged in Operation 'Kentucky Jumper' east of the A Shau Valley, Thua Thien Province, Republic of Vietnam during the period 17 April 1969 through 7 May 1969. Making repeated and daring assaults into the face of withering enemy fire, the officers and men of the brigade battled their way over mountainous terrain covered by triple canopy jungle into the heart of the largest enemy supply caches uncovered east of the A Shau Valley. With undaunted determination and exemplary personal fortitude, the men of the 3d Brigade, 101st Airborne Division (Airmobile) valiantly routed a well-equipped, well-entrenched and determined enemy force. In addition to inflicting heavy casualties upon the foe, they uncovered over 80 tons of supplies which dealt a severe blow to the enemy effort. With the pride and dedication, the skytroopers materially advanced the Free World military effort in the Republic of Vietnam. The men of the 3d Brigade, 101st Airborne Division (Airmobile) displayed extraordinary heroism and devotion to duty which are in keeping with the highest traditions of military service and reflect distinct credit upon themselves, their unit, and the Armed Forces of the United States.

Above: An 81mm mortar crew of Company D, 1st Battalion, 501st Infantry (Airmobile), 2nd Brigade, 101st Airborne Division (Airmobile), disembarks from a UH-1H during an operation west of Tam Ky on 1 June 1969.

On the LZ, command-controlled mines had been emplaced and aimed skyward against incoming helicopters, and the area was heavily booby-trapped. Most of these defences were destroyed in an artillery preparation immediately before the assault.

When the assault helicopters carrying C Company swept down on Veghel at 1700 hrs, four of the first five choppers to land took hits although none were destroyed. Bitter fighting ensued as the clouds closed over again, cutting off air support.

By midnight, the enemy had stopped returning fire, and the following morning C Company's sweep of the area was completed with little difficulty. Twelve NVA bodies had been left inside the perimeter and eight more were found along the enemy's line of withdrawal.

That afternoon the rest of the battalion joined C Company at Veghel and began a drive westward toward the border in pursuit. For the next 33 days the battalion fought tooth and nail with the retreating enemy, pushing them back yard by yard, from one position to the next, until finally they made a stand at Dong A Tay, the battle of 'Bloody Ridge'. Throughout this period, for the first time, PAVN units exhibited unusual determination to stand and fight in the face of major losses rather than flee to sanctuaries in Laos.

Meanwhile on 20 March, 2nd Battalion, 501st Infantry, was inserted into the Rao Nai Valley, southeast of the A Shau, and from there pushed out toward the Laotian border. They encountered light resistance along the way from small delaying squad or platoon-size elements.

The final phase of the operation began two days later; the 'No Slack' Battalion of the 327th Infantry was transferred from the control of 1st Brigade to 2nd Brigade and invaded the old airstrip on the floor of the valley. This had originally been the destination of the 1st Battalion, 502nd Infantry, before it was committed to Dong A Tay. Again, little resistance was encountered as the troops moved quickly southward to the Laotian border on three axes. Delays caused by bad weather coupled with allied forces' activity on the edges of the valley had apparently telegraphed the approach of the battalion, and the enemy units withdrew into Laos before they could be overtaken.

Once both battalions had reached the border they retraced their steps and conducted intensive search operations in their respective areas. In the next several weeks enemy base camps, hospitals, high-speed trails and supply caches were discovered and destroyed or removed. The 'No Slack' paratroopers found several trucks and bulldozers along a heavy-duty road that PAVN engineers had been constructing and improving only days before. D Company, 2nd Battalion, 501st Infantry, came upon a way-station hospital complex and drove off what was apparently a caretaker platoon. That night, after the company established its night positions in the complex, the enemy platoon returned with satchel charges, RPG fire and small arms. The attack was repelled, three sappers dying inside the perimeter.

A few days later the 'Drive On' troopers, following a high-speed trail, found caches that contained 120,000 AK-47 rounds, dozens of rifles, rocket-propelled grenades and mortar rounds. They continued to be harassed by booby-traps and snipers and cache security guards.

By this time the 1st Battalion, 501st Infantry, had completed another successful cordon operation on the plains and joined 'Massachusetts Striker'. On 10 April they combat-assaulted into Fire Base Thor and the area southeast, spearheading the brigade's move into Quang Nam Province in the direction of Da Nang.

1st Battalion, 502nd Infantry, after mopping up operations at Dong A Tay, was inserted on 16 April into Fire Base Lash astride the so-called 'Yellow Brick Road' (Route 614), an important North Vietnamese supply route. Encountering virtually no resistance, C Company had soon unearthed a huge, 100-ton cache of electronic equipment and medical supplies. Further probes uncovered 14 trucks, over 600 brand-new SKS rifles, Chinese-built radios and field telephones, large stocks of medicine, large quantities of assorted supplies and equipment, and documents indicating the location of another cache.

As discoveries such as these continued, it became apparent that the entire area of the extreme southern A Shau had been abandoned by the PAVN, who had left the bulk of their equipment and munitions behind in their hasty retreat. Furthermore the 'Yellow Brick Road' was interdicted and destroyed by the 2nd Brigade, hampering enemy plans for future offensives against Hue and Da Nang.

When Operation 'Massachusetts Striker' ended on 8 May, the paratroopers had killed 176 enemy, and captured 859 individual and 34 crew-served weapons.

With rucksacks almost empty, the 2nd Brigade flew back to the coastal plains and almost immediately began preparing for the next operation.

At the beginning of April the 101st Airborne initiated Operation 'Texas Star' in western Quang Tri and Thua Thien Provinces. It was a joint operation in conjunction with the 1st ARVN Infantry Division, and the purpose was to regain the initiative in the mountains east of the A Shau Valley. This effort ran until 5 September 1970; fighting was heavy throughout the entire period, but the intensity steadily increased during late June and early July culminating with the battle for FSB Ripcord.

In mid-May the 1st Battalion, 501st Infantry, and the 'First Strike' battalion was deployed to the Tam Ky area to fight with the Americal.

Operation 'Apache Snow'
10 May–7 June 1969

While the 2nd Brigade were winding down their operations in the extreme southern portion of the A Shau, division staff were busy amending the plans to exploit a massive 'warehouse' area pinpointed by Cavalry units while making a B-52 strike assessment.

Codenamed 'Apache Snow', the operation was designed to destroy those enemy forces occupying the steep mountains rising abruptly from the A Shau Valley that separated I Corps from Laos. A combined allied force was to block their likely escape routes into Laos along Highway 922 and interdict Route 548. Running the length of the valley floor, this was currently being used as an infiltration route into the coastal lowlands of Thua Thien and Quang Nam Provinces. RIF operations would then find the enemy and their caches and destroy them.

Weeks before the jumping off day, in order to confuse the enemy and mask true intentions, more than 30 landing zones were 'prepped' by the Air Force. 10,000 lb 'daisy-cutter' bombs fused to detonate above the ground were dropped on these locations, clearing vegetation without making craters. Then, only 16 hours before the assault, artillery batteries were placed at FSBs Bradley, Airborne, Currahee, Berchtesgaden and Cannon.

With the preparations complete, Operation 'Apache Snow' was initiated at 0730 hrs on 10 May with the largest single airmobile assault of the Vietnam War. Some 65 UH-1 'Huey' helicopters transported seven battalions of the 101st Airborne, 1st ARVN Division and 9th Marine Regiment, 3rd Marine Division, from FSB Blaze to their start lines. The

Below: Troopers undergo in-country training at Dong Da Thien during April 1969 under the guidance of members of Detachment 51, 5th Special Forces Group (Airborne).

H&HC, 3d Brigade, 101st Airborne Division cited in Department of the Army General Orders 16, 31 March 1972 (along with other attached units):

During the period 10-21 May 1969 the foregoing assigned and attached units of the 3d Brigade, 101st Airborne Division distinguished themselves by extraordinary heroism in action against the enemy in the vicinity of Dong Ap Bia Mountain, A Shau Valley, Republic of Vietnam. The 3d Brigade commenced Operation 'Apache Snow' by striking at the enemy on his ground. For 4 days the enemy harassed the men of the Brigade with mortar rocket-propelled grenades, and small arms fire. Undaunted by this enemy action, the units of the 3d Brigade continued to uncover huge amounts of enemy stores and equipment and to destroy his forces. After pinpointing a stronghold on Dong Ap Bia Mountain, the Brigade launched a series of determined attacks during the ensuing 8 days to drive the well-trained-and-equipped enemy from his entrenched positions. Each day the enemy continued to infiltrate reinforcements to help repel the determined American and Vietnamese forces. After 8 days of intense combat, units of the Brigade broke through the enemy defenses and overran his bunker complexes. The battle continued for another 36 hours while the men of the Brigade searched for and destroyed all remaining pockets of enemy resistance. During the 12 days of battle the 3d Brigade and attached units eliminated more than 500 enemy troops; seized large quantities of weapons, explosives, and other military equipment; and captured tons of rice. The determination, devotion to duty, indomitable courage, and extraordinary heroism demonstrated by the members of the 3d Brigade, 101st Airborne Division and attached units are in keeping with the highest traditions of the military service and reflect great credit on them and the United States Army.

choppers crossed the valley in the south and then, using the terrain as a screen, turned north along the Laotian border and headed for the selected LZs. Aircraft had already bombed the LZs for 50 minutes, artillery followed with a 15-minute barrage, and finally came aerial rocket artillery helicopter attacks.

Covered by AH-1 Cobra gunships, the lead elements of the 3rd Battalion, 187th Infantry, and 1st Battalion, 506th Infantry, were inserted over a 45-minute period, with Companies B, C, and D and the command post of the 1st Battalion on the ground by 0815 hrs. Within minutes the soldiers were pushing from the west – to the enemy's complete surprise. It was a flawless combat assault and an outstanding example of the capabilities of an airmobile unit. For the succeeding three days 3rd Battalion, 187th Infantry, watched trails in the surrounding area for signs of activity, but with one very significant exception, there were few contacts.

The Battle of Dong Ap Bia: Hamburger Hill

On 11 May 1969, B Company troops were climbing a hillmass called Dong Ap Bia (Ap Bia Mountain or Hill 937), when suddenly they began receiving automatic weapons fire. Unseen on the crest, entrenched in tiers of fortified bunkers with well-prepared fields of fire, were the 7th and 8th Battalions of the 29th NVA Regiment.

Little did either side know that this same hill would become the scene of one of the most savage battles of the Vietnam War, a bloody meat-grinder of a battle at a place quickly dubbed Hamburger Hill.

Responding to the contact, the battalion commander manoeuvred his companies along ridges leading to the top of the hill to determine the strength of the enemy. Realising that he had stumbled across a significant force, the division commander ordered the 1st Battalion Currahee to reinforce the 187th Infantry on the hill that evening. But as they moved off, the men almost immediately came under heavy fire from enemy gunners, and precious little progress was made. Three paratroopers were killed and another 33 wounded.

The next day, friendly fire from two Cobra gunships killed two and wounded 35 others. For three days thereafter the combat situation remained static. The PAVN units sat tight in their hilltop bunkers while the 101st Airborne probed and looked for weaknesses, under cover of continual bombardment by artillery, aerial rocket artillery and air strikes.

On 14 May a combined assault by companies B, C and D of the 187th Infantry was thrown back with the loss of 12 men killed and 80 wounded. On 15 May Companies A and B tried another assault, but this too proved fruitless as the North Vietnamese and Viet Cong forces withstood all attempts to dislodge them and inflicted 36 additional casualties. Regrouping once more, Zais now brought up two additional battalions, 2nd/501st and 2nd/3rd ARVN, along with A Company of the 2nd Battalion, 506th Infantry.

With the encirclement of the hill complete, and with the ARVN battalions posted to seal off escape routes, on 18 May two full battalions – the 3rd Battalion of the 187th Infantry and 1st Battalion of the 506th Infantry – assaulted the enemy bunker complex for a second time in an effort to drive out the North Vietnamese troops. Delta Company was within 25 yards of the top when a monsoon struck, rapidly turning the slopes into an unscalable mudbath, and forcing the paratroopers to move off the hill again.

After nine days of battle, there had been nine unsuccessful attempts to take the hill. At 1000 hrs on the 20th another was launched, this time a simultaneous four-battalion assault from multiple directions. Moving cautiously up the hill once more, under the cover of intense artillery and air strikes that had already turned the slopes into a deathscape of shattered trees and shell holes, the paratroopers made a slow, tortuous climb, fighting hand to hand through the bunkers. By early afternoon they had at last overcome the remaining defenders and secured the crest. The airborne at last had their victory.

Thus was ended the battle for Hamburger Hill. Decimated, the PAVN 29th Regiment limped back over the border to Laos. For 10 days it had bravely withstood the avalanche of fire that had been dumped on the hill (over 500 tons of bombs and 70 tons of napalm) and had been shattered in the process. So too had 187th Infantry, which had to be completely rebuilt.

As their comrades crawled up the hill at Dong Ap Bia, B, C and D Companies of the 2nd Battalion, 506th Infantry, combat-assaulted into the warehouse area discovered prior to the start of 'Apache Snow'. Their mission, to locate and destroy an enemy command post (CP) complex thought to be in the area, and capture food and munitions caches, soon bore fruit. Within days C Company discovered both the CP complex and a field hospital. In addition, more than 10 tons of rice and 75,000 rounds of ammunition for individual and crew-served weapons were captured during the sweep.

'Apache Snow' was terminated on 7 June. In all, the month-long operation accounted for 675 enemy killed, three prisoners, 241 individual and crew-served weapons captured, and more than 100,000 rounds of ammunition discovered. Allied losses were 56 US dead and five South Vietnamese, almost all of them at Hamburger Hill. The price of victory for taking Hamburger Hill was and is a major bone of contention. Critics charge that it was ambiguous as well as overly costly; the hill itself had no strategic or tactical importance and was abandoned soon after its capture. Many say that the battle wasted American lives and exemplified the irrelevance of US tactics in Vietnam. One Senator labelled the assault 'senseless and irresponsible'.

Below: The Battle of Hamburger Hill.

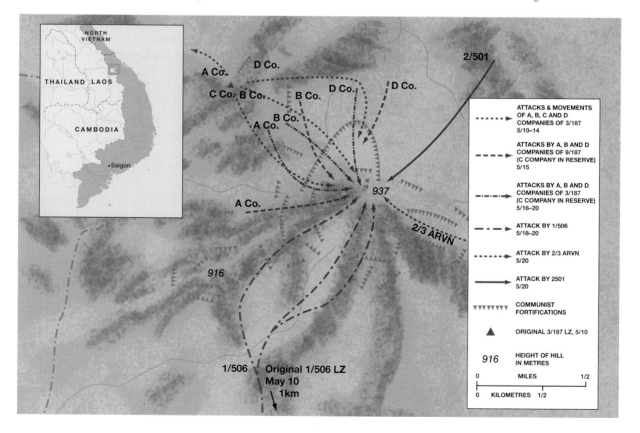

Defending the operation, the commander of the 101st acknowledged that the hill's only significance was that the enemy occupied it. 'My mission,' he said, 'was to destroy enemy forces and installations. We found the enemy on Hill 937, and that is where we fought them.'

Whatever one's opinion, it was the beginning of the end for American involvement in Vietnam. Washington ordered MACV Commander General Creighton Abrams to avoid such encounters in the future, and to accelerate the pace of Vietnamisation. It led indirectly to the limiting of subsequent US military operations. 'Hamburger Hill' was the last major search and destroy mission by US troops during the war (and the last major engagement fought by the 101st Airborne). From this point forth small unit actions predominated.

Operation 'Texas Star': Hill 882

Although overshadowed by the actions at Dong Ap Bia, another significant action was fought during May under Operation 'Texas Star' on Hill 882 in the mountains west of FSB Veghel. Hill 882 lay in the Nam Hoa mountain range of Thua Thien province (northern I Corps Zone), running along the northeast side of the A Shau Valley. 2nd Battalion, 502nd Infantry, was inserted onto the hill with the primary mission of establishing new LZs in the area, but after landing, they were repeatedly ambushed by PAVN regulars and had to be withdrawn because of heavy casualties.

At this time FSB Ripcord was under construction in the Coc Muen mountain range, Nam Hoa district, as part of the 101st Airborne defence network in Thua Thien. Nearly 3,000 feet high, Ripcord was located close to North Vietnamese sanctuaries in Laos, and in dominant terrain along which enemy infiltration routes to the populated lowlands had to pass. Fully aware of the threat that FSB Ripcord represented to their movements, the enemy had already begun to concentrate their forces in the area in preparation for an attack.

Soon after the withdrawal of the 2nd Battalion of the 502nd Infantry, B Company, 1st Battalion of the 327th Infantry was sent in. Unbeknown to them, they were an advance party sent in as a blocking force for FSB Ripcord.

Army intelligence had warned the commander of a possible PAVN sapper-battalion base of operations in the area and he had ensured the men were carrying extra machine-gun barrels and ammunition. Also, each squad was carrying a 90 mm recoilless rifle. Unknown to the troops, the sapper unit was part of a full PAVN division, which was massing for a planned attack on FSB Ripcord. The CO, Captain Terry Mills, split the company into three platoons, sending two off the hill into the surrounding jungle and try to locate the enemy while using the other platoon for command and control and to adjust possible air strikes and other firepower that was available.

On the fourth day, a reconnaissance patrol ran into a PAVN ambush. Their scout dog was killed by three hits from RPG-7 (rocket-propelled grenade) fire. Moving further down the trail that night the squad set up a night defensive perimeter within 50 yards of the NVA sapper base camp. The next morning, a recce team began to explore the surrounding area, and at noon it too walked into an ambush. All except one man were disabled in the sudden fusillade of fire. Using the squad radio, he tried to call in artillery support, only to watch the rounds fall harmlessly hundreds of yards away.

By this time the main force was also under attack as the PAVN probed the area trying to pinpoint the company position. The reconnaissance team withdrew, and after regrouping set up a defensive perimeter. A 'dustoff' was called for the wounded, and the company began withdrawing to the top of Hill 882.

After being resupplied the next morning, B Company was ordered to assault the PAVN base camp. As they advanced slowly to contact, there was a brief but intense small-arms exchange, before the airborne troops pulled back over a small finger of the hill. From this relatively safe position they called in Cobra gunship attacks on the enemy base camp, followed by 105 mm and 155 mm artillery fire from surrounding fire bases.

In the early afternoon, Air Force jets began dropping 500 lb bombs, and once these had gone, then came the napalm. On the second run, one of the pilots miscalculated, spreading the blazing liquid all over the company position. Many men were horribly burned. But the napalm had also devastated the sapper camp and the airborne troops took it without a fight.

After the battle, the company moved off the hill and set up recons in the valley that led to FSB Cannon. At night, the troops could plainly make out red flashlights as the PAVN moved into position to attack FSB Ripcord.

Operation 'Lamar Plains'

For a three-month period from mid-May, the 1st Brigade of 101st Airborne was under the operational control of the Americal Division; from 15 May it was engaged in Operation 'Lamar Plains' in the Chu Lai/Tam Ky area south of Da Nang. The 1st Battalion, 502nd Infantry, made two significant discoveries in the mountains southwest of Tam Ky. On 1 July, it found a cache containing 111 individual weapons, 33 crew-served weapons, three tons of ammunition and 17 bicycles. The second find was a 15-building hospital complex. 'Lamar Plains' ended on 14 August, and the brigade was returned to control of the 101st Airborne.

Other operations

In central Quang Tri Province the 3rd Marine Division continued their long-running Operation 'Kentucky' in the Con Thien area of the demilitarised zone. Initiated on 1 November 1967, the operation was aimed at preventing enemy infiltration through the barrier, and was terminated on 28 February 1969.

At the same juncture Operation 'Scotland II', initiated on 15 April the previous year, was rounded out. This long-running, multi-battalion sweeper operation centred in and around Khe Sanh, and engaged two battalions of the 4th Marine Regiment.

The 9th US Infantry Division continued Operation 'Speedy Express', a IV-Corps-wide effort to interdict lines of enemy communication and deny the enemy the use of base areas. It was started on 1 December 1968 and terminated at the end of May 1969, and although engagements were typically small, the division did fight several sizeable actions.

Throughout the early part of January 1969, PAVN/VC units continued to avoid major contacts with the Allies. However, on 23 February US Navy units and installations at Da Nang, Tan An, Ben Luc, Go Dan Ha and Tra Cu came under attacks that suggested a new enemy offensive, but since many units in these areas were poised to meet these attacks they caused only minimal damage.

SUMMER–AUTUMN 1969

9 June–31 October 1969

During the summer and autumn of 1969, conduct of operations was increasingly turned over to the South Vietnamese, while US troops withdrew in greater numbers amid reaffirmations of support for the Republic of South Vietnam's government from the Nixon administration. Nixon himself announced the phased reduction of

Below and Left: Troopers undergo in-country training at Dong Da Thien during April 1969 under the guidance of members of Detachment 51, 5th Special Forces Group (Airborne).

the US military presence in South Vietnam, which would be demonstrated initially by the withdrawal of 25,000 troops by 31 August 1969. In April 1969 American troop strength had peaked at 543,400; by mid-October this had dropped to 505,500.

Operation 'Montgomery Rendezvous'

Although enemy attacks now began to concentrate on South Vietnamese positions, as American units switched to small unit actions to avoid US combat deaths, there was still plenty of fighting for the 101st Airborne.

On 8 June, 'Montgomery Rendezvous', the third operation under the overall umbrella of 'Kentucky Jumper', jumped off in the familiar and feared terrain of the A Shau Valley. For the operation, the 3rd Brigade was once again teamed up with the 3rd ARVN Regiment. Their prime objective was to provide security for Engineer units constructing Route 547 into the valley, by seeking out PAVN forces in the high ground to the east.

The first objective for the engineers was to construct an airstrip on the valley floor near an abandoned French airstrip at Ta Bat. On the first day of the operation a company of infantry secured landing zones in the surrounding area, and a party of 326th Engineers was airlifted in. The following day CH-54 Tarhe 'Flying Cranes' and CH-46 Chinooks flew 48 sorties to bring in their heavy equipment. Drainage ditches were cut on either side of the strip, parts of the bog were filled in, trees were felled with explosives and cleared away. Fifty-four working hours later, the strip was complete, and ready to accept the first C-7A Caribou.

Below: An OH-6A 'Loach' of the 2nd Squadron, 17th Cavalry, flies 'nap of the Earth' to minimise enemy fire as it comes into land at Fire Base Victory on 16 October 1969. By late 1969, the firebase became the focus of divisional operations as the withdrawal of US forces accelerated. The division was now increasingly called upon to provide material support for ARVN formations.

For several weeks previously, engineers of the 27th Engineer Battalion, 18th Engineer Brigade, had been slowly cutting their way from FB Birmingham through the jungle to create a graded road all the way from Camp Eagle to the A Shau. Most of the road, Route 547, was cut into the sides of steep, tree-lined hills.

The mountainous terrain made for some difficult going, but by 20 June the road was ready for use. A column of 80 tracked vehicles of the 3rd Squadron of the 5th Cavalry, 9th Infantry Division, 7th Cavalry and 1st ARVN Division left FB Blaze and Cannon early in the morning. The lead APCs reached the new Ta Bat airstrip seven hours later without incident.

While the support command troops toiled away in the valley floor, 3rd Brigade combat operations were focused on the eastern highlands. Generally, contact with the enemy was light, with the exception of spirited sapper attacks on FSB Berchtesgaden and Currahee on the mornings of 14 and 15 June, respectively. At FSB Berchtesgaden, sappers armed with satchel charges managed to penetrate through the perimeter wire; one even made it into the mess hall, only to be killed by a cook. Eighteen PAVN troops were found inside the wire after the attack was repelled, and 13 more in the immediate vicinity.

The 1st Battalion, 506th Infantry, repelled another sapper attack on Fire Base Berchtesgaden launched in the early morning hours of 24 August. Approximately 90 enemy sappers, supported by mortar crews on the surrounding ridgelines, attacked the base at approximately 0320 hrs and were stopped cold just a few feet from the nearest bunker by well-coordinated base defensive fire. Aided by Cobra helicopters from the 4th Battalion, 77th Aerial Rocket Artillery, the troopers killed 31 PAVN and captured 19 weapons.

Ten days previously, on 14 August, 'Montgomery Rendezvous' had ended, having succeeded in bringing much-needed armour support to the A Shau Valley. The results of the two-month operation were 390 enemy killed and 185 individual and 43 crew-served weapons captured. US losses were 87 dead.

The conclusion of 'Montgomery Rendezvous' also brought the curtain down on Operation 'Kentucky Jumper'. After 167 days of combat in and around the A Shau Valley, more than 1,550 enemy had been killed and 41 suspects detained, 1,612 individual weapons, and 185 crew-served weapons captured.

Siege of FSB Ripcord

On 1 July 1970, the first enemy mortar rounds hit FSB Ripcord, ending a long period of anticipation for the men stationed at the isolated outpost. During the following three weeks they were subjected to intense artillery bombardment, and infantry attacks upon the perimeter. The battle reached a climax in the final week when a patrol ran into an enemy formation and lost 12 men and 50 wounded. Then, after a Chinook helicopter carrying a load of fuel took hits from a PAVN 12.5 mm anti-aircraft gun and crashed into Ripcord's ammo dump, exploding on contact, the decision was made to withdraw.

While supporting the extraction, the 101st Aviation Group was constantly exposed to heavy anti-aircraft and mortar fire from approximately 2,500 enemy troops of the 803rd and 6th PAVN Regiments. During the withdrawal, the commanding officer and two troopers were killed. All told, the 101st's losses were 61 killed and another 345 wounded.

For their bravery the 101st Aviation Group and its assigned units earned for themselves a Valorous Unit Award. In the words of the citation:

"Demonstrating aggressive determination and uncommon valour, the members of the 101st Aviation Group (Combat) (Airmobile), 101st Airborne Division (Airmobile) dauntlessly conducted the tactical redeployment of personnel and equipment from besieged FSB Ripcord. As a result of their unfailing tenacity and heroism in the face of massive enemy bombardment, the lives of numerous Americans were saved."

Quang Tri

In early autumn, plans were made for the redeployment of the 3rd Marine Division and on 30 September, the 1st and 2nd Battalions, 506th Infantry, were airlifted to Quang Tri Province to form a security screen for the move. Under the plan two airmobile battalions, supported by artillery FBs, were to be inserted along a line from the DMZ to just north of Khe Sanh in the southern portion of the province. These battalions would stop enemy movements from Laos and North Vietnam that could potentially interfere with the redeployment. On 2 October, the operation began when eight companies air-assaulted into two primary areas just south of the DMZ. First in was C Company, 1st Battalion, 506th Infantry, which was tasked with securing the area to be used as a battalion command post. All the others were landed without difficulty. Over the course of the next month, 3rd Brigade troopers stifled enemy attempts to disrupt the redeployment, encountering scattered contact with PAVN units, the bulk of which had already withdrawn to sanctuaries to the north and the west. On 8 November, as the Marines successfully completed their move, 3rd Brigade units closed down the northern AO. During the operation, a total of 59 enemy soldiers were killed and 22 individual and two crew-served weapons were captured.

By this time US operations had begun to take on a slightly different character, as efforts to Vietnamise the war gathered pace. Countrywide, the US Army initiated training programmes that aimed at raising the combat proficiency of South Vietnamese forces, and to allow them to assume greater responsibility for operations.

A relevant example of this is the pacification programme Operation 'Saturate', carried out by the 1st Battalion, 327th Infantry, in Phu Thu District of Thua Thien Province, from 5 October. Concurrent with the effort to Vietnamise the war, the battalion initiated a training programme for Regional Force companies in the district. It also organised a programme of medical care, with the emphasis on using Vietnamese nurses and doctors along with US personnel. Both of these were attempts to undermine the VC infrastructure known to be operating within Phu Thu, and damage its public credibility.

During the entire civic action and training programme, the hunt for the enemy went on as usual, but there were few contacts of any significance. However, the battalion sweeps did net dividends, as a significant number of enemy bunkers and booby traps were discovered and destroyed.

Below: Members of Company D, 1st Battalion, 502nd Infantry (Airmobile), 2nd Brigade, 101st Airborne Division (Airmobile) assault over the ridgeline of a hill during Operation 'Lamar Plain'. This operation was conducted by the division in conjunction with the Americal Division in Quang Tri Province between 16 May and 13 August 1969 and it resulted in 524 enemy casualties. Note (bottom) M79 grenade launcher. Known variously as the 'blooper' or 'thumper', the M79 40mm grenade launcher was a highly effective squad weapon.

WINTER–SPRING 1970

1 November 1969–30 April 1970

During this period, US and allied forces concentrated on operations to support the pacification programme. Particular effort was made in Vietnamisation through training and equipping RVN armed forces. Over the next few years, the ARVN was to be boosted to over 500,000 men. In turn this provided Nixon's administration with the necessary political means to recall three brigades of the US 1st Infantry Division and several major USMC units from Vietnam. At the end of 1969, America's fighting strength in Vietnam stood at 475,000; by the end of 1970 this had been reduced to 334,600.

During November a marked increase in enemy-initiated attacks signalled the start of the first phase of the Communist winter campaign. This was highlighted by intensified harassment incidents and attacks throughout the south. In November–December these were heaviest around Saigon, in III and IV CTZs, and were primarily directed against Vietnamese military installations in a clear attempt to disrupt the pacification programme. November was also marked by major attacks upon By Prang and Duc Lap in CTZ II (Central Vietnam).

By February 1970 the enemy had shifted their focus to I and II Corps. In the spring, attacks increased steadily, reaching a peak in April. Several efforts were made to take the offensive in the Central Highlands near I Corps CIDG camps at Dak Seang, Dak Pek and Ben Het. Dak Seang was attacked on 1 April 1970 and remained under siege throughout the month, until relieved by ARVN forces acting independently.

There were also numerous attacks by fire and several sapper attacks against US FSBs in I Corps through April and May.

In mid-November the 2nd Battalion, 501st Infantry, had just begun what was supposed to be a five-day stand-down at LZ Sally when it was ordered to deploy quickly to Quang Tri Province to assist elements of the 1st Brigade of the 5th Infantry Division. Many of the soldiers were being issued new clothing and cleaning their weapons and equipment when they were suddenly alerted for the move.

The eagerly anticipated opportunity to rest and relax rapidly was about to be rudely displaced by five days of heavy contact with the 27th PAVN Regiment in desolate hill country 20 miles west of Quang Tri. Within two hours of the alert, 18 CH-47 Chinooks were en route to Quang Tri Combat Base, with a 500-man force on board. There, over 40 UH-1 'slicks' took over the airlift and combat-assaulted their passengers into the area, where elements of the 1st Brigade, 5th Infantry, had been embroiled in fighting for several days.

In one notable action, B Company assaulted a large bunker complex only to become bogged down in a tit-for-tat firefight with the defenders. Under the eerie glow of flares and strobe lights, C Company launched a daring night manoeuvre to surround the fortified position. With Cobra gunships providing support, the airborne troops stormed the position, killing 29 PAVN troops.

Elsewhere, in a major series of engagements beginning on 28 January, 3rd Battalion, 506th Infantry, at that time OPCON to 173rd Airborne Brigade, battled the 8th Battalion of the 22nd PAVN Regiment in the area northwest of Bong Son, Binh Dinh Province, in northern II Corps area.

The firefights were initiated by PAVN troops hunkered down in the caves and crevices on Hill 474. Calling up air strikes by F-4 fighter-bombers and a massive artillery

Above: Members of Company E, 2nd Battalion, 501st Infantry (Airmobile), 2nd Brigade, 101st Airborne Division (Airmobile), service their quad .50-caliber M55 machine guns on 25 February 1970. These weapons proved fearsomely effective for the perimeter defence of fire support bases and other fixed installations. By this time dress regulations were increasingly lax and the boonie hat was the preferred choice of headgear.

bombardment, battalion troops manoeuvred by helicopter to block potential escape and then systematically cleared the enemy positions. The PAVN lost 90 dead as a result, in addition to 23 weapons and thousands of rounds of ammunition captured.

Operation 'Randolph Glen'

The launch of Operation 'Randolph Glen' on 7 December marked the start of a clear departure from the more conventional use of combat forces in South Vietnam. On the edge of populated lowlands in eastern Thua Thien Province, 2nd Brigade of the 101st Airborne and ARVN units staged a series of Civil Action programmes under which they provided technical assistance to government officials. These were accompanied by coordinated, limited military actions and ran until 31 March 1970.

The 'Street Without Joy'

In mid-February, the 101st Airborne troops were called on to help in another such programme – the resettlement of the infamous 'Street Without Joy' in Phong Dien District. In the early 1950s, this 20-mile-long strip of sandy flatland north of Hue was ravaged by fierce battles between the French and the Viet Minh. During Tet, the PAVN advance forced the inhabitants to evacuate their homes, and for two years they were housed in government refugee camps.

By early 1969, the area had been largely cleared of enemy troops and the 101st Airborne was able to begin a massive effort to resettle the refugees in their former homes. The 3rd/187th was ordered to the area in October of 1969 to eradicate the remaining VC infrastructure and began the arduous task of clearing mines and booby traps. Shortly thereafter, engineers from the 326th Engineer Battalion started repair work on the roads. By late April, more than 8,000 people had returned to their homes.

The Cambodian Incursion

In early 1970, Nixon directed that PAVN sanctuaries, staging areas, and storage depots in the strip of Cambodia bordering South Vietnam be eliminated. For years this area had provided a haven for enemy activities, and it was considered an intolerable threat to the US policy of Vietnamisation.

May Day, the traditional Communist holiday, was marked in 1970 by the massed assault of a combined Allied force of 15,000 US and ARVN soldiers across the southern border of Vietnam aimed at communist sanctuaries and supply bases inside Cambodia. Only a small task force from 3rd Battalion, 506th Infantry, 101st Airborne, participated in the Cambodian incursion. On 3 May the battalion, operating with the US 4th Infantry Division, was ordered to join Operation 'Binh Tay I', the mission to pacify west Cambodia. Its mission was to move into the former PAVN and VC sanctuaries in the Prek Drang base camp area of Cambodia, west of Pleiku City, and there to find, fix and destroy enemy personnel and equipment. By 1000 hrs on 5 May, the battalion was en route to the LZs. As they approached several aircraft received ground fire, and for several elements, alternative LZs had to be utilised.

Over the coming five days the troops skirmished intermittently with the enemy, and unearthed significant caches of arms and foodstuffs. On the morning of 10 May, B Company discovered a hospital complex with numerous hootches and a multitude of foodstuff and two tons of rice, before engaging a large enemy force in a pitched battle that lasted nearly two days. Having fought off sustained attacks by two PAVN companies, the following day D and B Company linked up and secured an LZ for extraction of B Company, which had sustained eight killed and 28 wounded, to FSB Currahee. A later sweep of the contact area by Delta Company revealed the bodies of 47 PAVN KIA and an unconfirmed number of wounded.

Below: Members of the 3rd Battalion, 187th Infantry, 101st Airborne Division (Airmobile), join the children of Ap Uu Thoung hamlet in a game of baseball. The troopers are members of a Battalion Action Team involved in pacification operations in Phong Dieu District, north of Hue, 15 January 1970.

Another sizeable cache of weapons and ammunition was discovered on 12 May by C Company. Among the captured equipment were small arms, rockets, artillery rounds, and thousands of grenades and mines of various types and descriptions.

There were no major ground activities in the area, but the enemy continued to be engaged in small actions for the next four days. On 16 May, the remainder of 3rd Battalion, 506th Infantry, began redeploying from Cambodia, returning to FSB Wildcat over the border in Vietnam.

At the end of June the remaining ARVN and US troops pulled out of Cambodia, having achieved little at a heavy price. From here on, there was little fighting in South Vietnam to speak of as US forces began a phased withdrawal. Although it never again fought a major engagement, the 101st Airborne was still engaged in ground operations and continued to distinguish itself in the field.

Operation 'Jefferson Glenn'

Following the conclusion of Operation 'Texas Star' on 5 September 1970, the 101st Airborne undertook the last major US military operation of the conflict: 'Jefferson Glenn'. Three battalions were tasked with establishing FSBs in the coastal lowlands of Thua Thien. The objective was to shield Thua Thien and Quang Tri by patrolling the belts of PAVN rocket launch sites that threatened critical installations.

Operation 'Lam Son 719'

At the end of January 1971, with US ground forces now operating largely in a support role, South Vietnamese forces launched a cross-border attack, with 101st Airborne Division support, into the border area of Laos adjacent to South Vietnam that had for many years been controlled by the enemy. The objectives of 'Lam Son 719' (named for the ARVN commander) were to disrupt an ongoing PAVN supply build-up at Tchepone in Laos, sever the Ho Chi Minh trail and destroy enemy staging areas. It was also seen as an important test of the airmobile concept.

Beginning on 8 February, the unit assisted in the airlift of 17,000 troops of the 1st ARVN Infantry Division and 1st ARVN Airborne Division from bases established on the Khe Sanh Plain into landing zones to the north and south of Route Nine. From here they were to attack an estimated 22,000 PAVN troops. Aided by heavy US artillery and air strikes, by 10 February the troops had seized the initial objectives of the operation. Soon enemy pressure bogged down the ARVN advance, and poor weather and heavy air defence opposition began to limit the air support available to relieve the pressure. This allowed the PAVN time to bring in massive armour and troop reinforcements from North Vietnam, South

Above: The last major campaign conducted by the 101st Airborne Division (Airmobile) in Vietnam was providing massive air support to the ARVN invasion of Laos – Operation 'Lam Son 719' – to cut the Ho Chi Minh Trail from 30 January to 6 April 1971. In conjunction with Operation 'Dewey Canyon II', a major air assault of six ARVN infantry battalions and an armoured brigade task force was launched into Laos on 8 February with all the US Army aviation units under the operational command of the 101st Airborne with the divisional air cavalry squadron, 2nd Squadron, 17th Cavalry, to the fore. 'Lam Son 719' proved to be a disaster and the policy of Vietnamisation was dealt a severe blow. Against the most intense anti-aircraft defences of the war with hundreds of heavy machine guns and more than 200 weapons ranging from SU-23-2 23mm cannon to the KS19 100mm gun, the US Army aviation units suffered heavy losses with 108 helicopters destroyed and 618 damaged but over 164,000 sorties were flown during the 67-day operation.

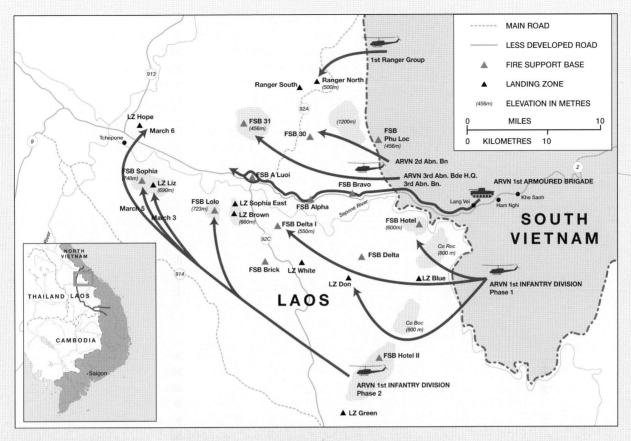

Vietnam and other parts of Laos. By 25 February, the invading forces had discovered enemy supply bases more than a mile square and had cut a major POL pipeline. However, over the coming days resistance stiffened considerably, and furthermore, the weather hindered tactical air movement. After enemy infantry overran Fire Base 31 General Lam, unable to continue the advance along Highway 9, decided to gamble on using his airmobile support to attack the main objective of Tchepone with a series of rapid air assaults.

After a very effective preparation of the area by B-52s, on 6 March two infantry battalions were lifted by 120 UH-1s for 40 miles into LZ Hope, north of Tchepone. This massive combat assault was carried out in what was considered to be the most hostile air

Above: 101st Airborne's role in the incursion into 'Lam Son 719' Laos.

defence environment ever encountered in the entire war. (A Company, 101st Aviation Regiment, had been conducting covert insertions into Laos for some time, and was well appraised of the extensive air defences the enemy had built up in the border area.) Despite this, only one Huey was hit and it made a safe landing in the objective area. The PAVN immediately increased pressure in the area and it was decided to withdraw to the east before the weather worsened.

The last elements of the ARVN 1st Infantry Division were extracted on 21 March and the remaining ARVN forces withdrew back into South Vietnam over the next few days, pursued by a PAVN force numbering some 40,000 men. During the extraction extremely heavy anti-aircraft fire was encountered along routes to and from the ARVN fire bases.

When the operation officially ended on 9 April, it was estimated that thousands of tons of enemy ammunition, petroleum, oils and lubricants, and other supplies and equipment had been destroyed. But the cost was tremendous; the invading units had been driven out by and lost half of their force. US aircrew losses were 176 killed, 1,942 wounded and 42 missing. Helicopter losses were put at 108 destroyed and 618 damaged.

Following the debacle of 'Lam Son 719', until the withdrawal at the end of the year, the infantry units made only a few scattered contacts with the enemy; most of the fighting was done by division artillery and aviation assets. On 14 April the ARVN 1st Infantry Division, supported by the 101st Aviation Brigade, launched Operation 'Lam Son 720' in the A Shau Valley to cut enemy supply lines.

CONSOLIDATION and WITHDRAWAL

1 July–30 November 1971

During this period the Vietnamisation programme continued apace, sustaining the progressive withdrawal of US troops. Pressure on the enemy was maintained by US air strikes on targets in the North. On 11 July South Vietnam assumed full control of defence for the area immediately below the demilitarised zone, a process begun in 1969. Secretary of Defense Melvin R. Laird announced completion of Phase I of Vietnamisation a month later, meaning that the US relinquished all ground combat responsibilities to the Republic of Vietnam. By early November, US troop totals had dropped to 191,000.

The participation of US forces in ground combat operations had not ceased; the remaining US manoeuvre battalions were still conducting missions. Until the operation was terminated in August, the 101st Aviation Brigade continued to support 'Lam Son 720'. In Thua Thien Province, other divisional elements increasingly turned responsibility for Operation 'Jefferson Glen' over to the ARVN 1st Infantry Division. Following the close of the operation on 8 October, the 101st began stand-down procedures.

On 12 November 1971, President Nixon put all remaining US troops on a defensive status. Heavy air attacks on North Vietnam were staged in December while both sides exchanged peace proposals. In early January 1972, Nixon confirmed that US troop withdrawals would continue but promised that a force of 25,000–30,000 would remain in Vietnam until all American PoWs were released. Secretary of Defense Laird reported that Vietnamisation was progressing well and that US troops would not be reintroduced into Vietnam even in a military emergency. US troop strength in Vietnam dropped to 136,500 by 31 January 1972, to 119,600 by 29 February, and then to 95,500 by the end of March.

Over that winter, the 101st Airborne Division finally returned home to Fort Campbell, and by the spring of 1972 the Vietnam War was at a low ebb. Although it dragged on for three more years, this brought the curtain down on the 101st Airborne Division involvement. At the official homecoming ceremonies on 6 April 1972 at Fort Campbell, Vice President Spiro T. Agnew and Army Chief of Staff General William C. Westmoreland (who had welcomed the 101st to Vietnam in 1965) were there to welcome the division home.

Above: The 101st Airborne Division (Airmobile) alone lost 68 killed with 261 wounded and 17 missing in action during 'Lam Son 719'. In the words of the assistant division commander, Brigadier General Sidney B Berry Jr: 'Every airmobile operation, even single ship resupply and aeromedical evacuation missions, had to be planned and conducted as combat operations complete with fire plan, escorting armed helicopters, and plans for securing and recovering downed crews and helicopter.'

EQUIPMENT, MARKINGS AND CAMOUFLAGE

This chapter provides brief details of the insignia, clothing and equipment typically worn by 101st Airborne troops in Vietnam, and of some of the weapons, personal equipment and aircraft they used. It is by no means an attempt at a definitive guide, for which I would recommend one of the specialist texts listed in the Bibliography.

INSIGNIA

There are a large number of 'unofficial' insignia associated with the 101st Airborne and its sub-units, and as these are far too prolific to list individually, I have instead restricted the following information to those official insignia that were common to all troops. For information on the former see the bibliography.

In common with all airborne qualified troops, 101st troops wore a *distinctive insignia* on the front of the left curtain of the garrison cap, consisting of an embroidered white parachute and glider on a blue disk with a red border approximately 2.5 inches in diameter overall. During the Vietnam War these were made by a variety of manufacturers (and occasionally hand embroidered).

There is another insignia, a *distinctive unit insignia* (DUI) specific to the 101st Airborne, which is worn on the upper sleeve of their dress uniform troops. It is a black cloth shield on which is embroidered the head of a bald eagle (NVA and Viet Cong reputedly referred to the 101st as the 'Chickenmen' because of this). Immediately above and touching the shoulder sleeve insignia (SSI), there is a black arc tab inscribed with the legend 'AIRBORNE' in yellow letters. Above the 101st shoulder sleeve insignia was often worn individual unit symbols. The design of the SSI recalls one of the traditions of the old Wisconsin 'Iron Brigade', this state being the territory of the original 101st Division after the First World War. The black on the shield represents the 'Iron', and the eagle is the famous bird nicknamed 'Old Abe' that was carried into combat during the American Civil War by one of the Iron Brigade regiments.

Enlisted men wore a variation on this DUI design near front-of-left curtain on their Garrison Caps. This was a gold coloured metal and enamel device consisting of a medium blue disc; superimposed on this is a black demi-eagle with a white head, wing details and eye and a gold beak in downward flight emerging from a white cloud. Above is a gold scroll bearing the motto 'Rendezvous with Destiny' in black letters.

The *combat branch or combat support branch insignia*, which for the 101st was the crossed rifles of the infantry, was worn on both lower lapels of the officers' dress jacket. On both upper lapels a small gilt 'U.S.' distinguished them as officers in the US Army.

Enlisted men wore a badge on the left upper lapel denoting their branch, and on the

Above: With the divisional insignia emblazoned on the ground of Camp Eagle, members of the 101st Airborne Division parade during a change of command ceremony on 17 May 1969 when Maj Gen John M Wright Jr superseded Maj Gen Melvin Zais. Camp Eagle was situated north of Phu Bai between Hue and Da Nang on Route 1, the fabled 'Street Without Joy'.

Far Right: Men of Company C, 1st Battalion, 327th Infantry (Airborne), 1st Brigade, 101st Airborne Division (Separate), carefully negotiate a stream in search of the elusive enemy during Operation 'Geronimo I' on 19 November 1966. The nearest trooper is equipped with the recently introduced Lightweight Rucksack that was standardised in November 1965 and issued to troops in Vietnam during 1966. The water resistant nylon bag and tubular aluminium frame weighed just three pounds. It featured one large compartment and three external pockets with twice the carrying capacity as its forerunner; it also had attachment straps for other items such as the one-quart plastic canteen shown here.

right upper lapel a small, round badge with the embossed legend 'U.S.' to distinguish them as soldiers in the US Army.

Variations on the US Army eagle insignia for general and warrant officers, and enlisted men, were worn on the garrison cap and on the front of the left breast pocket.

Rank insignia for both officers and enlisted men followed the pattern and positioning prescribed for all US troops on their dress and field uniforms: that is on the upper sleeve of both dress and field jackets for enlisted men, and on officer's shoulder epaulettes. All officers and NCOs also wore rank insignia near front-of-left curtain on their garrison caps. General, commissioned and warrant officers' caps had an edge braid of metallic gold, interwoven metallic gold and black, or interwoven metallic silver and black, respectively, and enlisted men an edge braid of black.

Medals, Combat and Special Skill Badges. Although not all men who served with the 101st were so qualified, those men entitled to Army Parachutist Wings wore them on the right lower side of the left breast pocket flap. On the dress uniform, medal ribbons were stitched in rows immediately above this flap, and in the same position above the right breast pocket, the unit citation ribbons (for a list of these see Appendix A). Above the medal ribbons on the left, the soldiers pinned their combat badges.

Finally, each man had a name badge on his right breast pocket flap, a subdued olive green version of which was produced for field jackets.

Field Uniform (Subdued) Insignia. On officers' and enlisted men's field uniforms, 'subdued' versions of some of these insignia were stitched. The insignia was produced in the same colour cloth as the uniform, and embroidered in black stitching. Officers wore the 'crossed rifles' combat branch patch on the right lapel. All ranks wore subdued name tags, rank insignia, Combat and Special Skill Badges (including Army Parachutist Wings), but in place of the medal ribbons there was a patch bearing the legend 'US ARMY'. Unique to the 101st Airborne was the subdued distinctive unit insignia patch that they were permitted to wear on the upper left shoulder.

Right: Laden down with equipment, a trooper of Company C, 2D Battalion, 502D Infantry (Airborne), 1st Brigade, 101st Airborne Division (Separate), treads carefully through a stream ever watchful for booby traps as his unit conducts a patrol in the 'boonies' during Operation 'Harrison' on 27 February 1966. Of interest, he is carrying several different types of hand grenades with the old World War II Mark IIA1 Fragmentation Grenade or 'pineapple' on his webbing belt next to an M8 white smoke and on his shoulder harness an M18 coloured smoke grenade. Under his left arm he is carrying a bag of demolition stores or M18A1 Claymore mines and under his right arm, next to his M16 rifle, boot socks stuffed with individual C-ration cans and other items of personal storage.

Right: A member of Company A, 1st Battalion, 327th Infantry (Airmobile), 1st Brigade, 101st Airborne Division (Airmobile), is presented with a medal by Major General Thomas Tarpley, the divisional commander, at Camp Eagle on 2 January 1972 during a stand down ceremony as the 'Screaming Eagles' return to the United States as part of Increment X of the US Army withdrawal from Vietnam. Divisional Headquarters closed on 10 March 1972 after 1,573 days in country as a full division. It suffered 4,011 killed in action – the third highest of any division in Vietnam – 18,259 wounded in action and its members were awarded 20 Medals of Honor.

Below: Happiness is a cold LZ – troopers of the 101st Airborne Division (Airmobile) rush to the treeline as their UH-1H Huey touches down in a jungle clearing; the trooper on the left is carrying an M19 60mm mortar tube. This weapon had a range of one mile and was capable of firing up to 30 rounds a minute, if sufficient ammunition was to hand. The total complement of helicopters in an airmobile division in Vietnam was 434 ranging from the tiny OH-13S Sioux to the gigantic CH-54 Skycrane.

CLOTHING

Dress uniform of the 101st Airborne Division was the standard US-Army-pattern uniform of the time, which consisted of a dark green, single-breast, waisted tunic and matching pleated trousers, with appropriate parade insignia, medal ribbons and so forth. In Vietnam it was rarely worn by troops except when on R&R.

Field uniform. In 1965 the US Army was still issuing the 'green sateen' field uniform to its troops. However, the demands of fighting in the hot and humid climate of Vietnam created a need for a different type of uniform, and a new pattern tunic and trousers were adopted. This older pattern tunic had two square breast and two lower pockets fastened by press studs. It had a distinctive round-cut collar.

These items were replaced in Vietnam by a new uniform based on the Second World War Para uniform, consisting of a tropical jungle jacket and matching trousers. Both jacket and trousers were made of tightly woven, quick-drying, wind-resistant poplin or Rip-Stop cotton fabric in olive drab army shade 107. They provided good protection against the sun, insects and other tropical hazards. Also, the loosely fitted garments provided body-heat ventilation and moisture dissipation.

The tunic was produced in three standard patterns, with differences of detail. All had two chest bellows pockets and two lower bellows pockets. In the field, tunic sleeves were commonly rolled up or cut off.

Three patterns of matching jungle trousers were issued. They had two front pockets, two hip pockets, two bellows cargo leg pockets, a small pocket inside the left cargo pocket for a survival kit, and draw cords at the bottom of the trouser legs. Although cool and comfortable, the trousers had a tendency to rip, especially at the knee.

Also issued was an olive-drab cotton T-shirt and a cotton–sateen utility fatigue shirt. The shirt was a shrink-resistant, heat-retentive and moisture-resistant garment with full-length sleeves, knitted cuffs and buttoned collar closure in olive drab.

Left: War is 90% tedium and 10% terror with hours of waiting for nothing to happen – Pfc Edward Horton spends his time reading a book while waiting to undertake a combat air assault during Operation 'Cook' on 8 September 1967. Attached to his M1956 Individual Load Carrying Equipment is an M26A1 fragmentation grenade and beside him is an M1 Steel Helmet with Leaf Pattern Camouflage Cover. The M1 helmet of paratroopers was fitted with the M1-C Parachutist's Liner with its distinctive web A-straps and chincup. Typically he wears his wristwatch attached to his OG107 utility shirt so as to avoid chafing and sores around his wrist in the hot and humid conditions of Vietnam.

BOOTS

Five types of combat boot were used in Vietnam. The standard all-leather combat boots that were first issued proved to be totally useless for fighting in the steamy jungles and swamps, and a purpose-designed jungle boot was soon introduced. This was manufactured in four patterns, all with leather and nylon sole and heel box, and canvas uppers and ventilation holes to speed drying. Air crew and chopper pilots tended to wear the older style right through the war because of fears about the nylon jungle boot sole melting in a fire.

Because of the numerous instances of immersion or trench foot among soldiers in Vietnam, particularly among those troops operating in the Delta for extended periods, 'comfort shoes' (otherwise known as 'bivouac slippers') were issued. The comfort shoe was constructed of an OG-106 nylon and rubber sole. They were fastened by an elastic velcro band, with two lace-up holes underneath the velcro band should this break. Comfort shoes were designed to be small and light enough to be folded up and stuffed into a pocket when not in use.

CLOTHING ACCESSORIES

I have omitted mundane but essential items such as socks and underwear. However, I include three items because they are commonly seen in period photographs; first is the tropical combat neckerchief, a popular item that was essentially a sweat cloth of highly absorbent, dark green cotton in army shade 409. This cloth was useful for wiping perspiration and dirt from the brow and hands, and for cleaning weapons and ammunition. It was worn over or around the head in a variety of bandanna, cravat and sweatband styles. There was also a knitted wool scarf, a seamless tubular scarf with reinforced ends that doubled as a cap or hand muff. The standard issue green field towel was also often worn around the neck to wipe the face free of sweat and protect the neck and shoulders from the chaffing of yoke straps or shouldered equipment.

HEADGEAR

Above: Booby traps – improvised explosive devices (IEDs) – were one of the greatest fears for the infantryman on the ground from the simple 'toe-popper' made from a single rifle round to the command-detonated US Air Force unexploded aerial bomb. All wrought havoc and destruction without a moment's notice to foot patrols and vehicles. This training patrol at the Screaming Eagle Replacement School at Bien Hoa remains prone and watchful as the point man investigates a suspected IED, affording us among other things, with an excellent view of his combat boots.

Based on the design of the WW2-pattern M1 helmet, the M1 of the 1960s had a lower profile but was otherwise unchanged. It was quite heavy to wear, particularly in the humid jungle of Vietnam. The two-part chinstrap was typically fixed up around the rear of the helmet. A helmet liner with nape strap or neckband was attached to the inside of the helmet and a reversible helmet cover to the outside, on which troops often wrote personal graffiti. For additional camouflage, the cover contained small slots for inserting natural foliage. An elasticated helmet band was designed to help hold the foliage in place, but was more commonly used to fasten field dressings, cigarettes, toilet paper, insect repellent or a spare magazine to the helmet so as to keep them dry and readily accessible.

There was also a standard issue tropical hat, made of either cotton poplin or rip-stop fabric. The hat featured an adjustable chinstrap, foliage loops and ventilation eyelets around the crown. An insect net was issued with it, but not often used. A visored, baseball style fatigue cap, made of polyester and dyed olive green, was available but was very unpopular with troops. Australian-style bush hats, cowboy-style hats and other non-regulation headgear produced locally were commonly worn.

Below: A Radio Telephone Operator (RTO) checks out his AN/PRC-25 FM radios in the field. The M1956 Load Carrying Equipment was configured to accommodate the Electrical Equipment Harness that incorporated the radio. Note the Spares Bag attached to the left of the radio that contained the seven-section long-range 'fishpole' antenna and a spare handset. Although highly reliable, the main shortcoming of the 'Prick 25' was its lack of a scrambler/descrambler device for secure transmissions, although this was rectified with a modified model that became the AN/PRC-77. Generally, communications security was poor in the US Army during the Vietnam war and many operations were compromised by the enemy's successful use of radio intercepts. Note, too, the helmets and other personal equipment on the grass beside him, and his 'Screaming Eagles' shoulder patch.

INDIVIDUAL EQUIPMENT

Combat troops were issued with basic, and more specialised, items of load-carrying equipment in or on which they carried such items as they needed to shelter, eat, fight and survive in combat. Until 1967 the M1956 pattern kit continued to be issued, with improvements in the detail of certain items. After this time a modernised version designed specially for Vietnam – the M1967 Load Carrying Equipment (LCE) – was introduced. The new equipment was essentially the same but replaced metal with plastic and canvas with nylon, which unlike the canvas was mildew resistant. The M1967 LCE did not entirely replace the earlier kit; the two were often mixed together to form composite webbing, since both types were fully compatible with each other.

The basic item was the pistol belt, to which were attached all other items. The M1967 Davis belt was essentially the same as the M1956 pattern, but was produced in both canvas and nylon and had the quick release 'Davis buckle'. The weight of kit mounted on the belt was distributed to the shoulders by means of suspenders (yoke straps), which attached from the front of the pistol belt to the buttpack (see below) or else directly to the back of the pistol belt to form an H shaped load-carrying system. The M1967 pattern suspenders had two fasteners to allow the buttpack to be mounted higher, and were made of padded nylon. There were also metal loops on each suspender for the attachments of small items. A single yoke version was produced.

To the belt were attached universal ammo pouches, the standard ammunition pouch for the Colt M16 magazine. The M1956 pouch was made of canvas, and there were carriers either side for grenades. A smaller canvas pouch was issued in late 1967 to early 1968. This was designed for easier access to the shorter M16 20-round magazine. M1967 ammo pouches were similar to this small version of the M1956 universal ammo pouch, but were made of nylon and had a quick release closure.

To strap his sleeping bag or poncho with liner rolled inside to the suspenders the soldier used the sleeping carrier. This complicated set of straps, also called 'spagette straps', was manufactured in canvas.

Below the sleeping carrier he attached the buttpack (also called the fanny pack), which was used to carry spare items of clothing, rations, cooking utensils and so forth. It has wings of canvas that fold inwards. The carry straps are underneath and clips on the rear attach it to the pistol belt. If required, the suspenders can be attached to the top through riveted holes on the flaps. An improved version issued from 1961 was a little larger and lined in plastic, and an adapter allowed the user to strap the buttpack higher on the shoulders, but neither design was particularly satisfactory.

In 1965 the design of the 'lightweight tropical rucksack' was standardised and it was issued in the following year to replace the M1956 and M1961 buttpacks. It consisted of a water-resistant nylon bag with one large compartment and three external pockets. This was fixed to a tubular aluminium frame. However, the rucksack prevents items being worn on the pistol belt, thus water canteens and first aid kits are located elsewhere, such as on the rucksack frame itself. A larger version known as the tropical rucksack was used, but soldiers in Vietnam generally found the X-frame to be uncomfortable over long periods of wear. More popular was the issue ARVN rucksack, originally produced for the South Vietnam Rangers and based on a North Vietnamese army pack. It became popular with US personnel because of its light weight and generous capacity. It was manufactured as a cotton duck pack with two external pockets and mounted on a sprung metal X frame, which kept the load high and away from the user's back.

Other items of belt kit included;

Compass pouch. A small pouch designed to hold either a lensatic compass or a field dressing.

Above: M114A1 155mm howitzers are prepared for action at Fire Support Base Ripcord situated in the A Shau Valley to support the operations of the 2nd Battalion, 506th Infantry (Airmobile) 101st Airborne Division (Airmobile) against the base areas of the 324th NVA Division during the ferocious fighting of July 1970. At this time, the 101st Airborne Division (Airmobile) was supported by two battalions of 155mm howitzers – the 2nd Battalion, 11th Artillery (155mm) and 1st Battalion, 39th Artillery (155mm). The latter was a self-propelled unit originally equipped with M109 155mm howitzers and latterly M107 175mm guns and M110 8-inch howitzers. Accordingly these M114A1 howitzers belonged to the 2nd Battalion, 11th

Artillery, – the Dragon Regiment – which arrived in Vietnam on 13 December 1966 and served with II Field Force Artillery and then Task Force Oregon before being assigned to the 101st Airborne Division (Airmobile) on 10 June 1968. During the summer of 1970 the US firebases were tempting targets to the enemy and the NVA repeatedly bombarded and attacked Fire Support Base Ripcord. In one three-week period 61 troopers of the 101st were killed and a further 345 wounded. Because of the heavy enemy pressure, FSB Ripcord was abandoned on 23 July with the loss of one CH-47 Chinook and damage to eight others out of a total of 14 involved in the evacuation.

Right: Members of Battery C, 2nd Battalion, 320th Artillery (105mm) (Airborne), 1st Brigade, 101st Airborne Division (Separate), fire their M102 105mm howitzer at maximum elevation from Fire Support Base Bastogne in support of combat operations on 16 April 1968. The M102 was specially designed for airborne and airmobile formations and was 1,500 pounds lighter than the M101A1. It could pivot through 360 degrees for faster engagement times.

Right: 'Hang it in the tube' – the crew of an M29 81mm mortar stand by for their next fire mission during a 101st Airborne Division (Airmobile) operation in February 1966. The M29 had a maximum range of 3,500 yards and a good crew could fire 30 rounds a minute but a normal sustained rate of fire was five or six a minute. There were three 81mm mortars per company and each had a six-man crew. The weapon fired High Explosive, White Phosphorous and illuminating rounds. An HE round weighed over 7lb so carrying rounds in the 'boonies' was a back-breaking task and mortars were often concentrated in firebases to provide immediate fire support to units in the field via an FOO (Forward Observation Officer) operating with the troops on the ground.

One-quart canteen and cover. A felt-lined, cotton-duck water canteen cover and polyethylene canteen, of which two were commonly carried. The M1967 pattern was fully nylon and had a small pouch for purifying tablets. The canteen fitted into a canteen cup and the cup inside the canteen cover. There was also a two-quart collapsible canteen in two patterns, consisting of a square, moulded-vinyl bladder and an M1910-pattern cap with chain. The bladder flattened when empty. The canteen could only be carried in a matching cover on the belt or in other positions, and took up a lot of space.

Entrenching tool and case. Until replaced, the M1951 pattern E-tool was used as the standard folding entrenchment tool. It had a wooden haft and could be adjusted to different angles. It was an excellent weapon and archaeological tool for digging trenches and filling sandbags. A heavier variant on this had an added pick. The 1967 pattern tri-folding E-tool was a great improvement on the old wooden-hafted E-tool. It had a hollow, triangular-shaped handle and single shovel blade, with one edge sharpened for cutting and the other serrated for digging. The blade could be adjusted to different angles in the same way as the M1951 E-tool. It folded twice for carrying and was stored in a stiff plastic case, which had slide attachments which allowed it to be mounted anywhere on the belt.

M1916 Pistol holster. Officers and chopper pilots were issued with the M1916 pistol holster, the standard black leather holster with 'US' imprinted on the flap. There was also a shoulder holster.

Shelter

For shelter on operations each soldier would carry a *half-man pup tent*, a tent pole that could be split into three sections and tent pegs. The tent was basically a panel with triangular flaps made in olive-green, water-repellent, mildew-resistant cotton duck. Two of these could be buttoned together to form a complete tent. In the event that the tent could not be used, a more immediate form of shelter was available in the *poncho*. The early item was in olive-green rubberised fabric, and very heavy when wet; when worn as a garment in humid Vietnam, it was also hot and sweaty. However, a useful feature of the poncho was that two could be snapped together to make a temporary shelter or 'hooch'. It was also commonly used as a ground sheet or a makeshift stretcher. A lightweight poncho, identical to the standard poncho but fabricated from a nylon-based fabric with polyurethane coating, was produced.

To sleep on the soldier had an olive green inflatable *air mattress* the same size and shape as the sleeping bag. It also doubled as a float for carrying items across streams and flooded land. Conditions permitting, the troops may also have used *jungle hammocks* to sleep on. The US Army's standard jungle hammock was made of water-repellent treated nylon supported by quarter-inch-thick polyester draw cords. The first soldiers to Vietnam had a heavy wool *blanket*, which became even heavier when wet and proved totally unsuitable. This was replaced by the *poncho liner*, a quick-drying, lightweight, quilted item made of rip-stop parachute fabric. This could be laced into the poncho to make a makeshift sleeping bag, although a purpose designed *sleeping bag* was also issued.

Eating

In the field the soldier used his self-contained aluminium mess canteen and utensils to prepare the food and drink contained in the individual C-ration meal. The 'Meal Combat Individual' consisted of a box containing a main meal (pork and beans, spaghetti and meatballs etc.), a B2 unit (crackers, candy, cheese), a dessert (canned fruit, pound-cake) and an accessory pack (pictured). The accessory pack contained a P-38 can opener, hot drink, gum, matches, toilet paper, salt, sugar, a plastic spoon and a small pack of cigarettes. LRRP units were issued with their own special ration packs.

Below: Pfc Oliver Crews struggles with an M79 grenade launcher during training at the Screaming Eagle Replacement Training School at Bien Hoa. Note the sighting mechanism above the barrel that allowed accurate fire out to a range of 400m. The weapon fired High Explosive, Smoke, Flechette and parachute illuminating rounds.

Medical

The standard medical kit was the Medical Instrument Supply Set, also known as a 'Unit One' bag. It was a 3-compartment bag made of heavy canvas, or of rubberised cotton after 1968. Nylon bags appeared in the early 1970s. Typical contents would include different sizes of dressings and bandages, an emergency instrument set, blood volume expanders, aspirin and anti-malaria tablets. Medical Bag No. 5 was a rectangular canvas rucksack with a large internal space for storing all the medical supplies a platoon would need, including an emergency surgical instrument set. It was issued with a Waterproof Carrier, which was produced in rubberised cotton, or nylon duck after 1967.

Gasmasks and fragmentation vests

CS and other gases were used extensively for tunnel-clearing, and two types of gas mask were issued. The first was the M17 Field Protective Gas Mask, a rubberised mask worn over the face to protect the face, eyes and respiratory tract. It was carried in a bag with straps that could be attached around the left leg, and came complete with spare eye lenses. The later M17A1 had a drinking tube in the front of the mask, which could be attached to the one-quart canteen by means of a special cap. A rubberised cotton mask hood could be worn over the gas mask to protect head neck and shoulders.

Body armour came in a variety of forms, all of them designed to protect the core of the body and vital organs. Given the high proportion of injuries inflicted by mines and booby traps, and the weight of the armour, many troops scorned its use. The most common was the M1952 fragmentation jacket, developed during the Korean War and used right through the Vietnam War. The vest contained a filler of semi-flexible layers of ballistic nylon cloth, with a quarter-inch layer of sponge rubber over the ribs and shoulders. This served as a shock-absorbing layer to alleviate contusions and fractures from the impact of missiles. The vest closed with a full-length zipper and could be adjusted by laced closures at both sides. It had two chest pockets, shoulder straps and two rows of web hangers for grenades and other equipment.

Above Left: With the divisional insignia on the pilot's door, a wounded trooper of the 1st Battalion, 506th Infantry (Airmobile), 3rd Brigade, 101st Airborne Division (Airmobile), is helped aboard an 'Eagle Dust Off' UH-1H during an operation near Hue. The 'medevac' helicopters were a great boost to morale for US troops in the frustrating type of warfare fought in Vietnam where the enemy could strike at any moment to cause casualties and then slip away into the hinterland before any significant retaliation was possible.

Above: Troopers of the 101st Airborne Division (Airmobile) progress along a chow line at Fire Support Base Victory near the Montagnard village of Mai Loc in the Central Highlands on 16 October 1969. Note the shoulder sleeve insignia of the Screaming Eagle. Most units produced a subdued version of their insignia but this was not favoured in the 'Airborne' and the 101st continued to display the full colour version. Units took great pride in their insignia and their titles such as the Screaming Eagles but equally units were highly disparaging of others – such as the nickname given to the 101st of the 'Vomiting Vultures' or 'Puking Buzzards'. To the NVA, the 101st were known as the 'Chicken Men' as few Vietnamese had ever seen an eagle.

Left: A UH-1H aeromedical helicopter brings in wounded members of Company D, 2nd Battalion, 502nd Infantry (Airborne), 101st Airborne Division, to Fire Support Base Berchtesgaden during Operation 'Somerset Plain' in August 1968. The aeromedical helicopters of the 101st Airborne Division (Airmobile) were attached to the 326th Medical Battalion and were known as 'Eagle Dust Off' whose unit motto was 'If we can't nobody else can.' (See also photo and caption on page 79.)

Right: Medical staff of the 326th Medical Battalion load a wounded trooper of the 2nd Battalion, 327th Infantry (Airborne) into an ambulance for transfer from the medical clearing station to a filed hospital. It was the proud boast of the medical facilities that if one was hit in the field it was possible to get the wounded man to a field hospital within 20 minutes; if seriously injured to a base hospital in Japan within 12 hours and if killed, the body would be home in a week thanks to the 'KIA Travel Bureau' of Graves Registration. Note the old French watchtower in the background.

Below: The crewchief of a UH-1H hangs on to the electrical hoist as he guides his pilot out of a tight Pick-up Zone as the aeromedical evacuation helicopter extracts wounded troopers of the 101st Airborne Division (Airmobile) during an operation near the DMZ on 16 October 1969.

The M1969 fragmentation jacket was basically an upgraded version of the M1952, with extra ballistic nylon layers and a semi-stiff three-quarter inch collar with three layers of ballistic filling, providing protection to the neck. In 1966 'body armour, small arms protective, ground troops' was introduced in an attempt to provide the soldier with a vest that not only acted as a fragmentation vest, but also protected against small arms fire. It consisted of a flexible shell of ballistic nylon felt, with pockets on both the front and rear to accommodate form-fitting ceramic composite armour plates. These plates had integrated web straps allowing them to be worn independently of the vest, and vice versa. However, with all the armour in place, the vest was very heavy, weighing around 22lb.

Weapons maintenance equipment and accessories

Basic accessories were the rifle sling and bipod. Later in the war certain troops were issued with 'Starlight' scopes. Perhaps the most important item of maintenance equipment was the cleaning kit, the contents of which varied according to weapon. Typically this contained: cleaning rod set, bore brushes, chamber brushes, a double-ended plastic toothbrush, cloth cleaning patches, a bottle of bore cleaner, compound solvent and a bottle of light small arms (LSA) gun oil. Miscellaneous items were carried in the *small arms accessories case* and *paratrooper's weapons case*.

In addition, there was a plethora of specialist equipment for machine guns and mortar crews, much of which had to be carried into the field. Machine gun crews, for example, had a special case for the spare barrel and gloves to change it.

In addition each man would most likely carry the following items in his equipment: sewing kit; personal hygiene kit; flashlight with a compartment containing coloured lens filters that could be attached to the front of the flashlight; sunburn cream; insect repellent; foot powder; first aid packet/field dressing; purification tablets (Puri-tabs).

WEAPONS

- *Pistols.* These included the M-1911A1 Colt .45in automatic pistol and L9A1 9mm (.45in) FN Browning High Power
- *Submachine guns.* The M1A1 Thompson .45 in, M3A1 .45in 'grease gun' and Model 45 9mm 'Carl Gustav' were used in the early part of the conflict
- *Rifles and carbines.* The first weapon issued to US troops in Vietnam was the M1 'Garand', a 0.3in self-loading rifle essentially unchanged from that carried by US infantrymen in the Second World War. This was replaced by the M-14, which fired the 7.62mm NATO cartridge, and subsequently by the M-16 5.56mm Assault Rifle (but only after some major teething troubles). A shorter carbine version designated CAR-15 was also issued.
- *Grenades and rifle grenades.* The Mk2, M26 and M61 were the standard Anti-Personnel Defensive Hand Grenades. The Mk2 could be launched by rifle. The M-79 was a dedicated shoulder-fired 40 mm grenade launcher; the M203 40mm grenade launcher attached to the underside of the M-16 barrel.
- *Machine guns, medium and heavy.* The M-60 7.62mm GPMG was the standard medium machine gun. Much loved by the troops for its impressive rate of fire, this weapon was also mounted on choppers and vehicles. Although best in the hands of a skilled gunner, for static base defence the 1919 vintage M2 .50-cal heavy barrel was highly prized.
- *Anti-armour weapons.* Although North Vietnamese armour was rarely encountered, it was occasionally engaged with anti-armour weapons. The most common was the man portable M72 66mm HEAT light anti-armour weapon (LAW). Although designed for use

Below: SP4 Robert Canfield of Company B, 1st Battalion, 327th Infantry (Airborne), 1st Brigade, 101st Airborne Division, (Separate), cleans his M16A1 rifle before going on patrol during Operation 'Wheeler' near Chu Lai in November 1967. The M16 required constant servicing for reliable operation in the field as a fellow trooper of the 101st, Pfc William Austin discovered during Operation 'Wheeler'. As he crossed a paddyfield he was charged by a water buffalo, one of the most irascible and dangerous animals encountered in Vietnam, scattering everyone in the patrol except Austin who was rooted to the spot. As he lifted his M16 to his shoulder, the buffalo knocked the weapon from his hands as it thundered by only to turn around and charge again. Retrieving his rifle from the mud, he pulled the trigger but nothing happened. Quickly clearing the jam, he fired again and the enraged animal fell pinning Austin to the ground. He screamed at his cowering colleagues to do something to which came the response – 'Olé!' On 18 November 1967, the 1st Brigade rejoined the 'Screaming Eagles' after the arrival of the division in November 1967. The brigade then lost its designation of 1st Brigade, 101st Airborne Division (Separate) and reverted to 1st Brigade.

against soft-skinned and lightly armoured vehicles, this proved particularly effective against bunkers. The standard infantry recoilless rifle was the M67 90 mm, a highly effective weapon that could be either tripod or vehicle mounted. In the former configuration, three men could carry it, but it was heavy and awkward and generally relegated to base defence. The first generation of aerial rocket artillery and some gunships employed the SS-11 wire-guided missile, which was flown to the target (usually a bunker) using a small joystick. Later in the war the impressive M151E2 127mm TOW was deployed. This was a wire-guided semi-automatic command-to-line of-sight-system with a high-explosive anti-tank (HEAT) warhead.

• *Mortars.* These ranged in size from the M2 and M19 60 mm tubes, which were

generally only used by reconnaissance teams, to the M1 and M29 81 mm (3.2 in), which were the standard US Army medium mortars and provided a significant amount of readily available firepower to the manoeuvring infantry. The 4.2 in M30 was also employed, but because of its size and weight this was left in the base camps or fire bases for static defence.

Above: Smoking can seriously damage your health but then so can a firefight with the 24th NVA Regiment as encountered by the 1st Battalion, 327th Infantry (Airborne), 1st Brigade, 101st Airborne Division (Separate), on the morning of 7 June 1966 during Operation 'Hawthorne' that was conducted to protect the Ruff Puff outpost of Tou Morong near Dak To and pre-empt an NVA offensive in Kontum Province. During its early years of service with the US Army the M16 5.56mm assault rifle suffered serious problems in the field with repeated stoppages that was attributed to inadequate cleaning and servicing by the troops. These problems led to the introduction of an improved model known as the M16A1 and thereafter it proved to be an excellent weapon for jungle operations although meticulous cleaning procedures remained vital.

HELICOPTERS

Helicopters used by the US Army were generally classified as 'utility', 'attack', 'observation', 'cargo' and 'heavy' – designations which are largely self-explanatory. The types used by aviation units assigned to the 101st Airborne are detailed below.

One of these aircraft in particular must be highlighted. That is the *Bell UH-1*, originally introduced in the utility role and, in the later of its many versions, used as to provide aerial rocket artillery and as a gunship. It was largely because of the Vietnam War that this aircraft became the second most numerous aircraft since the Second World War, and there was no significant clash of arms on the soil of South Vietnam in which the UH-1 did not participate. Crewed by three and designed to accommodate up to 15 troops (although this was regularly exceeded) it provided the backbone of US Army airmobility in Vietnam and was the helicopter most widely used by the 101st Airborne.

The other major type was the Bell *AH-1G Cobra*. This purpose-built gunship was the mainstay of the 101st's aerial rocket artillery units. It was operated by a crew of two sitting in tandem in a sleek fuselage with stub wings, with the gunner in the front position. Its weapons included 7.62 mm mini-guns, 40-mm grenade launchers, 20-mm cannon, anti-tank missiles and various rockets.

The observation and scout units flew the *Hughes OH-6 Cayuse*, a six-seater aircraft with a distinctive egg-shaped fuselage introduced in 1967 to replace the Bell H-13 Sioux. The OH-6 was itself eventually replaced by the *Bell OH-58A Kiowa*.

Two much larger helicopters were used by the 101st Airborne for heavy lifts. The more common was the Boeing Vertol *CH-47 Chinook*, a large tandem-rotor transport able to seat 44 fully-equipped troops or carry modest vehicles and artillery. A, B and C models were in use in the Vietnam conflict. Chinooks could fly in as slung loads all the

Right: One of the particular aviation assets of the airmobile divisions in the Vietnam war was the aerial rocket battalion within the Division Artillery. Equipped with UH-1 or AH-1 Cobra armed helicopters, the batteries provided the closest fire support to the ground troops, often delivering their 2.75-inch rockets within metres of friendly forces to suppress enemy fire and eliminate their positions. In the 101st, such fire support was provided by the 4th Battalion, 77th Artillery (Aerial Rocket) known as the 'Dragons'.

Below Right: A CH-47C Chinook of the 159th Aviation Battalion (Assault Support Helicopter) hovers over the POL point at Fire Support Base Tomahawk as it releases an underslung load of fuel bladders on 10 April 1971. Introduced in March 1968, the CH-47C featured an improved transmission and uprated engines that doubled the load and range of the original A model that first saw action with the 1st Cavalry Division (Airmobile) in September 1965. The white triangle on the forward rotor pylon indicates Company B – callsign Varsity – within the aviation battalion; A being a red triangle – The Pachyderms – and C blue which rejoiced in the callsign of Playtex as they provided 'support' for the division; indeed, one Chinook had a large pink bra painted underneath the fuselage. Company B had originally requested the callsign 'Mother Truckers' but the army deemed this to be unseemly.

Below: A striking image of the concept of airmobility as troopers of Company C, 1st Battalion, 327th Infantry (Airmobile), 1st Brigade, 101st Airborne climb aboard a UH-1H to return to Fire Support Base Birmingham on 15 April 1971. The helicopter provided extraordinary mobility in the area warfare of Vietnam, capable of inserting troops over scores of miles.

air-portable guns, ammunition and supply packages used in Vietnam, as well as such mundane items as trucks of drinking water. The other heavy lift helicopter was the Sikorsky *CH-54 'Tarhe'* (Flying Crane) aircraft. Almost the entire US Army inventory of this aircraft saw combat duty in Vietnam, carrying bulldozers, graders and light armour as slung loads, picking up and repositioning artillery, and also rescuing over 380 downed aircrew.

Among secondary US Army types in Vietnam were small numbers of older helicopters, including the Bell *OH-13 'Sioux'* and *OH-23 'Raven'* observation helicopters, the Piasecki (Vertol) *CH-21 'Shawnee'* and Sikorsky *CH-34 'Choctaw'* (designated the UH-34 'Dog' by USMC).

AVIATION UNITS

Detailed below are the aviation units assigned to 101st Airborne Division, with their call signs, aircraft type, and operating base.

158th Aviation Bn
HQ and HQ Company 158th Aviation Bn. 'Lightning' UH-1 Evans
A Company 158th Aviation Bn 'Ghost Riders' UH-1 Evans
B Company 158th Aviation Bn. 'Lancers' UH-1 Evans
C Company 158th Aviation Bn. 'Phoenix' UH-1 Evans
D Company 158th Aviation Bn. 'Redskins' AH-1G Evans

101st Aviation Bn
HQ and HQ Company 101st Aviation Bn. 'Mustang' UH-1 Eagle
A Company 101st Aviation Bn. 'Comanchero' UH-1 Eagle
B Company 101st Aviation Bn 'Kingsmen' UH-1 Eagle
B Company Gunships 101st Aviation Bn. 'Kingsmen' UH-1 Eagle
C Company 101st Aviation Bn. 'Black Widow' UH-1 Phu Bai
D Company 101st Aviation Bn. 'Hawk' AH-1G Phu Bai

2nd/17th Cavalry
HQ Troop.
Saber UH-1 Eagle

A Troop
Scout Platoon Assault '10-19' OH-6 Quang Tri
Gunship Platoon Assault '20-29' AH-1G Quang Tri
Aero Rifle Platoon Ground Element Assault '30-39' Quang Tri
Aero Rifle Platoon Flight Element Assault '40-49' UH-1 Quang Tri

B Troop
Scout Platoon Banshee '10-19' OH-6 Eagle
Gunship Platoon Banshee '20-29' AH-1G Eagle
Aero Rifle Platoon: Ground Element Banshee '30-39' Eagle
Aero Rifle Platoon: Flight Element Banshee '40-49' UH-1 Eagle

C Troop.
Scout Platoon Condor '10-19' OH-6 Phu Bai
Gunship Platoon Condor '20-29' AH-1G Phu Bai
Aero Rifle Platoon: Ground Element Condor '30-39' Phu Bai
Aero Rifle Platoon: Flight Element Condor '40-49' UH-1 Phu Bai

377th Artillery
A Battery 'Gunner' UH-1H & OH-6 Eagle

4th/77th Aerial Rocket Artillery
A Battery. 'Dragon' AH-1G Phu Bai
B Battery. 'Toro' AH-1G Eagle
C Battery. 'Griffin' AH-1G Evans

326th Medical Bn. 'Dustoff' UH-1 Eagle
1st Bde. 'Dead Bone' UH-1 Evans
2nd Bde. 'Brandy' UH-1 Phu Bai
3rd Bde. 'Thunder' UH-1 Eagle

163rd Aviation Bn 'Roadrunner' UH-1 Eagle

Heavy lift
159th Aviation Bn
A Company. 'Pachyderm' CH-47 Phu Bai
B Company. 'Varsity' CH-47 Eagle
C Company. 'Playtex' CH-47 Phu Bai

478th Aviation Company 'Hurricane' CH-54 Da Nang

PEOPLE

MAJOR GENERAL OLINTO MARK BARSANTI

Of all the men who commanded the 101st Airborne Division in Vietnam, the most celebrated is Major General Olinto Mark Barsanti. In his 31-year military career, Barsanti served in the Second World War, the Korean War and Vietnam. He earned more than 60 awards, medals and commendations, including the Distinguished Service Medal, the Distinguished Service Cross, the Distinguished Flying Cross and seven Purple Hearts.

Born on 11 November 1917 to Italian immigrants, Barsanti joined the US Army and was commissioned as a Second Lieutenant, serving initially with the 2nd Infantry Division. In June 1944 he participated in Operation 'Overlord' (the Normandy landings) as commander of the 3rd Battalion, 38th Infantry. Over the next eight months of battle Major Barsanti, at 26 years of age one of the youngest battalion commanders in the army, was awarded five Purple Hearts, a Bronze Star medal and three oak leaf clusters, and the Silver Star for his leadership in combat.

Barsanti remained in Europe until April 1945, when as a lieutenant colonel he returned to the United States for medical treatment. He attended and then taught at staff college, and at the outbreak of the Korean War was serving in General Headquarters, Far East Command under General Douglas MacArthur. Lieutenant Colonel Barsanti's most notable and courageous action during the war took place on 19 and 20 October. Driving alone behind North Korean lines and subjected to repeated attacks by soldiers using automatic weapons, Barsanti successfully completed a 190-mile mission to deliver secret orders to two South Korean infantry divisions. For this he was presented the Distinguished Service Cross, the second highest military service award, on 14 December 1950.

At 33 years of age, he was commanding officer of the 9th Infantry Regiment, the army's youngest regimental commander in Korea, and added the sixth Oak Leaf Cluster to his Bronze Star and a second Oak Leaf Cluster to his Silver Star. After

COMMANDERS OF 101st AIRBORNE DIVISION

Maj Gen Thomas L. Sherbourne, Jr.	23 May 1956–23 Mar 1958
Maj Gen William C. Westmoreland	2 Apr 1958–30 June 1960
Maj Gen Ben Harrell	30 June 1960–17 July 1961
Maj Gen Charles W. G. Rich	17 July 1961–25 Feb 1963
Maj Gen Harry W. Critz	25 Feb 1963–20 Mar 1964
Maj Gen Beverly E. Powell	20 Mar 1964–28 Mar 1966
Maj Gen Ben Sternberg	28 Mar 1966–1 July 1967
Maj Gen Olinto M. Barsanti	1 July 1967–19 July 1968
Maj Gen Melvin Zais	19 July 1968–May 1969
Maj Gen John W. Wright	May 1969–25 May 1970
Maj Gen John J. Hennessey	25 May 1970–1 Feb 1971
Maj Gen Thomas M. Tarpley	1 Feb 1971–6 Apr 1972

suffering injuries in battle, Barsanti returned to Japan in August 1951 and then to the United States.

During the 1950s he served in the Far East, United States and West Germany. Colonel Barsanti was reassigned to the United States in 1957, and served in a number of capacities in Washington before returning to combat duty in July 1963 in South Korea as Assistant Division Commander for Combat Operations, 7th Infantry Division. During this time he received notification of his promotion to Brigadier General, effective 1 September 1963. This made him, at 46 years of age, one of the youngest generals in the army.

Staff positions at HQ US Army Europe, HQ V Corps and United States Army Materiel Command followed, and in May 1967 came promotion to Major General. On 1 July General Barsanti assumed command of the 101st Airborne Division at Fort Campbell. Noted as a disciplinarian, Barsanti's training programme played a major role in preparing the 101st for combat in Vietnam. At the end of the year he oversaw the uplift of the division to Vietnam, and on 13 December reported to General Westmoreland that 'the 101st Airborne Division is present for combat in Vietnam'.

In Vietnam Barsanti was a regular visitor to the frontlines, where he sometimes became engaged in combat, and to the hospitals to encourage wounded troops. His personal courage and willingness to put himself in the line of fire is attested to by the two Purple Hearts he received. During his tenure the war in Vietnam was at its most intense; through some of its toughest battles he led the 101st with great skill and courage.

In July 1968 General Barsanti turned command of the 101st in Vietnam over to General Melvin Zais. On his return he was posted to Fort Sheridan, Illinois, as Chief of Staff of the Fifth Army, and on 31 August 1971 he retired from the army on medical grounds. He died on 2 May 1973, having lost a long battle with cancer.

GENERAL MELVIN ZAIS

General Barsanti's successor in command, Melvin Zais, led the 101st Airborne in Vietnam through the tough operations in the A Shau Valley: 'Nevada Eagle', 'Somerset Plain', 'Kentucky Jumper', 'Massachusetts Striker', 'Apache Snow', and 'Lamar Plain'.

Zais was born on 8 May 1916 in Fall River, Massachusetts. After formal education, he studied political science at the University of New Hampshire. In 1937 he was commissioned a Second Lieutenant in the US Army Reserve and fought in the Second World War. After the war he attended the US Command and General Staff College, and was also a graduate of the Armed Forces Staff College and the National War College. On 1 June 1964, Zais was promoted to Brigadier General. His first command was the 1st Infantry Division (the famed Big Red One; Spearhead 6) in 1966, after which he returned to Washington as Director of Individual Training, Office, Deputy Chief of Staff for Personnel. In May 1967 he was promoted to Major General, and in July 1969 took command of the 101st Airborne Division (Airmobile). During his time as commander of the unit he proved both a worthy and able leader who is, perhaps unfairly, best remembered for the controversial decision he made at Dong Ap Bia (Hamburger Hill) to defeat the enemy at any cost. After formally handing over to John W. Wright in May 1969, Zais stayed on in Vietnam for another year as commander XXIV Corps, and was Director for Operations, J-3, Organization of the Joint Chiefs of Staff in Washington from 1970 to 1972.

His awards and decorations include the Distinguished Service Medal with three Oak Leaf Clusters, Silver Star with Oak Leaf Cluster, Legion of Merit with Two Oak Leaf Clusters, Distinguished Flying Cross with Oak Leaf Cluster, and Bronze Star Medal.

Top: General John Hennessey.

Above: General Melvin Zais.

Left: General John Cushman.

COLONEL DAVID M. HACKWORTH

Another famous – and controversial – veteran of the 101st Airborne Division is Colonel David H. Hackworth, America's most decorated living soldier, with more than 100 awards, including two Distinguished Service Crosses, 10 Silver Stars, eight Bronze Stars for Valor and eight Purple Hearts. Of the 26 years he spent in the army, seven were in combat theatres. Assigned to the 101st Airborne in January 1965, he led the 1st Battalion, 327th Infantry Regiment, into Vietnam in July and through Operations 'Highland', 'Gibraltar', 'Van Buren' and 'Hawthorn'. However, by the early 1970s he had become totally disillusioned with the way the war was being conducted and one of its most vocal public critics.

Hackworth suffered a rough childhood, and ran off to join the US Merchant Marine at the age of 14, towards the end of the Second World War. After the war, aged 15, he enlisted in the US Army and was assigned occupation duty in Trieste. The start of the Korean War found him a sergeant. Hackworth volunteered for duty and was assigned to 25th Infantry Division, winning not only a battlefield commission as a lieutenant, but medals for valour, as well as Purple Hearts. He subsequently volunteered for a second tour in Korea, serving with the 40th Infantry Division.

After the war ended, Hackworth retired from the army, and spent some time at college. Life as a civilian bored him and, using his connections, he rejoined the expanding 'cold war' US Army. Hackworth climbed the peacetime career ladder dutifully, and was a battalion commander in the 101st Airborne Division when it was sent to Vietnam in 1965. Although he led his battalion with great skill, he became rapidly soured with the conduct of the war.

Assigned to the Pentagon at the end of his one-year tour, he spent much of that assignment accompanying Brigadier General S.L.A. Marshall on a research trip. Despite mounting disillusionment, Hackworth refused to resign, feeling it was his duty as a field-grade officer to wage the campaign as best he could.

There followed a tour as commander of a training battalion of the 9th Infantry Division at Fort Lewis, Washington, which served only to convince Hackworth of the ineffectiveness of the training given to soldiers sent to Vietnam. In 1969 he returned to Vietnam, serving in a number of positions including as a senior advisor to the ARVN. His unflinching view that the US Army was not learning from its mistakes, and that the South Vietnamese ARVN officers were essentially corrupt, got him in trouble with his superior commanders. Hackworth returned home in June 1971, as the army's youngest colonel.

His disenchantment erupted in a television interview with the ABC programme *Issues and Answers*, aired on 27 June, during which he said, 'This is a bad war. ... It can't be won [and] we need to get out'. In that interview, he also said that the North Vietnamese flag would fly over Saigon in four years, a prediction that turned out to be right on target. The interview enraged senior US Army officers at the Pentagon, who ordered an investigation into his conduct in Vietnam. Although Secretary of State Robert F. Frohlke ordered this to be dropped, Hackworth was harassed and ostracised within the army, and in September retired with the rank of colonel.

After a period of self-imposed exile in Australia, Hackworth returned to the United States in the mid-1980s, where he now works as a defence analyst for the broadcast and print media, and is a vocal spokesman for veterans.

Top: General Ben Sternberg.

Above: General Thomas Tarpley.

Right: President Nixon and MoH Sgt Gordon Roberts.

MEDAL OF HONOR WINNERS

Twenty men from the division were awarded the Medal of Honor, the highest award for bravery the United States bestows on it soldiers, during the Vietnam War. Their names are given here. Posthumous awards are starred.

Sgt. 1st Class Webster Anderson
Captain Paul W. Bucha
Sp4c. Michael J. Fitzmaurice
Cpl. Frank R. Fratellenico*
1st Lt. James A. Gardner*
Staff Sgt. John G. Gertsch*
Sp4c. Peter M. Guenette*
Sp4c. Frank A. Herda
Staff Sgt. Joe R. Hooper
Sgt 1st Class Lawrence Joel
Pfc. Kenneth M. Kays
Sp4c. Joseph G. LaPointe Jr.*
Pfc. Milton A. Lee
Pfc. Carlos J. Lozada
Lt. Col. Andre C. Lucas*
Pfc. Milton L. Olive III
Sgt. Robert M. Patterson
Staff Sgt. Clifford C. Sims*
Sgt. Gordon R. Roberts
Sp4c. Dale E. Wayrynen*

MEDAL OF HONOR CITATION
ROBERTS, GORDON R.

Rank and organization: Sergeant (then Sp4c.), U.S. Army, Company B, 1st Battalion, 506th Infantry, 101st Airborne Division. Place and date: Thua Thien Province, Republic of Vietnam, 11 July 1969. Entered service at: Cincinnati, Ohio. Born: 14 June 1950, Middletown, Ohio. Citation: For conspicuous gallantry and intrepidity in action at the risk of his life above and beyond the call of duty. Sgt. Roberts distinguished himself while serving as a rifleman in Company B, during combat operations. Sgt. Roberts' platoon was maneuvering along a ridge to attack heavily fortified enemy bunker positions which had pinned down an adjoining friendly company. As the platoon approached the enemy positions, it was suddenly pinned down by heavy automatic weapons and grenade fire from camouflaged enemy fortifications atop the overlooking hill. Seeing his platoon immobilised and in danger of failing in its mission, Sgt. Roberts crawled rapidly toward the closest enemy bunker. With complete disregard for his safety, he leaped to his feet and charged the bunker, firing as he ran. Despite the intense enemy fire directed at him, Sgt. Roberts silenced the 2-man bunker. Without hesitation, Sgt. Roberts continued his 1-man assault on a second bunker. As he neared the second bunker, a burst of enemy fire knocked his rifle from his hands. Sgt. Roberts picked up a rifle dropped by a comrade and continued his assault, silencing the bunker. He continued his charge against a third bunker and destroyed it with well-thrown hand grenades. Although Sgt. Roberts was now cut off from his platoon, he continued his assault against a fourth enemy emplacement. He fought through a heavy hail of fire to join elements of the adjoining company which had been pinned down by the enemy fire. Although continually exposed to hostile fire, he assisted in moving wounded personnel from exposed positions on the hilltop to an evacuation area before returning to his unit. By his gallant and selfless actions, Sgt. Roberts contributed directly to saving the lives of his comrades and served as an inspiration to his fellow soldiers in the defeat of the enemy force. Sgt. Roberts' extraordinary heroism in action at the risk of his life were in keeping with the highest traditions of the military service and reflect great credit upon himself, his unit, and the U.S. Army.

ASSESSMENT

The 101st Airborne was the last army division to leave the Vietnam war zone, after almost seven years in combat. For the greater part of this time the division fought in I Corps, scene of most of the toughest fighting and where most casualties occurred. 4,011 men were killed and another 18,259 wounded. The 1st Brigade spent a total of about 2,200 days in combat, while the full Division (including the 2nd and 3rd Brigades spent a total of 1,573 days.

The 101st Airborne Division came to war in Vietnam with a very illustrious history and many laurels. But past glories do not win battles. It is to the credit of the division that it did not rest on its laurels, instead re-igniting the legendary airborne *esprit de corps* within the ranks to fight difficult battles in trying circumstances in a war that many believe the United States could not win. Nevertheless, despite the misgivings that many of the men must have had, countless acts of courage have been documented and undoubtedly many more went unrecorded. Statistics can never tell the full picture, but one worth noting is that 17 Medals of Honor were awarded to 101st Airborne troops during the Vietnam War. Another statistic that speaks volumes about the character of these men is that almost 2,000, mostly in infantry battalions, extended their Vietnam tours by six months.

One measure of any unit is the regard in which it is held by its enemy. According to divisional lore, many enemy commanders warned their men to avoid the 'Chicken Men' at all costs, because any engagement with them would surely be lost. In the end, perhaps the final word should go to one of their number. In his farewell to the 101st Division, Barsanti stated:
"I have pushed hard and demanded much, always knowing what the results would be – success and victory. During the last six months you have established records that other units have not surpassed in much longer periods of time. This is a tribute to your dedication, 'will to win,' and discipline as an airborne division."

UNIT CITATIONS

Republic of Vietnam Cross of Gallantry with Palm for Vietnam 1968-1969
Republic of Vietnam Cross of Gallantry with Palm for Vietnam 1971
Republic of Vietnam Civil Action Honor Medal, First Class for Vietnam 1968-1970

Presidential Unit Citation (Army), Streamer embroidered Dak To, Vietnam 1966
Presidential Unit Citation (Army), Streamer embroidered Dong Ap Bia Mountain

Valorous Unit Award, Streamer embroidered Tuy Hoa
Valorous Unit Award, Streamer embroidered Thua Thien
Valorous Unit Award, Streamer embroidered Thua Thien

Meritorious Unit Commendation (Army), Streamer embroidered Vietnam 1965-1966
Meritorious Unit Commendation (Army), Streamer embroidered Vietnam 1968
Meritorious Unit Commendation (Army), Streamer embroidered Vietnam 1968-1969

POSTWAR

Today, the 101st Airborne (Air Assault) is the US Army's and the world's only air assault division, and continues to develop and exploit the doctrine of air assault.

In January 1991, during the first Gulf War, the 101st Airborne made the deepest and largest combat air assault in history, when 2,000 men, 50 transport vehicles, artillery, and tons of fuel and ammunition were airlifted 50 miles into Iraq. Remarkable, the division suffered no soldiers killed in action, and captured thousands of enemy prisoners of war. Since that time its soldiers have supported humanitarian relief efforts in Rwanda and Somalia, and more recently supplied peacekeepers to Haiti and Bosnia. When the US 'War on Terror' began after the events of 11 September, elements from the 101st went into Afghanistan as part of Operation 'Anaconda' to drive the Taliban regime from power and the al Qaeda organization out of the country. At the end of February 2003, the division deployed to Kuwait and took part in the subsequent invasion of Iraq. It has since been occupied on occupation duties in that country under Operation 'Enduring Freedom'.

Left: SP4 Dale Wayrynen won his Medal of Honor posthumously. On 18 May 1967, during combat operations near Duc Pho, his platoon came face to face with the enemy and during the fighting, a live enemy grenade landed in the centre of the tightly grouped Americans. Wayrynen threw himself on the grenade at the moment it exploded.

Below: A CH-47E Chinook helicopter comes in for a landing at Udairi air base in Kuwait as a UH-60 Black Hawk waits for clearance to move onto the runway on 29 March 2003. All the aircraft are from the 101st Airborne Division (Air Assault) based at Fort Campbell, and deployed in support of Operation 'Iraqi Freedom'.

REFERENCE

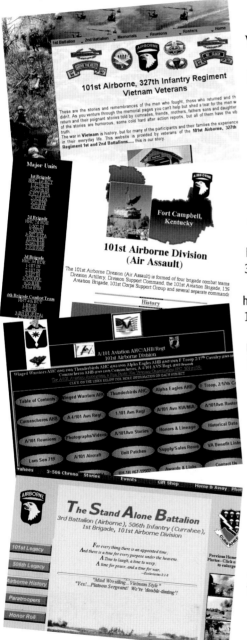

WEBSITES

UNIT WEBSITES/HISTORIES
http://www.army.mil/cmh-pg/matrix/Matrix.htm
Details of 101st insignia, commanders and history.

http://screamingeagles-327thvietnam.com/
101st Airborne, 327th Infantry Regiment Vietnam Veterans site. Good information on the battles fought by this unit plus good photographs of fire bases.

http://www.b2501airborne.com/
Company B, 2nd Battalion, 501st Infantry website.

http://www.currahee.org/
3rd Battalion, 506th Airborne Infantry, 1st Brigade, 101st Airborne Division.

http://www.a101avn.org/
101st Aviation Battalion website.

Unit histories
http://www.campbell.army.mil/division.htm
Details units currently stationed at Fort Campbell, including those of 101st Airborne.

http://101_lha.tripod.com/101st_lha/id6.html
History of 101st Airborne in Vietnam.

http://www.angelfire.com/rebellion/101abndivvietvets/page15history101.html
History of 101st Airborne in Vietnam.

http://www.screamingeaglesthroughtime.com/id119.html
Month by month diary of actions.

http://screamingeagles-327thvietnam.com/second/trung_luong/20_jun.htm
A very detailed account of the Battle for Trung Luong, fought by the 2nd Battalion of the 327th Regiment, by Colonel (Ret.) Tom Furgeson.

REFERENCE

GENERAL HISTORY

http://www.vietnamwar.com/
Good general background to the war.

http://members.aol.com/veterans/warlib6v.htm
Comprehensive page of links to Vietnam resources.

http://www.cc.gatech.edu/fac/Thomas.Pilsch/Vietnam.html
Another excellent page of links.

http://www.screamingeagle.org
101st Airborne Division Association, the Screaming Eagles Veterans' Website.

MISCELLANEOUS

http://www.army.mil/cmh-pg/
Homepage of the US Army Center for Military History.

http://www.vietnamtripledeuce.org/PresidentialUnitCitation.pdf
Presidential citation for Operation 'Hawthorne'.

http://vietnamresearch.com/unif/
Excellent table showing relevant US Army rank insignia.

http://www.quanonline.com/military/military_reference/american/american.html
Information on clothing and insignia.

http://www.3rdmarines.net/Vietnam_Operations_by_Name.htm
Brief details of US military operations in Vietnam (from 1966).

http://www.ehistory.com/vietnam/pdf/101airborne.pdf
Official post-battle report form, Dong Ap Bia (Hamburger Hill).

The online archive of the Vietnam Project at Texas Tech University is also an extensive resource for reference works published by the US Government and US Army.

BIBLIOGRAPHY

BOOKS AND ARTICLES

Bowman, John S. (ed.): *The Vietnam War – An Almanac*, World Almanac Publications, 1985. The bulk of the volume is a detailed chronology.

Burns, Richard R.: *Pathfinder – First In, Last Out*, Ballantine, 2002. Burns was in the Pathfinder detachment, Headquarters Company, 101st Aviation Battalion from December 1967 to December 1968.

Clodfelter, Michael: *Mad Minutes and Vietnam Months*, Zebra Books, 1989. Clodfelter served in Vietnam with the 101st Airborne from July 1965 to December 1966.

Chinnery, Philip D.: *Vietnam – The Helicopter War*, Naval Institute Press, 1991.

185

Far Right: Three soldiers from the 101st Airborne Division, one armed with a 5.56mm Colt M4 carbine equipped with the Knights Armament Company (KAC) Modular Weapon System (MWS), observe movement from atop a fortified bunker position at the Kandahar, International Airport, Afghanistan, during Operation Enduring Freedom, January 2002.

Below Left and Right: The six-colour 'chocolate chip' desert camouflage uniform was introduced in the late 1970s following the creation of the Rapid Deployment Force. This trooper of the 101st Airborne Division (Air Assault) is cleaning his M16A2 5.56mm assault rifle at the outsell of Operation 'Desert Storm' in February 1991 with the Kevlar PASGT 'Fritz' helmet on his head that replaced the venerable steel M1 helmet of World War II and the Vietnam era. As part of US XVIII Airborne Corps, the 101st Airborne Division (Air Assault) was deployed to the western edge of the Coalition Forces as the flank protection for the major assault of the armoured and mechanised divisions of US VII Corps. Using its awesome aviation assets, the division air assaulted deep into Iraq as far as the Euphrates river valley. Here (left), AH-64A Apache attack helicopters and their companion OH-58D Kiowa observation helicopters wait for their next mission during Operation 'Desert Storm'.

Gadd, Charles: *Line Doggie – Foot Soldier in Vietnam*; Presidio, 1987.
Gadd served a one-year tour with the 1st Battalion, 501st Infantry, starting in December 1967.

Grant, William T.: *Wings of the Eagle – A Kingsmen's Story*, Ivy, 1994.

Gregory, Barry: *Vietnam Helicopter Handbook*; Patrick Stephens, 1988.

Hackworth, Col. David H. and Sherman, Julie: *About Face – The Odyssey of an American Warrior*, Simon & Schuster, 1989.

Kelly, Michael P.: *Where We Were in Vietnam – A Comprehensive Guide to the Firebases, Military Installations and Naval Vessels of the Vietnam War, 1945–1975*; Hellgate, 2002.

Lepore, Herbert P.: 'The Coming of Age – The Role of the Helicopter in the Vietnam War'; *Army History*, No. 29, Winter, 1994, pp. 29–36.

Nolan, Keith William: *Ripcord – Screaming Eagles under Siege, Vietnam 1970*; Presidio Press, 2000.

Rosser-Owen, David: *Vietnam Weapons Handbook*; Patrick Stephens, 1986
Stanton, Shelby L.: *Vietnam Order of Battle*; US News Books, 1981.
Foreword by General William C. Westmoreland. A vital reference work listing US units, with dates and locations of Vietnam service, etc.

Tucker, Spencer C (ed.): *The Encyclopedia of the Vietnam War – A Political, Social and Military History*; OUP, 1998.

MAGAZINES AND PERIODICALS
In Combat, Marshall Cavendish Magazine Collection.
The Vietnam Experience, Orbis Magazine Collection.

MONUMENTS

In June 2004 a new monument was unveiled at Fort Campbell to honour the soldiers who have served in the 101st Airborne Division throughout its history.

The monument, directly in front of the division headquarters building, is a large, jet-black granite obelisk with panels that depict the division's storied history: in the Second World War, the Vietnam conflict, Operation 'Desert Storm' and recent operations including Operations 'Enduring Freedom' and 'Iraqi Freedom'.

Abbreviations

1/5th	1st Battalion 5th Cavalry Regiment	H&HC	Headquarters and headquarters company	Pink Team	A scout helicopter and a gunship
AHC	Assault helicopter company	HEAT	High-explosive anti-tank	PT	Physical Training
AIT	Advanced infantry training			PZ	Pickup zone
AMTF	Airmobile Task Force	IED	Improvised explosive devices		
AO	Area of operation			Red Team	Two gunships
ARA	Aerial rocket artillery	IMR	Improved military rifle	Regt	Regiment
ARVN	Army of the Republic of Vietnam			RPG	Rocket-propelled grenade
		KBA	Killed by artillery	RTO	Radio telephone operator
ASHB	Assault Support Helicopter Battalion	KIA	Killed in action		
				Sfc	Sergeant first class
		LAW	Light anti-tank weapon	SLT	Swing landing trainer
BAC	Basic Airborne Course	LCE	Load carrying equipment	Sp4c	Specialist fourth class
'Blues'	Rifle platoons	LDA	Lateral drift (while parachuting)	Sqn	Squadron
Bn	Battalion			SSI	Shoulder sleeve insignia
Bty	Battery	LFT	Light fire team		
		LRRP	Long-range reconnaissance patrol	TAC	Tactical air control
CIDG	Civil Irregular Defense Group	LZ	Landing zone	USARV	US Army Vietnam
Co	Company	LOH	Light observation helicopter	USMC	US Marine Corps
CO	Command Post	Loach	Hughes OH-6A Cayuse		
C&C	Command and control			VC	Viet Cong
CTZ	Corps tactical zones	MACV	Military Assistance Command Vietnam	White Team	Two scout helicopters
DEROS	Date Eligible for Return from Overseas	MIA	Missing in action	WIA	Wounded in action
DMZ	Demilitarized zone	MLCE	Modernized load-carrying equipment	WP	White Phospherous
DUI	Distinctive Unit Insignia				
		NVA	North Vietnamese Army		
FB	Fire base				
FFAR	Free flight aerial rocket	PAVN	People's Army of Vietnam		
FOO	Forward observation officer	PF	Popular Forces		
FSB	Fire support base	Pfc	Private first class		

INDEX